Dedicated to
Amb. Wendy

[signature]
Washington DC, June 2017

Egyptians in Revolt

Egyptians in Revolt investigates the political economy of the Egyptian labor and student movements. Using elements of social movement theory within a broad political economy framework, it assesses labor and student mobilizations in four eras of contemporary Egyptian history: the pre-1952 era, the Nasser era, the Sadat era and the Mubarak era.

Egyptians in Revolt examines how both student and labor groups responded to the political economy pressures of the respective eras. Within the context of social movement theory, the book argues that political opportunities and threats have had a significant impact on both student and labor mobilizations. In addition, the book explores how the movements have, at times, been able to affect government policies. However, the argument is made that the inability of both groups to sustain momentum in the long term is due to co-optation efforts by established political forces and the absence of viable and enduring organizational structures that are autonomous of state control.

By combining analysis to include both labor and student movements, *Egyptians in Revolt* is a valuable resource for understanding the Egyptian political economy and its impact on mobilizations. It will therefore be of interest to students and scholars of Middle East Studies, as well as those interested in social movement more broadly.

Dr. Adel Abdel Ghafar is a joint fellow at the Brookings Doha Center and Qatar University, specializing in political economy. He holds a Ph.D. in Political Science and International Relations from the Australian National University.

Routledge Studies in Middle Eastern Democratization and Government

Edited by: Larbi Sadiki

Qatar University

This series examines new ways of understanding democratization and government in the Middle East. The varied and uneven processes of change, occurring in the Middle Eastern region, can no longer be read and interpreted solely through the prism of Euro-American transitology. Seeking to frame critical parameters in light of these new horizons, this series instigates reinterpretations of democracy and propagates formerly 'subaltern,' narratives of democratization. Reinvigorating discussion on how Arab and Middle Eastern peoples and societies seek good government, *Routledge Studies in Middle Eastern Democratization and Government* provides tests and contests of old and new assumptions.

7 **Political and Constitutional Transitions in North Africa**
Actors and Factors
Justin O. Frosini & Francesco Biagi

8 **Al Jazeera and Democratization**
The Rise of the Arab Public Sphere
Ezzeddine Abdelmoula

9 **Revolutionary Egypt**
Connecting Domestic and International Struggles
Edited by Reem Abou-El-Fadl

10 **Oil States in the New Middle East**
Uprisings and Stability
Edited by Kjetil Selvik & Bjørn Olav Utvik

11 **Politics of the Islamic Tradition**
The Thought of Muhammad Al-Ghazali
Mohammed Moussa

12 **The Arab Lobby and the US**
Factors for Success and Failure
Dania Koleilat Khatib

13 **Hamas and the Media**
Politics and Strategy
Wael Abdelal

14 **Egyptians in Revolt**
The Political Economy of Worker and Student Mobilizations 1919–2011
Adel Abdel Ghafar

15 **US Hard Power in the Arab World**
Resistance, the Syrian Uprising and the War on Terror
Layla Saleh

16 **Palestine in EU and Russian Foreign Policy**
Statehood and the Peace Process
Malath Alagha

Egyptians in Revolt

The political economy of labor and student mobilizations 1919–2011

Adel Abdel Ghafar

Routledge
Taylor & Francis Group
LONDON AND NEW YORK

First published 2017
by Routledge
2 Park Square, Milton Park, Abingdon, Oxon OX14 4RN

and by Routledge
711 Third Avenue, New York, NY 10017

Routledge is an imprint of the Taylor & Francis Group, an informa business

British Library Cataloguing in Publication Data
A catalogue record for this book is available from the British Library

Library of Congress Cataloging in Publication Data
Names: Abdel Ghafar, Adel, author
Title: Egyptians in revolt : the political economy of labor and student mobilizations 1919–2011 / Adel Abdel Ghafar.
Other titles: Routledge studies in Middle Eastern democratization and government ; 14.
Description: Milton Park, Abingdon, Oxon : Routledge, 2017. |
Series: Routledge studies in Middle Eastern democratization and government ; 14 Includes bibliographical references and index.
Identifiers: LCCN 2016016003| ISBN 9781138656109 (hardback) |
ISBN 9781315622132 (ebook)
Subjects: LCSH: Labor movement–Egypt–History. | Student movements–Egypt–History. | Egypt–Economic conditions–20th century. | Egypt–Economic conditions–21st century. | Egypt–Economic policy.
Classification: LCC HD6863 .A64 2017 | DDC 962.05–dc23
LC record available at https://lccn.loc.gov/2016016003

ISBN: 978-1-138-65610-9 (hbk)
ISBN: 978-1-315-62213-2 (ebk)

Typeset in Times New Roman
by Wearset Ltd, Boldon, Tyne and Wear

MIX
Paper from responsible sources
FSC www.fsc.org FSC® C013056

Printed and bound in Great Britain by
TJ International Ltd, Padstow, Cornwall

This book is dedicated to my late father, Ismail Abdel Ghafar (1950–2008), an extraordinarily kind man who had supported and encouraged me in my studies and endeavors across five continents. May he rest in peace.

Contents

Figures

Tables

Preface[1]

On January 25, 2011 at approximately 4 p.m., I was standing with a group of protestors in Tahrir Square. The acrid stench of tear gas surrounded me, and the sounds of bullets, screams and sirens were deafening. By that afternoon, several thousand protestors had occupied the square, and our group was protecting one side of it from the police on Qasr al-Aini Street. Suddenly, a squad of Central Security riot police started charging toward us, shields raised and batons drawn. Several protestors had fallen to the ground and were being brutally beaten by the riot police. I started running with the group as we tried to scramble away from the carnage and escape the riot police. As I ran, I saw a dying protestor, his skull cracked open, his brains slowly pouring out. Suddenly, a man next to me stopped and shouted "don't run! Egyptians, when will you stop running away? Turn around and let's face them once and for all!" He grabbed my shirt, and I stopped. I grabbed the shirt of the person next to me, and he stopped. Slowly, our entire group came to a halt. The riot police continued to run toward us and were getting dangerously close. The front row of police were menacing in their riot gear, as tear gas canisters were lobbed at us from the officers behind them. We stood still. I briefly contemplated what had brought me to this point.

That day, January 25, 2011, had started like any other day. It was a national holiday to commemorate Police Day, in remembrance of the Egyptian police officers who had died in Suez at the hands of British forces on the same day in 1952. Like thousands of other Egyptians, in mid-2010 I had joined the 'We Are All Khaled Said' Facebook page, set up after the police murdered a young man in cold blood in Alexandria. It had disgusted me how police brutality had taken this young man's life, and how the regime of Egyptian President Hosni Mubarak had so blatantly tried to cover up his death. Protests against the police were being planned via social media to coincide with Police Day, which I planned to attend with friends. I joined the protests early in the day not thinking that they would escalate to this unimaginable scale, and thus I found myself in the position I was in by 4 p.m. in Tahrir Square facing a squad of riot police.

As the police neared us with their armor and batons raised high, they noticed something different: we were not moving. They may have never witnessed something like this before. The line of soldiers started to slow down until they abruptly stopped, just a few meters before us. For a moment, both crowds stared at each other, polar opposites on an urban battlefield. That moment will be etched in my memory forever; time almost seemed to stand still.

Then the most incredible thing happened. The riot police, having seen us stand our ground, turned back and started running for their lives. We started chasing them, even capturing a few—we took away their weapons and helmets, then released them. They ran back to their lines, psychologically broken. Although they would still fight us in the coming days, we all knew that something profound had just taken place. There was a raised collective consciousness amongst us. A realization. An epiphany. Simply, we will no longer be afraid. We drew strength, courage and resolve from one another, from our numbers, and from our conviction. Our small group right there reached that conclusion, as other Egyptians had reached it across the country that day. And in that moment, the Mubarak regime had lost its most significant weapon: fear. Eighteen days later, Mubarak stepped down.

During those days in Tahrir Square I saw an unlikely convergence of workers and students, men and women, rich and poor, old and young, Muslim and Copt, all united to oppose Hosni Mubarak. As I observed and interacted with the people around me, I was immensely curious to understand how and why these events were unfolding. I was particularly interested in how groups from different socio-economic backgrounds such as workers and students would come together to challenge the state. My experience during the uprising motivated me to pursue this research to answer some of these questions. Initially, I sought to specifically research the 2011 uprising, but as I read further I became aware of the deeper history of worker–student mobilizations against the state in Egypt and the various political and socio-economic factors. This led me to broaden the scope of my study to include Egyptian mobilizations from 1919, ending with the 2011 uprising, with a focus on the labor and student movements.

Note

1 The preface is based on my testimony of my participation in the events of January 25, 2011 published in Adel Abdel Ghafar, "The First Hours of the Egyptian Revolution," *New York Times Lede Blog*, January 25, 2012, http://thelede.blogs.nytimes.com/2012/01/24/the-first-hours-of-egypts-revolution/ (accessed October 1, 2014) and Adel Abdel Ghafar, "January 25th: The Day the Barrier of Fear Broke Down," in Asaad Al Saleh (ed.), *Voices of the Arab Spring: Personal Stories of the Arab Revolutions* (New York: Columbia University Press, 2014).

Acknowledgements

Research is a solitary endeavor, so it's prudent that I start by thanking my family for all their support over the years. In particular, I am indebted to my late father Ismail Abdel Ghafar to whom I dedicated this book to, as well as my late grandfather and namesake Adel Shams el Din Abdel Ghafar. Both men have supported me in immeasurable ways over the years and to them I am eternally grateful. I would also like to thank my sister, confidant and friend Lina Abdel Ghafar for her support and encouragement throughout this work. Throughout my life she has always been the voice of reason, and continues to be so—whether I actually listen to her advice is a completely different matter. During my doctoral studies at the Australian National University (ANU), I was lucky enough to meet my wife, Jane. An avid traveler and scuba diver like myself, our adventures continue to take us across the globe. I am tremendously indebted for her love, encouragement and support.

This book is based on my doctoral dissertation, so it's apt to also thank the chair of my panel and supervisor, Associate Professor Matthew Gray. Matthew provided tremendous and invaluable support throughout my time at the ANU and it has been a true privilege to have been supervised by him. I am also indebted to Professor Bob Bowker and Dr. Noah Bassil as members of my supervisory panel for all their diligent feedback, comments and suggestions. At the Centre of Arab and Islamic Studies at the ANU where I was based, I also received exemplary support and mentorship from Professor Amin Saikal and Dr. Kirill Nourzhanov for which I am also very grateful.

I am also indebted to a number of academics that supported me over the years. I would like to thank Professor Ahmad Shboul, who supervised my M.A. thesis at the University of Sydney and has provided encouragement and mentorship throughout my time in Australia. I would also like to thank Professor Gennaro Gervasio for all his support, as well as all the intellectually stimulating shisha outings in downtown Cairo. I am also indebted to the support I received in Cairo from Dr. Hala el Said, Dean of the Faculty Economics and Politics at Cairo University, and Dr. Rabab el Mahdy at the American University in Cairo.

During my research, I was fortunate enough to personally meet Timothy Mitchell, Khaled Fahmy, Hani Shukrallah, Gilbert Achcar and Abdel Khaleq Gouda, all scholars and intellectuals whom I immensely respect and admire. I am indebted to them for illuminating and sometimes challenging discussions about my research, which helped me further crystalize my ideas.

Finally, I would like to thank my generation, the Egyptian youth of the January 25 uprising. I am eternally proud to have been standing with them shoulder to shoulder in Tahrir Square from January 25 to February 11, 2011 as we challenged tyranny. While we were not entirely successful in creating the progressive, inclusive and prosperous Egypt we aspired to live in, nonetheless together we wrote a powerful chapter in Egypt's long-term struggle for freedom and prosperity. I wish the best of luck to the coming generation in writing the next chapter.

Note on Arabic transliteration and translation

This book uses a number of Arabic words, including names of people, places and organizations, as well as general descriptive words used in colloquial Egyptian Arabic. For the sake of simplicity, names of people and places are used as they appear in English publications (for example, Abdel Nasser instead of ʿAbdul-Nāṣir; Cairo instead of al-Qāhira). Arabic words will otherwise be transliterated according to the *International Journal of Middle East Studies* system, by which the letter *ʿayn* is represented by (ʿ) and *hamza* by (ʾ) (for example, *ʿashwaʾiyyat*). Arabic words, phrases and book titles will be followed by an English translation in parentheses.

Abbreviations

AISCD	Alexandria Iron and Steel Company in Dekhila
ASU	Arab Socialist Union
AUC	American University in Cairo
CAPMAS	Central Agency for Public Mobilization and Statistics
ECES	Egyptian Centre for Economic Studies
EFITU	Egyptian Federation of Independent Trade Unions
EMNL	Egyptian Movement for National Liberation
ERSAP	Economic Reform and Structural Adjustment Program
ESOP	Employee Stock Ownership Plan
FDI	foreign direct investment
GAFI	General Authority for Investment and Free Zones
GFC	Global Financial Crisis
GFETU	General Federation of Egyptian Trade Unions
HADETU	Democratic Movement for National Liberation
IMF	International Monetary Fund
ISI	import substitution industrialization
MENA	Middle East and North Africa
NAM	Non-Alignment Movement
NCWS	National Committee for Workers and Students
NDP	National Democratic Party
RCC	Revolutionary Command Council
RYC	Revolutionary Youth Coalition
SCAF	Supreme Council of the Armed Forces
SFD	Social Development Fund
SLD	state-led development
WTO	World Trade Organization

1 Introduction

> Men journey together with a view to particular advantage, and by way of providing some particular thing needed for the purposes of life.
>
> Aristotle[1]

Introduction

The question of why people collectively act has long been a pertinent one. From the Spartacus slave uprising to the French Revolution, to the anti-globalization movement and most recently to the events that have become known as the 'Arab Spring', people throughout the ages have sought to challenge the status quo for a variety of reasons, and with varying degrees of success. Mobilizations have long occurred in Egypt, with archaeologists showing that the first recorded labor strike occurred in ancient Egypt under the reign of Ramses III, when the builders of Deir el Madina stopped working to demand more food and better living conditions.[2]

It is in the contemporary era of Egyptian history that movements coalesced around specific demands, formed organizations and adopted a variety of tactics to press for their demands and challenge the authorities. State–society relations have developed considerably since the Mohammed Ali era (1805–1848) when Egypt began its transformation from a semi-feudal society toward a capitalist mode of production.[3] In addition to that socio-economic transformation, from the late nineteenth century to the early twentieth century a strong national identity was being consciously and unconsciously developed and consolidated in opposition to colonialism,[4] beginning the era of large-scale mass mobilizations in contemporary Egypt. Despite the postcolonial authoritarian state constructed in the decades after the 1952 Free Officers' *coup d'état*, Egyptians would protest and mobilize in response to varying socio-economic and political conditions over the following decades, and with varying degrees of success.

Research questions and aims

This book explores the mobilizations of the labor and student movement from 1919 to 2011. It uses a political economy framework and elements of social movement theory to answer the following research questions: within the context of state–society relations in Egypt from 1919 to 2011, what was the impact of political economy on mobilizations by the labor and student movements? How did the movements respond to political opportunities and threats? How did the movements cooperate and what were the limitations of such cooperation?

At the broadest level, the political economy framework I apply is Richards and Waterbury's three-point model, used to analyze the political economy of the Middle East.[5] The three variables of the model are:

1 economic growth and structural change;
2 state structure and policy; and
3 social actors.

The use of this framework to analyze Egyptian political economy and its impact on mobilizations provides a practical lens by which to explore each of the variables, their interactions and their impact on one another.

In terms of case studies, I chose the labor and student movements as the focus of the investigation to shed light on how how social actors from different socio-economic backgrounds are affected by political economy, how they cooperate at certain junctures and the limitations of such cooperation. To that end, I utilize elements of social movement theory to further the understanding of the impact of the two variables on the social movements in question. The social movement theory elements employed are political process theory, framing, spillover and diffusion. Within political process theory, I specifically use the opportunities and threat model developed by Goldstone and Tilly.[6] The following opportunities and threats facing both movements will be analyzed:

Opportunities[7]	Threats[9]
• Institutional access	• State-attributed economic problems
• Elite conflict	• Erosion of rights
• Regime weakness	• State repression
• International dynamics[8]	

Argument summary

In this book, I have five interrelated arguments. First, I argue that political economy dynamics have had a direct impact on the labor and student movements and their mobilizations. Moreover, despite the authoritarian nature of the state, the labor and student movement were at times able to affect government policies, as well as challenge the regime itself (as seen in 2011).

Second, and within the context of social movement theory, I argue that various opportunities and threats had an impact on mobilizations by the labor and student movements. Third, I argue that at certain junctures of contemporary Egyptian history, the movements have combined their efforts to challenge the state, and have exhibited spillover and diffusional processes in their cooperation.

The book aims to show how at times this cooperation was coordinated, and at other times it was haphazard. Fourth, I argue that framing processes could be observed in the mobilizations by the movements.

Finally, I argue that there were two interrelated factors that inhibited the cooperation between both movements. The first factor is the attempts by the authorities as well as other political forces to co-opt the movements to their own advantage. The second factor is the inability of both movements to build enduring organizations that are autonomous of state control. Ultimately, the book seeks to illuminate the role of worker and student activism in Egyptian mobilizations from 1919 to 2011.

Research scope and selected mobilizations

The book situates mobilizations within the four epochs of modern Egyptian history from 1919 to 2011. Despite the book's broad scope, it does not attempt to provide a complete chronology of Egyptian mobilizations; rather, the main reason for using this historical approach is that such analysis allows the research to deduce patterns, as well as highlight differences. The four eras to be analyzed in their respective chapters are:

- The pre 1952 era (Chapter 2): the 1946 protests against the British presence in Egypt and *al-Lajna al-Ṭullābiyya wa al-ʿUmmāliyya* (the student and worker committee).
- The Nasser era (Chapter 3): the 1968 protests against the lenient sentencing of air force generals who were being held to account for the 1967 War defeat.
- The Sadat era (Chapter 4): the 1977 'Bread Intifada' protests against the removal of subsidies by the Sadat regime.
- The Mubarak era (Chapters 5 and 6): the 2011 uprising.

Two caveats are necessary at this juncture. The first is that this book seeks to illuminate the role of the labor and student movements in the selected mobilizations, however it does not attribute each of these mobilizations solely to these movements. There were a variety of people and groups involved in each of these mobilizations in addition to the workers and students. Therefore, the book seeks to illuminate the role of each movement in the selected mobilizations, but not to provide an all-encompassing analysis of the role of all the individuals and groups who participated.

The second caveat relates to the selection of the dates of the title of the book from 1919 to 2011. Even though the analysis of the diffusional processes in Chapter 2 focuses primarily on the worker and student movements during the 1946 protests, the chapter also critically discusses the involvement of these movements in earlier mobilizations, such as the 1919 uprising and the 1935 and 1936 student protests. This is why the title of the book and its scope extends from 1919 to 2011, rather than from 1946 to 2011.

Book contribution

This book contributes to the broader area studies literature on the Middle East and North Africa (MENA) region and specifically on Egypt to further the understanding of Egyptian political economy and its impact on social movements. This book is the first of its kind to apply the hybrid theoretical model of political economy and social movement theory to research twentieth and twenty-first century Egyptian mobilizations. By selecting four main episodes of contention occurring through four different eras, the book aims to shed light on the process of mobilization, on how the labor and student movements have challenged successive regimes (with varying degrees of success), and on the different spillover and diffusional processes and mechanisms involved between these movements.

Given the current transitions occurring across the MENA region and particularly the continued challenges in Egypt's transition, an understanding of the broader socio-economic and historical context of mobilizations arguably contributes to the understanding of events currently unfolding. Thus, in addition to contributing to scholarly literature on mobilizations, in a practical sense the book also aims to provide policy-makers and the informed public with a deeper understanding of socio-economic drivers of protests and instability in Egypt.

In addition, there is a tendency when analyzing Egyptian mobilization or activism to focus either on the middle-class student and youth movements or on the predominantly working-class labor movement. By combining analysis to include both movements, the book makes an original contribution that furthers the understanding of cross-movement cooperation in Egypt.

Finally, the book also seeks to contribute to the social movement theory literature by analyzing the impact of political economy on social movements in authoritarian settings. When compared to some other regions of the world, there is a dearth of scholarship when it comes to applying social movement theory to countries in the MENA region and this research attempts to fill some of these gaps.

Why use political economy and social movement theory?

In my search for a framework to analyze labor and worker mobilization in Egypt, there were several options available. Using a normative political science approach in examining social movements within the context of the authoritarian state would have been beneficial, but it would not have taken economic factors and their impact on social movements fully into consideration. Following from that, what then would have been the unit of analysis? Was it the state or the social movements themselves? In the context of Egyptian political economy, there are a variety of state-centric studies, which focus on the state structure as well as on the ruling elites.[10] At the other end of the spectrum, there are a variety of studies where social actors are the focal point.[11] A framework was needed that gave equal analytical attention to both state and society.

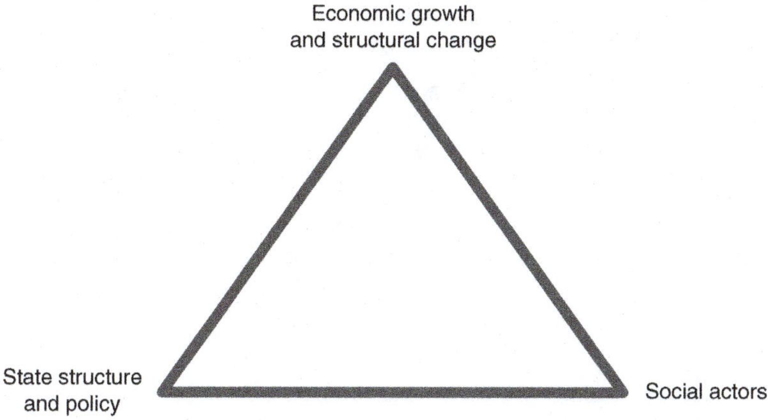

Figure 1.1 Richards and Waterbury's political economy model.

To that end, I chose to apply the political economy framework proposed by Richards and Waterbury (see Figure 1.1).[12] This is for three main reasons: first, the model is constructed with enough scope to allow for the analysis of the state, its construction and its policies, and also the possibility of independently analyzing social groupings. Second, the model treats economic growth and structural change as its own variable, rather than incorporate it as a natural by-product that fits within analysis of the state. This is beneficial in the sense that it allows the book to independently assess the socio-economic policies of the state and its direct quantifiable impact on economic growth and social actors.

The framework gives agency not only to the state (to impact the economy) but also to social actors (to impact both the state and the economy). Finally, the framework helps the research to investigate the complex interaction between political and economic processes as they unfold in society, the distribution of wealth between different groups and individuals, and the processes that transform these relationships over time.[13]

Having selected the political economy framework, the third variable of the model, that of 'social actors,' needed further analysis to understand how and why social actors 'act.' By using specific concepts from within social movement theory, the book will be able to incorporate the labor and student movements as actors and agents, showing how they act and react to their surrounding economic, social and political conditions (see Figure 1.2).

More specifically, the political opportunity and threat model helps explain the mobilizations of the labor and student movement by analyzing changes in the external environment of movements that may lead to increased contention and mobilizations against the state. To that end, Tarrow argues that:

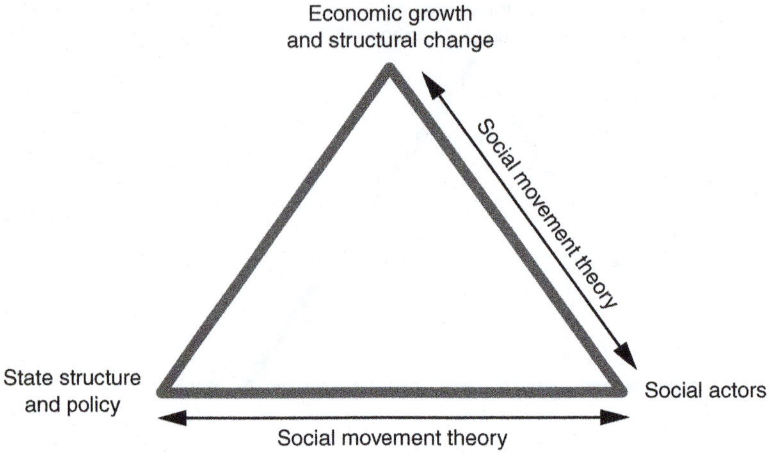

Figure 1.2 Richards and Waterbury's Middle East political economy model incorporated with social movement theory.

> Contention increases when people gain external resources to escape their compliance and find opportunities in which to use them. It also increases when they are threatened with costs they cannot bear or which outrage their sense of justice. When institutional access opens, rifts appear within the elites, allies become available, and state capacity for repression declines, challengers find opportunities to advance their claims. When combined with high levels of perceived costs for inaction, opportunities produce episodes of contentious politics.[14]

Also from within social movement theory, the concept of framing allows us to analyze how movements construct and present their grievances, and how this resonates not only from within the movement itself, but also with other movements and the general public. A frame denotes "an interpretive schemata that simplifies and condenses the 'world out there' by selectively punctuating and encoding objects, situations, events, experiences, and sequences of action within one's past or present environment."[15] Issues are 'framed' within the symbols and history of a specific culture, aiming to create and foster a feeling of solidarity among a group to attempt to galvanize them behind a cause that may lead to mobilization.[16]

Finally, the social movement theory concepts of spillover and diffusion help investigate how at times movements cooperate to reach their goals and how they affect each other, but also shows the limitations of such processes. As Meyer and Whittier argue:

> Social movements are not distinct and self-contained; rather, they grow from and give birth to other movements, work in coalition with other movements, and influence each other indirectly through their effects on the larger

cultural and political environment. Because social movements aspire to change not only specific policies, but also broader cultural and institutional structures, they have effects far beyond their explicit articulated goals. The ideas, tactics, styles, participants and organizations of one movement often *spill over* its boundaries to affect other social movements.[17]

'Labor' and 'student' movements in the Egyptian context

The origins of the Egyptian labor and student movements will be explored fully in Chapter 2, however the term 'labor movement' in the Egyptian context can be misleading at times. This is because many workers do not join collective actions, while others join in their individual capacities and not as part of a 'movement.' For the purposes of this research, the labor movement is understood as those Egyptian industrial workers in the private or public sector who are active in official or unofficial unions, as well as those non-unionized workers who also take part in collective action according to the prevailing conditions of the time.

Similarly, the term 'youth movement' can be construed in a variety of ways. Every student is a youth, but not every youth is a student. Generally speaking, youth are students for a set period of time during their formal school and university education. Some have argued that in the first decade of the twentieth century, the Egyptian student movement can be analyzed as its own class as they eventually became *Effendis* (the middle class that grew in the early twentieth century and locally educated and trained for roles in the government and public sector).[18] It becomes increasingly difficult during the Mubarak era to differentiate between the activism of youth and students as many organizations such as the April 6th Movement contained university students and recent graduates. For the purposes of this research, the term 'student movement' will be used as an overarching description when describing campus-based activism, and 'youth movement' will be at used in the final two chapters when university students and recent graduates both participated in mobilizations.

It is worth noting that one of the main differences between the labor movement and the student movement is that eventually students grow up and join the workforce, while workers in general tend to continue being workers as blue-collar jobs arguably provide for less social mobility. A worker can move from being unskilled to skilled to highly skilled and move up in the ranks of the factory, nonetheless he or she would continue to be described as a worker. Students, on the other hand, face a necessary rupture in their role (i.e., their graduation), meaning that the student movement is continuously transient. However, the movement's effects are not transient as students might continue their political activities beyond university or college. The book observes that a number of Egyptian student leaders later became prominent politicians—for example, Hamdeen Sabahi and Abdel Monem Aboul Fotouh (two of the most prominent candidates in the 2012 Egyptian presidential elections) were both student activists and leaders in the 1970s. Many student leaders became involved in politics and activism after their university education. This is particularly pertinent to many student leaders of the 1990s, who would form networks among themselves that would facilitate the 2011 uprising, as will be discussed in Chapters 5 and 6.

Mobilizations, revolutions and uprisings

What does this book mean by the term 'mobilization'? Mobilization is used herein to denote a protest movement united to achieve a common goal. Mobilizations can be deliberately planned or an ad hoc response to specific socio-economic or political issues. Within the Egyptian context, as the book explores, the goal can be specific (such as workers protesting for higher wages, or students protesting against the presence of security forces on campus) or broad (for example, calling for the removal of the British in the pre-1952 period—see Chapter 2; or calling for accountability for the 1967 War as seen in 1968 during the Nasser era—see Chapter 3).

The word 'mobilization' gives the analysis a certain flexibility, which allows it to view protests broadly as the terminology otherwise employed remains polarizing to this very day. For example, the 1977 protests against price increases were infamously labeled by Sadat as 'the intifada of thieves,'[19] while others labeled it the 'Bread Intifada.'[20] More recently setting aside the theories of pro-Mubarak and pro-regime supporters that the 2011 uprising was a 'foreign conspiracy,'[21]—we find that the terminology is divided between 'revolution' and 'uprising.' In her seminal volume, Theda Skocpol differentiates between a social revolution and a rebellion:

> Social revolutions are rapid, basic transformations of a society's state and class structures; and they are accompanied and in part and carried by class-based revolts from below. Social revolutions are set apart from other sorts of conflicts and transformative processes above all by the combination of two coincidences; the coincidence of societal structural change with class upheaval; and the coincidence of political with social transformation. In contrast, rebellions, even when successful, may involve the revolt of subordinate classes—but they do not eventuate in structural change.[22]

Furthermore, in Skocpol's view a revolution is a process in which "a mass based movement, coalescing with the aid of ideology and organization, consciously undertakes to overthrow the existing government and perhaps the entire social order and if it wins, undertakes to establish its own authority and program."[23] While Skocpol's view is deeply rooted in the Marxist tradition, it carries apt observations for non-Marxist analysis as well. Viewed three years later, and in light of the overthrow of the President Mohamed Morsi in 2013, it is clear that the Egyptian army is in control of the machinations of the state, and indeed was always in control, raising doubts as to whether the 2011 protests against the Mubarak regime can truly be described as a 'revolution.' They may be considered a 'revolutionary episode,' but they did not result in the deep structural changes described by Skocpol and so do not meet the criteria of a revolution.

Following the same logic, what makes the Urabi officer movement a revolution?[24] Or the 1919 uprising a revolution? Neither resulted in the change seen, for example, in the Russian or French revolutions. Arguably, using the term 'revolution' to describe a mobilization can be highly subjective and primarily outcome based. However, it is not the goal of this book to deny the agency of the Egyptian people in mass movement. Quite the opposite: this book seeks to highlight how at times the labor and student movements were successful in challenging the state at various historical junctures. To maintain a balanced and nuanced view, the book uses term 'uprising' to describe the various mobilizations.

Methodology

Interviews

This book uses material from a number of interviews that I conducted from December 2012 to September 2013 during fieldwork for my doctoral dissertation, when I was based in Cairo as a Visiting Fellow at the American University in Cairo (AUC). The interviews were conducted in Cairo, Alexandria and Mahallah and included a wide range of participants: government officials, academics, economists, opposition leaders, student activists, labor activists and workers.

I was able to meet activists who took part in mobilizations from the 1960s onwards, but in writing Chapter 2, which investigates mobilizations prior to 1952, I had to rely solely on secondary sources as many participants had passed away. All interviews were semi-structured; some were recorded; others were off the record. Some interviewers consented to be named, while others preferred anonymity.

Despite the sample's relatively modest size, it nonetheless provided a valuable set of detailed qualitative ideas and recollections from a cross-section of Egyptian society and has purposefully included participants from various political currents and different socio-economic backgrounds. The qualitative data is also supplemented by quantitative data and analysis by scholars, think tanks and international organizations to support the findings of the qualitative data. Furthermore, as the interviews were semi-structured and extended discussions, interviewees had agency to emphasize what they wanted and to contribute personal stories, anecdotes, recollections of moods and emotions, so not only state simple facts.

Participant observation

Within the broader genre of political ethnography,[25] I used participant observation[26] as a method in the research for the Conclusion (on the 2011 uprising). While the book does use a variety of primary and secondary sources that focus on the 2011 uprising, my own observations, recollections and notes were also helpful in corroborating some of the other material.

A limitation of both the interview and the participant observation methodologies also needs to be state clearly. There is potential for researcher bias, as I was an active participant in the events of 2011. To that end, I employed some of the tactics advanced by Shenton.[27] These included the triangulation of the data, which involves the combination of several methods of data collection such as interviews, personal observations and corroborating the data with supporting research.[28] Another form of triangulation is selecting different interviewees from various backgrounds, which I have also done here. This insures that individual viewpoints and experiences "can be verified against others and, ultimately, a rich picture of the attitudes, needs or behavior of those under scrutiny may be constructed based on the contributions of a range of people."[29]

Finally, I used the strategy of 'peer scrutiny' to negate any perceived researcher bias. This was accomplished by submitting chapters of the book for review by a number of academics for constructive feedback. 'Peer scrutiny' is important as it allows others to challenge the assumptions I have made as my proximity to the subject may have inhibited my ability to view the project with complete detachment.[30]

Secondary sources

A variety of journals and books were consulted and are utilized and referenced throughout the research. The book also uses various CAPMAS data sets, reports from the World Bank, the IMF, as well as several UNDP Human Development Reports. Reports by various NGOs and think tanks in Egypt such as the Land Centre for Economic Rights and Egyptian Centre for Economic Studies (ECES) were also utilized.

Book structure

The current chapter introduced the research and its aims, made the relevant definitions and highlighted the book's contribution, methodology and structure.

Chapter 2 critically sketches the structural changes that the Egyptian economy underwent from the time of Muhammad Ali until the early twentieth century and its impact on society. It provides the historical background of the development of the labor and student movement. It utilizes elements of social movement theory to critically assess changes in the opportunities and threats faced by the labor and student movements. Finally, it uses the 1946 uprising and *al-Lajna al-Ṭullābiyya wa al-ʿUmmāliyya* (The National Committee for Students and Workers) as the case study to assess the diffusion and spillover processes that have occurred between the movements.

Chapter 3 focuses on the Nasser era. It first provides background to the development of the Egyptian political economy under the Free Officers and during the Nasser presidency. It investigates the labor and student movements and their complex relationship with the new regime. It highlights the major opportunity structures of that era, including the 1967 defeat,[31] as well as analyzing the threat environment. Finally, it investigates the diffusion and spillover processes between the labor and student movements and critically assesses how successfully the movements were able to challenge the state during the 1968 uprising.

Chapter 4 examines the Sadat era and starts by providing the background on the development of Egyptian political economy as the regime sought to solidify its power. It investigates the student and labor movements and their evolving relationships with the Sadat regime. It seeks to highlight the major opportunity and threat structures of that era. Finally, it assesses the diffusion and spillover processes between the labor and student movements and critically evaluates how successful the movements were in challenging the state during the 1977 uprising.

Chapter 5 focuses on the first two decades of the Mubarak era (1981–2001) and provides the background on the development of Egyptian political economy under the Mubarak regime. It discusses the economic situation at the time, and investigates some of the economic decisions made by the regime. It analyzes the student and labor movements and their relationships with the regime, as well as the impact of Egyptian political economy. It seeks to highlight the major opportunity and threat structures of that era. Unlike previous chapters, Chapter 5 will not have a section on diffusion between movements in the first two decades of the Mubarak era, as arguably such diffusion was tenuous at best. During the final decade of the Mubarak regime we do see clear processes of diffusion, which will be discussed in the final chapter.

Chapter 6 focuses on the last decade of Mubarak's rule and starts with an analysis of the political economy of the regime in its last decade. It investigates the student and youth movements within the context of Egypt's budding democratization movement that appeared in opposition to *mashrūʿ al-tawrith* (the hereditary project that denotes the Mubarak family and their inner circle's ambition and plan for Gamal to become president). It focuses on the resurgent labor movement as it moves from its corporatization to directly challenging the regime. Finally, it analyzes the January 25 uprising within the context of opportunities, threats, resource mobilizations and diffusional/spillover processes.

The final section of the book concludes and briefly summarizes the main points of the book, highlighting the findings as well as their limitations. The conclusion will also present implications of the research, as well as comment on potential future lines of inquiry to build on this work.

Notes

1 Aristotle, *Nicomachean Ethics*, viii.9.1160a.
2 Paul Frandsen, "Editing Reality: The Turin Strike Papyrus," *Studies in Egyptology* 1 (1990): 166–199.
3 Nazih Ayubi, *Overstating the Arab State: Politics and Society in the Middle East* (London: I.B. Tauris, 1995), 100.
4 For an understanding of the multifaceted origins of Egyptian nationalism, see for example Juan Cole, *Colonialism and Revolution in the Middle East: Social and Cultural Origins of Egypt's Urabi Movement* (Cairo: The American University in Cairo

Press, 1999), Jamal Mohammed Ahmed, *Intellectual Origins of Egyptian Nationalism* (London: Oxford University Press, 1960) and Abdel Aziz Ramadan, *Taṭāwur al-ḥarakat al-waṭaniyya fi misr, 1918–1936* (The Development of the Egyptian Nationalist Movement, 1918–1936) (Cairo: Dār al-Kitāb al-ʿArabī, 1968).

5 Alan Richards and John Waterbury, *A Political Economy of the Middle East*, 3rd edn (Boulder: Westview, 2006), 7.

6 Jack Goldstone and Charles Tilly, "Threat (and Opportunity): Popular Action and State Response in the Dynamics of Contentious Action," in Ronald Aminzade, Jack Goldstone, Doug McAdam, Elizabeth Perry, William Sewell, Sidney Tarrow and Charles Tilly (eds.), *Silence and Voice in the Study of Contentious Politics* (Cambridge: Cambridge University Press, 2001), 179–194.

7 Listed in Paul Almeida, "Opportunity Organizations and Threat-Induced Contention: Protest Waves in Authoritarian Settings," *American Journal of Sociology* 109, no. 2 (September 2003): 345–400.

8 See Anthony Oberschall, "Opportunities and Framing in the Eastern European Revolts of 1989," in Doug McAdam, John D. McCarthy and Mayer N. Zald (eds.), *Comparative Perspectives on Social Movements* (Cambridge: Cambridge University Press, 1996), 93–121.

9 Ibid., 351–353.

10 See John Waterbury, *The Egypt of Nasser and Sadat: The Political Economy of Two Regimes* (Princeton: Princeton University Press, 1983), Robert Springborg, *Mubarak's Egypt: Fragmentation of the Political Order* (Boulder: Westview Press, 1989) and Raymond A. Hinnesbuch Jr, *Egyptian Politics Under Sadat: The Post-Populist Development of an Authoritarian–Modernizing State* (Cambridge: Cambridge University Press, 1988).

11 For examples of this with regards to the Islamist movement, see Carrie Rosefsky Wickham, *Mobilizing Islam: Religion, Activism and Political Change in Egypt* (New York: Columbia University Press, 2002). With regards to the labor movement, see Joel Beinin and Zachary Lockman, *Workers on the Nile: Nationalism, Communism, Islam and the Egyptian Working Class, 1882–1954* (Princeton: Princeton University Press, 1987). With regards to the student movement, see Ahmad Abdalla, *The Student Movement and National Politics in Egypt, 1923–1973* (London: Saqi Books, 1985).

12 Richards and Waterbury, *Political Economy of the Middle East*, 7.

13 UNDP, *Political Economy Analysis*, UNDP Oslo Governance Centre (UNDP, n.d.), www.undp.org/content/undp/en/home/ourwork/democraticgovernance/oslo_governance_centre/analysis_and_learning/political_economyanalysis.html (accessed October 1, 2014).

14 Sidney Tarrow, *Power in Movement: Social Movements and Contentious Politics* (Cambridge: Cambridge University Press, 1998), 17.

15 David Snow and Robert Benford, "Master Frames and Cycles of Protest," in A.D. Morris and C.M. Mueller (eds.), *Frontiers in Social Movement Theory* (New Haven: Yale University Press, 1992), 137.

16 See for example Robert Benford and David Snow, "Framing Processes and Social Movements: An Overview and Assessment," *Annual Review of Sociology* 26 (2000).

17 David S. Meyer and Nancy Whittier, "Social Movement Spillover," *Social Problems* 41, no. 2 (May 1994): 277.

18 A.J.M. Craig, "Egyptian Students," *Middle East Journal* 7, no. 3 (Summer 1935): 293–299.

19 Raymond William Baker, *Sadat and After: Struggles for Egypt's Political Soul* (Cambridge, MA: Harvard University Press, 1990), 120.

20 Riyad Moharam, "*Dhikra intifādāt al-khubz 18–19 January 1977*" (The Memory of the Bread Intifada, 18–19 January 1977), *al-Hiwar*, www.ahewar.org/debat/show.art.asp?aid=241223 (accessed October 1, 2014).

21 According to Mubarak's lawyer, Farid el Dib, the January 25 uprising was a

"US–Qatari–Turkish-Muslim Brotherhood" conspiracy that aimed at overtaking Egypt. Such comments and allegations became increasingly popular in public discourse after the ouster of President Mohamed Morsi in 2013. See Suha Yahyia, "*al-Dīb: 25 Yanayer Mu'amara Amrīkiya Qaṭariya Turkiya Ikhwāniya Tastahdif Maṣr*" (El-Deeb: 25th of January was a US Qatari Turkish Brotherhood Conspiracy Targeting Egypt), *al-Dostor*, September 27, 2014, www.dostor.org/684910 (accessed October 1, 2014).

22 Theda Skocpol, *States and Social Revolutions: A Comparative Analysis of France, Russia and China* (Cambridge: Cambridge University Press, 1979), 4.

23 Ibid., 14–15.

24 The description *Thawrat 'Urabī* (Urabi's Revolution) is widely used in Egypt to describe Urabi's officer movement. Non-Egyptian scholars have also used the term 'Revolt.' See Donald Malcolm Reid, "The 'Urabi Revolution and the British Conquest, 1879–1882," in M.W. Daly (ed.), *The Cambridge History of Egypt* (Cambridge: Cambridge University Press, 1998), 217–238.

25 For an elaboration on political ethnography, see Gianpaolo Baiocchi and Brian T. Connor, "The *Ethnos* in the *Polis*: Political Ethnography as a Mode of Inquiry," *Sociology Compass* 2, no. 1 (2008): 139–155.

26 See Andra Gillespie and Melissa R. Michelson, "Participant Observation and the Political Scientist: Possibilities, Priorities, and Practicalities," *PS: Political Science and Politics* 44, no. 2 (April 2011): 261–265.

27 Andrew K. Shenton, "Strategies for Ensuring Trustworthiness in Qualitative Research Projects," *Education for Information* 22 (2004): 63–75.

28 Ibid., 65.

29 Ibid., 66.

30 Ibid., 67.

31 As established by Tarrow, a defeat is a major opportunity for regime challengers. See Tarrow, *Power in Movement*, 178–179.

2 The pre-1952 era

> It is almost never when a state of things is the most detestable that it is smashed, but when, beginning to improve, it permits men to breathe, to reflect, to communicate their thoughts with each other, and to gauge by what they already have the extent of their rights and their grievances. The weight, although less heavy, seems then all the more unbearable.
>
> Alexis de Tocqueville, *The Old Regime and the Revolution*[1]

Introduction

Napoleon Bonaparte's invasion of Egypt in 1798 ushered in an era of European colonialism in the Middle East. This era can be seen retrospectively within the context of the earlier failure of the second Ottoman siege of Vienna in 1683. The subsequent, if gradual, Ottoman retreat signaled the beginning of a significant reversal of fortune to the advantage of European powers. Henceforth the Middle East would come to fatefully experience the weight of the encounter with several rising and expanding European powers.

The French occupation of Egypt ended in 1801, when a joint Ottoman–British expedition succeeded in expelling the French forces, and Egypt reverted to nominal Ottoman control. Muhammad Ali, an Albanian commander, was able to consolidate his power over Egypt and was recognized by the Sublime Porte in Istanbul as *Wali* (viceroy) of Egypt. Termed 'the founder of modern Egypt,'[2] Muhammad Ali began modernizing agriculture, industry and the Egyptian army.

By the late nineteenth century, deep changes were unfolding in all aspects of Egyptian society. Economic activity was becoming further integrated into the newly emerging global economy, society was experiencing a transformation and the labor and student movements were coming into being as independent movements, but also as part of the broader nationalist movement. This chapter provides background to the changing nature of Egyptian political economy, and critically examines the emerging labor and student movement and their role in mobilizations in the decades prior to the 1952 *coup d'état*.

The development of the Egyptian economy

During Muhammad Ali's reign (1805–1848) the Egyptian economy began to be integrated in the global economy. Using innovative and sometimes brutal methods,[3] he was able to institute modern agrarian practices and grow cotton at industrial levels for foreign export. It is under his reign that the Egyptian economy began to enter its capitalist phase, as he focused on export cash crops. Grain and cotton in particular became a boon for the Egyptian economy, opening new horizons of trade with European countries and many European traders and farmers came to Egypt with the latest advances in European agricultural technology.[4] Even though Muhammad Ali had set the Egyptian economy on its capitalist course, ensuring the centrality of the state in this transformation, it was not yet thoroughly capitalist in its operation. Wahba argues that "the state created by Muhammad Ali represented an imitation of the industrial states of Europe. It was 'capitalism without capitalists.' The superstructure of a strong bureaucracy and industrial monopolies existed, but not the relations of production."[5] This is a reflection of the fact that the *Wali* himself was the main capitalist business owner and producer, and the European traders had to deal directly with Muhammad Ali and his representatives. Workers at that time were conscripted as farmers, workers or soldiers in a semi-feudal system.

Muhammad Ali needed agricultural exports to finance his plans for modernizing the Egyptian army, creating a manufacturing base as well as modernizing the state bureaucracy, all while attempting to move away from tutelage to the Ottoman Sultan. Egypt's external trade was nominal during the French occupation but under Muhammad Ali it was the engine of growth for the Egyptian economy.[6] Egypt at the time had a lower population and thus reached self-sufficiency in food, an accomplishment no ruler of Egypt has been able to achieve since then.[7] There are four key economic and social factors that characterized the reign of the Muhammad Ali dynasty and that would have a lasting effect on Egyptian political economy: one-crop export economy; external borrowing; economic dominance of foreigners and finally population growth and urbanization.

One-crop export economy

Within the state structure and policies variable outlined by Richards and Waterbury is the strategy of agro-export led growth, where the export of agricultural produce becomes the centerpiece of economic strategy.[8] This is relevant to the Egyptian case as agriculture and more specifically cotton became the engine of growth for the Egyptian economy from the Muhammad Ali era onwards and would dominate the pre-1952 years. Cotton had been growing in Egypt, albeit at in smaller quantities, for a long time but production had been limited and was of lower quality. A French engineer named Jumel who worked in a state-owned factory first brought the economic potential of cotton to the attention of Muhammad Ali. After noticing the long staple cotton variety in a Cairo garden, Jumel began growing it on an experimental basis in his own garden. After he presented his findings to Muhammad Ali, the *Wali* began a campaign to grow it on an industrial scale. By 1821, cotton was cultivated on 100,000 to 150,000 *feddans* (one *feddan* equals 1.038 acres).[9]

Due to the dependence of cotton cultivation on huge amounts of water, in the early years, the farming of cotton was limited to the fields adjacent to the Nile. By 1830, Muhammad Ali had built a network of canals that made it possible to grow cotton on a much larger scale, such that by 1836 it was growing on 320,000 *feddans*.[10] Before cotton was mass-produced, its exports were negligible. However, as the quality of the cotton became globally known, coupled with higher demand and higher prices, by 1836 cotton began to account for more than 80 percent of total Egyptian exports.[11] Egypt thus became a one-crop export economy that over-relied on cotton, fitting within Richards and Waterbury's description of the agro-export led growth development model.[12] This would have three main adverse effects: first, it put Egypt firmly in the eyes of colonial powers (particularly the British, who sought cotton as a raw material for their mills). Second, after colonizing Egypt, the British administration strongly resisted diversification efforts, ensuring that the economy would continue to rely heavily on cotton. Third, the economy was vulnerable to external price shocks and the fluctuations of global cotton prices, putting it through several cycles of boom and bust.

External borrowing

The second factor affecting Egyptian political economy in the nineteenth and early twentieth century that also falls within the state structure and policies variable was the reliance of the successors of Muhammad Ali on external debt. Ironically, Muhammad Ali himself disliked relying on external debt, and was able to finance his expansions through a manufacturing base of small industries, exporting cotton and foodstuffs to Europe. During his reign, there were occasional deficits in the budget to finance certain projects, or to pay the *jizya* (tax) to the Sultan in Istanbul, but soon the budget was back in surplus. It is under his heirs that external borrowing and all that this entails in terms of loss of agency began to manifest strongly in the Egyptian economy. Crouchley argues that manufacturing and exports afforded Muhammad Ali a degree of autonomy unprecedented in modern Egyptian history.[13] This autonomy was lost as Muhammad Ali's successors began to borrow heavily to finance projects, while relying less on international trade as a source of revenue.

Under the short reign of Said Pasha (1854–1863), Egypt accrued what can be construed as its first ever substantial European debt. In 1862 the German Oppenheim Bank lent the Egyptian treasury 2.5 million British pounds at 11 percent interest rate collateralized by the Nile Delta land tax.[14] Said Pasha only received 84 percent of the loan after fees and charges, and the loan was payable over 30 years making the compounded interest payment and original loan valued at 8.2 million British pounds, approximately four times the value of the amount handed to him.[15] However, unlike Muhammad Ali, who spent on grand projects to attempt to modernize Egypt, Said Pasha directed minimal money at modernization, while spending copious amounts of money on his palaces and personal expenses, at one stage even building himself his own personal railroad line between Alexandria and Marriout.[16]

It is under the reign of Ismail Pasha (1879–1863) that unprecedented levels of borrowing from European bankers materialized. Initially, international events had some positive impact on the Egyptian economy. The American Civil War had started in 1861, two years before Ismail assumed power. By the first two years of his reign, the US cotton industry had almost ground to a halt, leading the price of Egyptian cotton to increase by 100 percent as well as trebling Egyptian cotton exports, creating a windfall for the treasury.[17] However, after contributing to the financing of the Suez canal and Ismail's extravagant spending throught his rule, Egypt's external debt reached 91 million Egyptian pounds (EGP) with the annual interest and charges reaching an astonishing 80 percent of the overall budget.[18] Global economic changes were also having a local impact. As the century progressed, the economy would prove no less susceptible to the international economic situation.

Due to the outbreak of World War I, the Egyptian economy grew on the back of rising global cotton prices. During the war years, the economy saw a 139 million EGP budgetary surplus,[19] although its majority went to servicing the debt that had been accumulating since the time of Khedive Ismail. As time progressed, the social and economic situation became characterized by unemployment, unequal distribution of wealth and the growing marginalization of large segments of the population. The Egyptian economy of the 1930s and 1940s had not been immune to the Great Depression. As Mabro writes:

> While capital was flowing out of the country, Egypt's population and her need for complementary resources were growing. An increasing shortage for land called for larger investments to offset diminishing returns, but this was not forthcoming. By the 1930s the misery of the *fellah* (peasant) had become intolerable and underemployment a permanent feature of the economy.[20]

The deep class divisions that stratified the masses of the poor from a small but extremely wealthy elite were becoming ever more apparent. This elite class included landed gentry, modern agrarian capitalists, the Egyptian capitalist bourgeoisie (commerce, banking and 'captains' of industry), and closely connected foreigners.

Foreign dominance of the Egyptian economy

The third factor affecting Egyptian political economy in the nineteenth and the first half of the twentieth century was the foreign dominance of the economy. Europeans had strongly exerted their influence in Egypt since the time of the

Khedive Ismail; by the late nineteenth century, foreigners controlled a large part of the economy. Such foreign control manifested itself in three main areas: national debt carried in Egypt's public finances, a legacy of Khedive Ismail's over-spending; land ownership, where at one stage foreigners owned 50 percent of the country's agricultural land; and foreign monopolies over entire industries.[21]

After being invited by Khedive Ismail and subsequent rulers to be involved in economic development, foreigners took full advantage of the invitations and had increasingly begun to reside in Egypt and some even became Egyptian citizens, making their presence felt in the local economy and business associations. When the Egyptian Federation of Industry was established in 1922, all 11 of its directors lived in Egypt, but only three were Egyptian citizens.[22] Moreover, foreign control of the economy was not limited to major industries, as foreigners also established a lead in small business enterprises. Lord Cromer, British Consul General to Egypt from 1883 to 1907, wrote, "Boot mending, as well as boot making, is almost entirely in the hands of the Greeks and Armenians. The drapery trade is controlled by Jews, Syrians, Europeans, the tailoring trades by the Jews."[23] Even though Lord Cromer was able for the first time in years to balance the Egyptian budget and bring it back to solvency, nonetheless the British ensured the Egyptian economy would rely on agriculture and not industry. Afaf Marsot writes:

> By the turn of the century Cromer had rendered Egypt solvent, albeit at the expense of Egyptian industry, and had transformed agriculture into a monoculture, cotton, to feed the mills of Lancashire. The cultivation of tobacco was prohibited and an excise tax imposed on imported tobacco helped to balance the budget. Attempts to set up local industries were discouraged by Cromer, who loaded them with tariffs equal to the taxes paid on imported goods, rendering them non-competitive. Textiles, which should have thrived using Egyptian cotton, were deliberately discouraged so that cotton could be exported. Egypt was relegated to becoming a provider of raw materials for Britain.[24]

Throughout the early twentieth century, the economy continued to rely heavily on agriculture, with some primitive industries taking hold. The heavy reliance on the export of cotton remained and exposed the economy to outside shocks. Even though import substitution industrialization (ISI) became the dominant economic strategy of the post-1952 state, elements from within the Egyptian capitalists were advocating diversification away from cotton and into industry. Even though many capitalists from the era had long-standing partnerships with European banks and industries,[25] nonetheless they recognized there was a clear need for an Egyptian bank. The capital necessary for such a shift, however minor, from agriculture to industry became available after the foundation of Banque Misr by Talaat Harb Pasha in 1920. The bank was founded as an attempt by Egyptians to have more influence in their own economy and to be able to diversify investment activities beyond the cotton industry.[26] To that end, it attracted local capital that would have been idle or that would have gone as deposits into European banks. Parallel to the banking operations, the bank also conducted research into the economy. A 1929 Banque Misr report was an early advocate of industrial substitution, calling for "a ten year industrial development plan, joint public private ventures, and a state sponsored industrial development bank," which differed little from the plans Nasser implemented 30 years later.[27]

The British occupation had acted as a barrier to Egyptian industrialization. The British had opposed industrial development in Egypt by working against the construction of large-scale industries such as textile mills that would be able to use local raw material to produce a finished product, fearing increased competition for their own mills. Lord Cromer's stated policy was the exportation of raw Egyptian cotton and the importation of finished British goods. He argued that Egypt was a predominantly agricultural country that did not need an industrial base.[28] To that end, the British formulated laws to attempt to derail any Egyptian industrial development. They cancelled laws that protected local industry and raised taxes on the importation of industrial machinery, meanwhile allowing certain industries that fed cotton exports, such as small factories preparing raw cotton for manufacturing.[29]

In response to the political and economic situation, there were stirrings of nationalism from the late eighteenth century onwards, as Egyptians began to resist colonialism. This began with the Urabi uprising in 1879, originally led by the army, which could be considered the first mass mobilization in modern Egyptian history after segments of the population rallied around Urabi's army movement.[30] Saʿad Zaghloul and the Wafd Movement emerged in 1919 with huge support from various segments of society. Large segments of the population were opposed to British occupation, including students, workers and members of the army itself. Even after nominal independence from the British in 1922, there was still widespread social unrest, magnified by the inability of King Farouk's regime and street protests to move British troops out of Egypt and the Canal Zone.

Even though the Anglo-Egyptian Treaty of 1936 had recognized Egypt's nominal independence, only three years later, after the outbreak of World War II, Britain again increased its political and economic dominance of Egypt. The Suez Canal would prove vital to the war effort, held by the Allies and coveted by the Axis powers. Italy's interest in the canal had been growing since it invaded Ethiopia in 1935, seeking to create a colonial empire in East Africa that included Eritrea and Somalia. Egypt's people, economy and resources would be enlisted in the war effort.

In 1940, the Sabry government issued a law extending the *imtiaz* (concession) of the British-backed Ahly Bank for 40 years, which gave the bank the power to print Egyptian banknotes—effectively giving control of the economy to the British, who through it were now able to control fiscal policy. The printing of banknotes meant that the British inadvertently increased inflation, restricted foreign trade and controlled the price of cotton and other agricultural produce. Even part of the war effort was funded by Egypt, for the Ahly Bank issued banknotes in lieu of supplies needed for the Allied troops stationed in Egypt, creating a debt of 450 million British pounds. All these factors contributed to reduce the purchasing power of the Egyptian pound.[31]

Population growth and urbanization

The fourth factor effecting Egyptian political economy in the nineteenth and early twentieth century was population growth, which helped contribute to the related problem of over-urbanization that would develop over the coming decades. The population of Egypt in 1800 was estimated to be nearly 2.5 million. With development of agricultural practices and irrigation facilities in the nineteenth century, the population steadily increased such that by 1882 when the British occupation of Egypt began, the population reached 6.8 million. Table 2.1 highlights the population growth and rural migration to the city from 1821 to 1907. Each census since 1897, however imprecise, showed a further increase, and by the 1937 census, the population totaled 15.9 million, and by 1947 was estimated to be approximately 17.3 million.[32]

The Egyptian economy had remained mostly agrarian as the population grew, in contrast to the situation in Europe, where the increase in population was accompanied by industrialization. The actual area under cultivation did not grow proportionally to accommodate the population growth: in 1882, cultivated land amounted to 4.7 million *feddans*; by the 1897 census, this area amounted to 5.0 million *feddans*; in 1937, the area rose to 5.3 million. Owing to the great expansion of perennial irrigation, the crop area increased from 4.8 million *feddans* in 1882 to 8.3 million in 1937.[33] As the population increased at a much faster rate than either the cultivated area or the crop area, the holdings were rapidly fragmented, forcing many rural dwellers to move to the cities. Deep structural changes were unfolding in society as rural migration to urban centers began to increase exponentially, in part due to greater education and job opportunities.

The continued expansion of education and state services resulted in an influx of migrants from the rural areas of Egypt to urban centers. The rate of employment and urban infrastructure were unable to match the rate of the migrant influx, and many rural migrants were unable to adapt to city life. Ibrahim describes the migrant population as urban villagers who "live in, but are not of the city."[34] A large segment of these urban villagers are "floating internal refugees with no homes but city streets. They attend no school, do no work, have no cash, and buy no goods."[35]

Table 2.2, which is based on data from the 1947 census, shows that by the end of the 1940s five million out of a total population of 19 million resided in urban centers, the largest being Cairo and Alexandria,[36] and that this trend would continue over the coming decades. The combination of population growth, urbanization and lack of services and jobs in urban centers, all occurring under the British occupation, would be key factors in facilitating mobilization against colonial rule, and also against future regimes in Egypt. Within the context of Richards and Waterbury's third variable, 'social actors,' Goldstone and Tilly postulate that:

Table 2.1 Population of towns over 20,000 inhabitants and selected other important towns (1821–1907)

	1821–1826	*1846*	*Average annual growth rate (%) (1821–1846)*	*1882 census*	*Average annual growth rate (%) (1846–1882)*	*1897 census*	*Average annual growth rate (%) (1882–1897)*	*1907 census*	*Average annual growth rate (%) (1897–1907)*
Lower Egypt Inland									
Cairo	218,560	256,679	+0.65	374,830	+1.0	570,062	+12.5	654,476	+1.3
Tanta	10,000	19,500	+2.6	33,750	+1.5	57,289	+3.5	54,437	–0.5
al-Mahallah	17,000	20,000	+0.65	27,823	+0.9	31,100	+0.7	33,547	+0.7
Mansoura	8,500	9,886	+0.60	26,942	+2.8	36,131	+2.0	40,279	+1.0
Damanhour	–	8,000	–	19,624	+2.5	32,122	+3.3	38,752	+1.9
Zagazig	–	–	–	19,815	–	35,715	+3.9	34,999	–0.2
Bilqas	–	–	–	–	–	19,469	–	25,473	+2.7
Minuf	–	–	–	16,293	–	19,726	+1.3	22,316	+1.2
Shibin al-Koum	–	4,500	–	16,250	+3.6	20,512	+1.5	21,567	+0.5
Lower Egypt Coastal									
Alexandria	12,528	164,359	+10.3	231,396	+0.95	319,766	+2.1	332,247	+0.3
Damietta	13,600	37,089	+4.0	34,044	–0.20	31,515	–0.5	29,354	–0.7
Rosetta	13,400	18,300	+1.2	16,666	–0.26	14,286	+1.0	16,810	+1.6
Suez	2,900	4,160	+1.4	10,559	+2.6	17,173	+3.2	18,374	+0.7
Port Said	–	–	–	15,560	–	42,095	+6.2	49,884	+1.7
Middle Egypt									
Al Fayoum	–	–	–	25,799	–	31,262	+1.2	37,270	+1.8
Minya	–	–	–	15,900	–	20,404	+1.7	27,221	+2.9
Bani Suwayf	–	–	–	10,085	–	15,297	+2.8	23,357	+4.2
Mallawi	–	–	–	10,777	–	15,471	+2.4	20,249	+2.8
Upper Egypt									
Assiut	17,000	20,000	+0.4	31,389	+1.24	42,012	+1.9	39,442	–.06
Akhmim	–	–	–	18,792	–	27,953	+2.6	23,795	–1.6
Qena	–	–	–	15,402	–	24,364	+3.0	20,069	–1.9
Girga	–	7,500	–	14,819	+1.9	17,271	+1.0	19,893	+1.4
Aswan	–	–	–	–	–	13,005	–	12,618	–0.3
Total Population	4,423,396	4,476,439	+0.4	7,840,271	+1.6	9,734,405	+1.4	11,287,359	+1.5

Source: Mohammed Chaichian, “The Effects of World Capitalist Economy on Urbanization in Egypt, 1800–1970),” *International Journal of Middle East Studies* 21, no. 1 (February 1988): 26.

Table 2.2 Total population of urban places in Egypt arranged by rank order of descending size (census of 1947 data)

Name	*Population*	*Rank*	*Administrative function*
Cairo	2,090,654	1	Governorate
Alexandria	919,024	2	Governorate
Port Said	177,073	3	Governorate
Tanta	139,926	4	Province capital
Mahallah	115,758	5	Province capital
Suez	107,244	6	Governorate
Mansoura	101,965	7	Province capital
Assuit	90,103	8	Province capital
Damanhour	84,352	9	Province capital
Zagazig	81,813	10	Province capital
Fayoum	73,642	11	Province capital
Al Minya	70,298	12	Province capital
Ismailia	68,229	13	Governorate
Giza	66,516	14	Province capital
Beni Suif	57,106	15	Province capital
Damietta	53,631	16	Governorate
Sohag	43,168	17	Province capital
Qena	42,929	18	Province capital
Shebin al Koum	41,636	19	Province capital
Dawahi Misr	41,390	20	Industrial district
Kom Ombo	39,235	21	Agricultural
Tahta	37,095	22	District center
Benha	35,880	23	Province capital
Malawi	35,624	24	Province capital
Akhmim	34,788	25	District center
Belqas	34,771	26	District center
Guerga	33,631	27	District center
Menuf	31,475	28	District center
Dessuq	31,334	29	District center
Edku	30,033	30	Agricultural
Qalyub	30,021	31	District center
Rosetta	29,558	32	District center
Mit Ghamr	29,030	33	District center
Biala	28,757	34	District center
Luxor	27,457	35	District center
Zefta	27,404	36	District center
Aswan	26,343	37	Province capital
Edfu	26,192	38	District center
Abu Tig	25,952	39	District center
Esneh	25,811	40	District center

Source: Janet L. Abu-Lughod, "Urbanization in Egypt: Present State and Future Prospects," *Economic Development and Cultural Change* 13, no. 3 (April 1965): 318–319.

Sustained population growth in excess of economic growth frequently alters the relationships among states, elites, and popular groups in ways that undermine stability. If increased demand produces inflation, real revenues to the government will fall unless taxes are raised; but that may be seen as

> highly unreasonable if peasants have less land, and workers are finding jobs scarce and their pay declining due to increased competition for jobs and resources. Urban population may increase disproportionately—and faster than urban administrations can increase housing, health, and police services—if the agricultural sector cannot absorb the population increase.[37]

From the early twentieth century onwards, the main Egyptian cities would strain under the pressure to absorb substantial numbers of rural migrants creating stress on all services. Abu Lughod argues that

> studies made in regions containing cities varying widely in size indicate that the per capita cost of providing municipal and private services may sky rocket, once population exceeds an optimum point of several thousand. Super-cities cost in new investment, overhead and municipal housekeeping many times more than their population would require if decentralized.[38]

The development of the Egyptian working class

The rise of the industrial working class in Egypt is intrinsically linked to the eighteenth-century Industrial Revolution in Europe. The appearance of mechanized technology in factories had led to increased demand and urban availability of non-agrarian jobs, which in turn yielded the subsequent increase in migration from rural to industrial areas. This was a phenomenon that first occurred in Europe, but which spread to the rest of the world, albeit somewhat later. Industrial relations began to develop between factory owners and factory workers. The latter did not own the means of production, but relied on selling their labor to the factory owners in return for wages.

Table 2.3 Growth of population in Egypt (1800–1957)

Year	*Population*	*Percentage increase during decade*
1800	2.4–3 million	–
1836	3–3.25 million	–
1871	5,250,000	–
1882	6,804,000	–
1897	9,715,000	–
1907	11,287,000	16.2
1917	12,751,000	13.0
1927	14,218,000	11.5
1937	15,933,000	12.1
1947	18,947,000	18.9
1957	26,080,000	36.8

Source: Charles Issawi, "Egypt Since 1800: A Study in Lop-Sided Development," *Journal of Economic History* 21, no. 1 (March 1961): 25.

The development of paid work in industrial manufacturing in the developing world coincided with the colonial period. As more advanced industrial countries exhausted internal development prospects, they set their eyes on the developing world as a source of raw material, as well as the perfect market for manufactured goods. Waves of European colonization began in Africa, forming a phase that can be considered the beginning of the development of the capitalist system in the global south. Until that period in the early eighteenth century, the economic modes in many of these countries were mostly agrarian, including also small artisans and hand workers. These traditional modes of production retreated in the face of capitalist development.[39]

Modern industry in Egypt also traces its beginnings to the time of Muhammad Ali, who first constructed mechanized factories and who effectively had a monopoly on all industrial production in the country. As factory work became available, many farmers, including those who had lost their land, began to sell their labor in factories. These new industrial factories were arguably the fraught nucleus of the industrial Egyptian working class: starting from the era of Muhammad Ali, workers toiling in the factories were effectively slaves owned by the *Wali*. By the turn of the twentieth century workers were no longer slaves per se, but were exposed to terrible working conditions exemplified by long hours, insufficient pay and unsafe working environments. The disparity in wages between Egyptian and foreign workers was high, and Egyptian workers were not able to get the promotions and career mobility that was afforded to some European workers.[40]

Despite these challenges, as the number of Egyptian workers grew, they were able to organize and coalesce around demands such as improving the working conditions and increased pay. After World War I, there was an exodus of European workers, and slowly Egyptian workers began to fill this void. The number of workers in the industry and transport sectors was 457,451 in 1907; by 1917 that number had reached 639,929 and continued to grow exponentially during the war.[41] It is during those years that the struggle of the Egyptian working class was no longer an economic one, but became part of the wider nationalist movement of the time that culminated in the 1919 uprising.

Unions

Labor activism has a long history in Egypt, with collective action starting as early as the beginning of the 1900s. Although Egypt at the time was predominantly an agrarian economy, some industries began to take hold which gradually brought with it labor activism. The first industrial action taken in Egypt was not by Egyptians but by foreign workers, predominantly Italians, who initiated a series of strikes at tobacco factories between 1899 and 1907 to demand better pay and working conditions.[42] At that stage, foreign workers enjoyed advantages over local workers in their working conditions and pay and sought to protect and increase those rights.

The main cause of the 1899 strike was the deployment of new machines to roll cigarettes, which led to widespread firing of foreign workers in tobacco companies. The foreign workers were able to leverage on their experience in industrial action gained in Europe and strike in opposition to the new machines and lower wages, and also preventing replacement workers from taking their place. The strike leaders had planned to stop work until the cigarette stocks were depleted, in order to force factory owners to negotiate a settlement. The strike was successful in its demands and the first union of cigarette rollers was formed.[43]

Even though European workers had more advantages than their Egyptian counterparts, the working conditions disadvantaged workers as a whole in terms of union protection and legislative frameworks. The participation of some Egyptian workers in these strikes arguably served as training for their own unionizing and bargaining. In 1900, Egyptian coal dockworkers in Alexandria went on strike to increase their wages and decrease their long working hours. As the century progressed, Egyptian workers began to unionize and take collective action in an organized fashion across the country. In the first decade of the twentieth century, tram workers in Cairo and Alexandria organized themselves into a loose union and (unsuccessfully) demanded better pay and conditions. These workers were met with British repression.[44]

World War I was a double-edged sword for Egyptian workers. The budding unions halted its activities in light of the imposed wartime anti-protesting laws; thousands of workers were also relocated in British facilities and bases situated in Palestine and Iraq. The working class also suffered from higher prices and rising unemployment. On the other hand, the war provided an opportunity for Egyptian industry to develop as imports were drastically reduced, leading to the further development of the industrial and trading base. The end of the war signaled the return of collective action by Egyptian workers, reigniting efforts to form unions and increase wages. The period from 1917 to 1919 witnessed a huge increase in strike action, which began to take national shape. Two main advocacy trends within the union movement began to appear: one toward building strong but separate local unions, and the other toward building a single large national workers' union.[45]

The labor movement and the 1919 revolution

The years before 1919 saw wide social discontent against the British occupation from all segments of society. Rich landowners were unhappy with the rules implemented by the British regarding the marketing and selling cotton. The growing educated *effendi* class was unhappy with the lack of job opportunities. The rural poor, many of whom had lost their work and moved to the cities in search of work, found the combination of price increases, inflation and lack of jobs to be particularly crushing. The *fellahin* were under constant threat of conscription to serve the British.[46] The situation was ripe for an uprising and the labor movement provided its initial fuel, to the extent that it is hard to differentiate between the series of strikes by the tram and rail workers in 1919 and the rest of the mobilizations that occurred afterwards. The workers had joined the protests at times in their individual capacities and other times as part of organized strikes and factory sit-ins.

The 1919 revolution in effect had two main currents, the first focused on ending the British protectorate and the other focused on improving the lives of the working class. Even though the currents differed in their composition and support base, they were able to agree that the main fight was against the colonizers. Recognizing its potential, various political forces (such as the Wafd) attempted to co-opt the labor movement from 1919 and continued to do so right through to the beginning of World War II. They did so in an effort to create unions that would be loyal to them alone. Even though the Wafd's main interest lay in protecting the middle class and landed elites, nonetheless it sought to bring the labor movement under its umbrella. In part this was due to:

- The fear that the labor movement would eventually be controlled by the growing communist movement, which had a radical economic agenda. The workers' chants in 1919 started with anti-British sentiment but grew to call for the nationalization of the Suez Canal, an end to landed estates, free education and the freedom to form unions.[47]
- The Wafd saw itself as representing the whole nation, and in that regard did not want a single segment of society representing itself.
- After witnessing the strong mobilizations by workers during the 1919 revolution, the Wafd recognized this power and sought to use it to augment its power and further its agenda.[48]

On May 19, 1924, the Wafd decided to form a Union of Nile Workers, led by Abdel Rahman Fahmy. The union's stated goals were to bring workers under one broad umbrella and try to improve the livelihood of its members and their families. This is considered one of the first attempts to form a national union in Egypt. Unfortunately, after the assassination of Sir Lee Stack and the resignation of the Wafd government, the Union of Nile Workers collapsed.[49] Political forces continued their efforts to co-opt the budding union movement. The Free Constitutionalist Party in 1930 formed a union of industrial workers led by Daood Rateb and the Wafd itself formed another union under the leadership of Abbas Halim.[50]

Many of the unions backed by political parties soon lost steam and were hemorrhaging members, as their support base was not built on solid ground from the working class. The leaders of these unions often came from political parties, were not elected by union members, and the centralized hierarchal structure of the unions all but guaranteed their control was secured by the political parties.[51] The political parties' efforts to control the unions in the pre-1952 era could be construed as a precursor to the complete corporatization that would occur in the Nasser era. Fearing communist influence, the Wafdist government of Sa'ad Zaghloul (January–November 1924) worked to suppress the unions' activities when it could not control them. Ginat argues that the government:

rejected the communists' and the workers' demands for radical change in the government's social policy. Zaghlul was determined to exercise his power over the communists and workers by employing severe measures intended to stamp out their anti-government activities and destroy their organizations. The strikes were suppressed and the government dissolved the communist-oriented General Confederation of Trade Unions and replaced it with the Wafd-led National Labour Union.[52]

The labor movement and World War II

Industrial production grew during World War II as Egypt was cut off from global markets, leading to the creation of small industries and the revival of major industries that had fallen away before the war due to international competition. Factories and workers were concentrated in large industrial areas, such as al-Mahallah al-Kubrah and Shubra al-Khimah. Even though there was a huge growth in industrial production, it only constituted 12 percent of GDP. Even so, it had a positive impact on the labor movement as the numbers of workers grew.[53]

The end of the war signaled a rapid decline in many of the industries that had supplied Allied forces—leading to massive unemployment, with an estimated 376,000 workers being forced out of work.[54] The existing labor laws were insufficient to protect worker's rights, with no minimum wage, no social insurance or safety net, and constant attacks on unions by the government and factory owners. The post-World War II unemployment levels also affected university graduates who were unable to find work.

Despite the continued government efforts to co-opt and suppress the labor movement, however, a select number of unions were able to stay partially independent and became increasingly politicized. Although the Trade Union Act of 1947 prohibited general federations, there was one conspicuous attempt by a group of trade unionists to thwart both the spirit and the letter of the law. Early in 1946, an organization calling itself the Workers' Committee of National Liberation (later simply the Workers' Congress) began to identify itself with national issues and to collaborate with student political groups. Along with a call for the evacuation of British troops, the Congress demanded higher wages, better working conditions and a reorganized labor administration.[55]

The development of the Egyptian student movement

The development of school and university education

The development of modern education can also be traced to the reign of Muhammad Ali, who sent educational missions to Europe whose participants returned to create an educational system that followed European (especially French) models of education. Between 1813 and 1847, such educational missions were sent to Italy, France and England. The first missions had the aim of learning military sciences, shipbuilding, navigation, engineering, mechanics and irrigation; only later were missions sent to learn law and humanities.[56]

The mode of traditional education in Egypt, which had not changed for centuries, involved a child starting in the *Kuttāb* (Quranic schools) to learn reading, writing, basic mathematics and Quranic recitation. The student would then have the option to enroll at al-Azhar to learn Islamic studies. Primary schools modeled on the European ones were established in 1830, and in 1837 a Ministry of Education was founded to manage these schools. The *Kuttāb* and al-Azhar remained outside the jurisdiction of the ministry, creating a dual system that Egypt would suffer from in the years to come.

With the influx of new ideas and schools of thought, Egyptian society began to experience what Moaddel terms a "cultural duality."[57] At an organizational level and as a consequence of the colonial experience, a two-tiered system began to take hold. In the field of law, Western court systems based on European laws appeared alongside traditional courts based on *Shariah*. In education, Western systems of schooling appeared with European curriculums next to traditional systems like the *Kuttāb*s, *Madrasa*s and al-Azhar. The two regimes were totally unconnected to each other, but an emerging trend began an attempt to synthesize both, albeit with limited initial success.

From 1816 to 1839, Muhammad Ali built schools and colleges that would be the cornerstone of the Egyptian higher education system. These included vocational schools of human medicine and nursing, engineering, management, veterinary science, agriculture and accounting. Later, Egyptian attempts to build an institute of higher learning were initially opposed by the British. Reid writes:

> Fearing that a European-style university would fan political unrest, Cromer pleaded a shortage of funds and tried unsuccessfully to deflect demands for more education into interest in simple elementary schooling for the masses. A committee of private citizens took the matter into their own hands, and, since Cromer himself had long preached private initiative and self-help, his objections to the university were unconvincing.[58]

The committee was formed in 1906 and was initially lead by the then-prince Ahmad Fouad to plan for the development of an Egyptian university, including its funding, building, staffing and management. A key goal of the committee was to differentiate the university from the vocational schools and colleges that had existed since the time of Muhammad Ali. Reid notes that after the university gained prominence, many factions would later claim it was their idea. Members of the Muhammad Ali dynasty would claim it was Prince Fouad's idea, as he chaired the committee. Supporters of the nationalist party (*al-hizb al-watani*) would claim that it was their idea, pointing to Mostafa Kamel's 1900 article calling for the establishment of a 'grand school' and of his 1904 article calling for the establishment of a faculty to be named after Muhammad Ali. Meanwhile, the Umma Party would claim that the university was the idea of Saad Zghloul, Qasim Amin and Muhammad ʿAbduh, arguing that an independent university was one of the goals of the nationalist movement.[59]

Regardless of whose idea it was, by 1908 the 'Egyptian University' (as it was initially known) was established despite strong opposition from the British, who understood the potential danger of an educated, urban middle class. In a 1947 cable to the British foreign office, embassy staff warned:

> The Effendis (by whom I mean the educated and the semi-educated products of Eastern universities and schools) seem in fact to be rapidly developing into a professional middle class destined to claim for itself a definite position in the social order of the Arab world and to play an increasingly important part in shaping the political destinies of the Middle East. The very fact that they are, by reason of their scholarship, breaking away from the practices of their ancestors, must necessarily encourage a feeling of restlessness which is no doubt intensified by their growing realization of the social inequalities of the society in which they live and in which the remuneration for the posts and careers open to them is, in most cases, still very poor. It is not surprising that in such circumstances the great bulk of the Effendis should have a strong feeling of social grievance. The question of the growing importance of the Effendis and their probable future role in the Middle East would seem indeed to deserve careful examination.[60]

University education and social mobility

University education was important not only because students would acquire new knowledge, but because (alongside advancement in the army) it provided one of the main opportunities for social mobility. From the time of Muhammad Ali to that of Sadat, the state was the largest employer of university graduates.[61] Secular education had been identified with government jobs since its introduction in the nineteenth century. The British had cemented this connection between education and public service through their incentives to acquire a formal education. During his time in Egypt, Lord Cromer had made the school certificate not only a prerequisite for a job, but a guarantee of one as more civil servants were needed in the expanding state bureaucracy.[62]

Education as a vehicle of social mobility became the goal of thousands of Egyptians across the country. This was reflected in higher enrolment numbers and the continued migration of students from rural areas to Cairo, Alexandria and other urban hubs: the chance of a permanent government job provided not only stability and income but also respectability and the possibility of joining the growing middle class. The connection between education and government jobs reinforced the centrality of the state. A key failure of government policies since the nineteenth century and arguably to date was the inability or unwillingness to stress the importance of vocational training to avoid overcrowding universities and subsequent unemployment. The lure of the prestige of a university education further stigmatized vocational training; many students would come to Cairo and Alexandria from rural areas, sometimes with their families, and endure horribly adverse conditions to fulfill their dream. A.J.M. Craig, a British visiting scholar at Cairo University from 1950 to 1951 who had become close with many students, noted:

> Sacrifices are made to acquire education. In a shack built on the roof of our house there lived, throughout the winter, part of a provincial family which had come to Cairo so that the two sons may be educated. The *ménage* consisted of the elder boy who was at Cairo University, the younger who was at a secondary school, the grandmother who had come to look after them, and their young sister who had been sent as an afterthought to run errands and spare the crone's weary legs. All of them lived on beans and bread and various scraps, financed by the distant father, a peasant working in his fields.[63]

Politicization of students

This restlessness observed by A.J.M. Craig can be viewed within the context of the political conditions of the time. As previously discussed, there had been nationalist stirrings in various segments of Egyptian society since the end of the eighteenth century. In 1879 the first political party, *Al-Hizb Al-Watani*, was formed, but the British were successful in stopping institutionalized politics from taking hold for a few years after the Urabi uprising. Nonetheless, by 1890 a new non-military based nationalist movement was beginning to take shape under the leadership of Mostafa Kamel and the Ummah Party.[64] The 1919 revolution had provided further impetus for the liberation struggle, and many were still unsatisfied even after the nominal recognition of Egyptian sovereignty in 1922. The year 1923 ushered in what some scholars define as the 'liberal' age, the first homegrown experiment in democracy. That liberal era also advocated the hiring of a locally trained middle class for roles in the government and public sector. The 'effendis,' as they became known, were supposed to fill the employment gap. Abdalla argues that "the newly emerging industrial bourgeoisie struggled to introduce educational changes which were a prerequisite for fulfilling its very different needs for accountants, engineers, technicians and managers."[65] As part of that push, new schools and universities were opened to educate a growing middle class.

As more students joined the universities, many of them began to be increasingly politicized within the context of the growing nationalist movement. The students had come to understand many of the reasons behind the oppressive conditions surrounding them. In a secret cable to the Foreign Office in London, Arnold Smith, another British scholar in Egypt, noted:

> During the past two years, in which I have been lecturing to the 3rd and 4th year students at the Egyptian University, I have become convinced that there is a widespread and growing awareness among educated youth here of the

> almost hopeless backwardness of the present social and economic set-up in Egypt. Students, young professional men, young army officers, etc. are becoming increasingly dissatisfied with their *status quo*—and who can blame them?[66]

The student movement joined workers on strike and pressured Egyptian politicians to take a harder stance against the British presence. They were also becoming acutely aware of the prevalent economic conditions, and had begun to make demands relating to jobs and income. Abdalla writes that:

> the spread of liberal education gave students a numerical strength while the country's low level of economic development frustrated their ambitions for future careers. The rocky course of the country's constitutional life led increasing numbers of them to doubt the adequacy of its political system. The regime's inability to achieve the complete independence for which the nation had revolted in 1919 was the concrete proof of its overall failure.[67]

During the 1930s and 1940s, the student movement became increasingly militant. In 1936 the students marched on the palace to support Nahas Pasha's call for the resignation of the Nassim government and to demand non-cooperation with the British. The police tried to stop them, and many were arrested and injured; one student was shot to death, creating further impetus for the movement.[68] In 1946, a national strike and a 'day of evacuation' were called against the British, and the students marched toward the British barracks in downtown Cairo. The British garrison opened fire with machine guns on the students, killing approximately 23 demonstrators and injuring 120.[69] In the early 1950s, some groups within the movement went from being militant to being actually militarized. Some student groups were given military training and arms and had joined the *fedayeen* in the Suez, attacking British positions at the canal.[70]

To the students, much like blue-collar workers, the nationalist movement was their vehicle for achieving the expulsion of the British from Egypt and gaining access to higher jobs then monopolized by foreigners living in Egypt. The students of the faculties of commerce, law and some of the technical schools all went on strike in 1936 to demand improvements in the education system and access to jobs after graduation. As the students began to exert their power, the government took note. Abdalla argues that

> foreign nationals were so widely employed in commercial and industrial firms that Egyptians had little chance of being employed in them. The government was compelled to tighten up the immigration regulations, and no foreigners were permitted to enter the country to take up employment until proof had been given that no suitable Egyptian candidate could be found.[71]

Similar to the workers' movement, political powers such as the Wafd sought to co-opt the student movement. Gorgas argues that following the proclamation of Egypt's first constitution on April 19, 1923, student participation in politics acquired a new dimension. As student participation in anti-British demonstrations increased exponentially, the Egyptian Wafd Party hoped to steer and benefit from this energy. Education ministers became increasingly reluctant to punish demonstrating students, while party leaders and state officials flattered and encouraged student patriotism. Furthermore, the students became one of the most effective election agents due to their ability to spread political propaganda all over the country and organize meetings and street demonstrations.[72]

It is noteworthy that even though the student movement acted in unison, it was by no means unified. There were many currents competing within the movement, and at the time they were generally divided into three groups: the Wafdists, Muslim Brotherhood, and communists. While they occasionally conducted coordinated action, at times they withheld support pending approval from various senior members of their respective organizations. It is these schisms that the Free Officers would later use to further divide the student movement. The Wafdist students were initially considered the nucleus of the student movement, as their activism and mobilizations dated back to the 1919 revolution and thus to the Law School of Cairo University.[73] Increasingly, the Wafd relied on students to convey its messages across the country.

The Egyptian left: a bridge between the labor and the student movements

During World War II, Egypt became an arena for various ideologies. British and US discourse was anti-Nazi in nature and espoused democratic values of self-determination, even though the British had colonies across the world. Nazi propaganda had attempted to portray the Allies as colonialists and promised that under Germany many of the oppressed peoples would be liberated. Segments of the Egyptian nationalist movement had succumbed to German propaganda as a reaction to the British presence, viewing Rommel's onslaught on Al-Alamien as a potential liberation. Soviet propaganda at the time had a unique opportunity, for at that stage it was not viewed as the antithesis of the Western model and was in fact championed by the Allies during the war. In the period following 1945, Soviet propaganda aimed to highlight the social and economic advances of the socialist model, and Marxist ideas predictably took hold in segments of Egyptian society unhappy with the existing state of affairs.[74]

The Egyptian communist movement had begun to find traction in the years following World War I. The Egyptian Communist Party was founded in 1921, declaring itself the true representative of the Egyptian working class, and by the end of 1921 had 1,500 members in Cairo and Alexandria.[75] Its program called for the nationalization of the Suez Canal, the liberation and unification of Egypt and the Sudan, repudiation of all state debts and foreign capitulation agreements, an eight-hour work day, and equal pay for Egyptian and foreign workers. It also called for the abolition of land tenancy in which the *fellah* paid half the crop as rent and the cancellation of debts for *fellahins* who owned less than ten *feddans*. It also called for a restriction on land ownership to a maximum of 100 *feddans*.[76]

It took several years for the party to find appeal beyond the urban intelligentsia and to reach into the working class. In 1924 the party issued a call for a general strike, which was heeded by workers in Alexandria who occupied a British-owned textile company. After Saʿad Zaghloul made promises to the workers, they called off the occupation, but the party was sidelined in favor of the Wafd, who recognized the workers' power.[77] While the Communist Party continued to lose members and lost its organizational capabilities, many of its members went on to form and join other left-wing organizations in Egypt. The communist current did not get much initial traction because it was viewed as a foreign ideology, many of its members (including some of its leaders[78]) also being foreigners residing in Egypt. The 1940s (and especially during World War II) saw concerted efforts to 'Egyptianize' communist organizations. Among the first indigenous Egyptian communist organizations was the *khubz wal-huriya* (Bread and Freedom) group,[79] which was among the first organizations to begin building networks and contacts directly between workers and students, without the interference of other nationalist forces.

1935 student uprising

The roots of the 1935 uprising can be traced to the 1930 Sidqi government, which saw the suspension of the 1923 constitution, disbanding of parliament and a return to autocratic rule. The Egyptian economy, like economies everywhere at the time, suffered from the Great Depression. The price of a ton of cotton fell by more than half, reducing it to ten pounds after a 1926 high of 26 pounds.[80] The decline in cotton prices had a deep impact on farmers as well as industry workers, and any protests were met with repression by the Sidqi government, which sought to crush any dissent. By 1934 there was massive discontent against the government, so the king forced its resignation and Mohammed Nessiem was appointed prime minister. Yet all sectors of society, including the students' movement, called for a return to parliamentary life and the reinstitution of the 1923 constitution, which the Nessiem government resisted.

In the morning of November 13, 1935, high school and university students began arriving at the Faculty of Law at Cairo University to protest for the reinstitution of the 1923 constitution, a return to parliamentary life and the expulsion of the British from Egypt. Their numbers grew and soon the protest headed downtown toward the British embassy and parliament. Protests had spread to several schools across Cairo, including one from the Nahda School led by a young Gamal Abdel Nasser, who would be injured later in the day.[81] Over the following days, the protests would spread across Egypt with hundreds of injuries and 50 casualties.[82] The student protests helped galvanize opposition to the Nessiem government, which was forced to resign in 1936. This led to the formation of a new Wafdist government by Nahas Pasha, which that same year signed the Anglo-Egyptian treaty that began the withdrawal of British troops from

Egypt (except the area surrounding the Suez Canal). The 1935 student uprising can be construed as the maturation of the student movement still coming to terms with its growing power, demonstrating both its ability to influence national politics and its susceptibility to manipulation by political powers. Gorgas argues that the student protests that unfolded in 1935 and again in 1936 occurred for two main reasons:

> Firstly, several political parties were manipulating the students. Secondly, the students were protesting against their living conditions and unemployment. As early as the 1940s, the rapid expansion of facilities at the secondary and university levels bore no relation to the needs of Egypt in terms of either numbers or specializations and created serious political problems. For example, in 1937, 11,000 university graduates were unable to obtain any employment at all.[83]

Assessing the opportunity environment

As previously outlined, the political opportunity model focuses on opportunities in the political environment that provide incentives for members of a movement to collectively act. The analysis here focuses on opportunities such as institutional access, international dynamics and the availability of a master frame. Several of these opportunities can be observed in the pre-1952 period within the context of the labor and student movement. There are other elements of political opportunity that are relevant to the study (for example media access and information flow), but these will become more important in later Egyptian mobilizations.

Institutional access: the labor movement

Increased institutional access for the labor movement can be clearly observed in Egypt's so-called liberal age from 1923 to 1952. Unions began to form after the 1919 revolution, reaching a total of 38 by 1931, but they were not formally legalized until the Trade Union Law of 1942 issued by the government of Nahas Pasha.[84] The law was a groundbreaking legal instrument recognizing and regulating union activity, enabling workers to organize and bargain collectively. As of December 31, 1947, there were 441 active unions with a total membership of 91,604. Though this number may appear high, it actually represents a decline both as to the number of unions and total membership from November 30, 1945, when there had been 489 trade unions with 139,546 members.[85] The main reason for this rather sharp decrease (amounting to a difference of 48 unions and 47,942 members in three years) was that many of the unions registered in 1945 turned out, on investigation by the Egyptian Labor Office, to be 'paper unions' having fewer than the minimum of 50 members required by the Act. Others were dissolved because of their failure to maintain proper accounts and records.[86] Of all the established unions of the 1940s, the industrial workers' union was among the strongest, owing to its close work with other factory workers and the resulting constant interaction between the union and its members. The codification of labor laws proved a political opportunity, and the clustering of factories allowed for closer proximity and coordination of the labor movement in the decades to come.

Institutional access: the student movement

The goal of the government in establishing universities was to educate students so they could be employed in the state apparatus and private enterprise when available. An unintended consequence of such educational policies was that over time, university campuses became hubs of activism and opposition to the government. This did not happen overnight, but was a process that unfolded after establishment of Cairo University. Besides enduring hardships to acquire education, many young Egyptians from rural areas had not yet been exposed to political ideas. University campuses, as well as the dense surrounding urban settings, provided for a growing consciousness of the socio-economic and political conditions of the time. During his time in Egypt, A.J.M. Craig observed:

> Undoubtedly, much of the students' restlessness is due to the dismal life, which many of them lead. Despite the long line of motorcars parked every day outside the gates of the various buildings, the majority of the students are from poor homes. A large proportion come up to Cairo from the villages and live in lodgings that are almost always dreary and occasionally squalid. Hostels exist (there is a special house for students from foreign countries and more are being built), but the number of students is so large (about 20,000 at the University of Cairo) that the government's task is immense. Nor is there the social life that is to be found at a Western university. Although there are fine playing fields, they are not so well used as they might be, and there are almost none of the clubs and societies that make British universities every night a hive of debate and entertainment. Lack of money may be partly responsible but lack of initiative is surely the main reason.[87]

Craig would continue to observe the restlessness and politicization of students. He concluded:

> Until the Suez Canal question is settled, all their attention and their enthusiasm will be directed towards a fiery nationalism. But afterwards much will depend on how the government approaches the central problem of the Egyptian universities: what to do with the students once they have been graduated.[88]

Students were increasingly politicized not only because of university campuses, but also because of their close proximity to each other in university halls and dorms. The social movement literature investigates several case studies that highlight the impact of the campus environment on mobilizations, as in the cases of the US,[89] Filipino,[90] Russian[91] and Chinese student movements.[92] The ecology[93] and the layout of the campus prove to be a key factor in mobilization. In his study of the 1989 student movement in Beijing, Zhao found that the ecology of the campus was a determinant factor in student activism in five major ways that are wroth quoting here in full:

- It facilitated the spread of dissident ideas before the movement and the transmission of news about a particular event during the movement.
- It nurtured many dormitory-based student networks. These networks were the basis of mutual influence, even coercion, among students and, therefore, sustained a high rate of student participation.
- It shaped students' spatial activities on the campus, creating a few places that most students had to pass or stay daily. These places became centers of student mobilization.
- The concentration of many universities in one district encouraged mutual imitation and interuniversity competition for activism among students from different universities.
- The ecology also facilitated the formation of many ecology-dependent strategies of collective action.[94]

Aspects of these dynamics can be observed in the case of Cairo University, starting with the 1919 uprising from the Faculty of Law. As more universities were established (Alexandria University in 1942; Ein Shams University, first known as Ibrahim Pasha University, in 1950), they too became hubs of activism. Zhao's observation about the walls around university campuses facilitating activism holds especially true for Cairo University. Because of the walls, the roads on campus were no longer part of the public road system, and police could not get inside a campus without clear consent from school authorities. Even when school authorities were unsympathetic to the movement, they might not be inclined to call the police to handle the students as that would alienate the students and encourage more troubles in dealing with students after the police left. The simple existence of walls around the university created a lower risk environment that facilitated student mobilization.[95] This ecology was a contributing factor for the labor movement as well, as the clustering of factories in industrial areas (for example in Helwan and al-Mahallah) was also conducive to union activities, allowing workers and unions from different factories in a single area to network with others.

International dynamics

The social movement literature has investigated the impact of changes in the international system on social movements.[96] In Egypt, this dynamic can be viewed in the lead up to World War II, which provided political opportunities to the overall nationalist movement. By 1935, European politics began to take a turn for the worse. Nazi Germany was being re-militarized and becoming more assertive. The Italian fascists had been looking toward the Middle East and the Arab world to establish influence. To British dismay, Italy had supported Egypt's nationalist claims and in February 1933 the king and queen of Italy had visited Egypt, an event that was viewed as important both in Italy and in Egypt.[97]

Italy's control over Libya and influence in East Africa had been increasing and by 1935 its utilization of the Suez Canal was second only to the British, due to the massive numbers of soldiers, workers, equipment and livestock that was passing southward to its bases in East Africa. In October of the same year, hundreds answered Italy's call for volunteer fighters from the Italian community in Egypt. As we now well know, Italy at the time was going on a war footing. Mussolini's plans to invade Abyssinia became known after the Walwal incident.[98] This was the case even though both Italy and Ethiopia were signatories to the League of Nations, and should have been bound by article X that forbids aggression between member states. In January 1935, Emperor Haile Selassie appealed to the League for arbitration and a meeting was convened in Geneva to decide on its position regarding the potential invasion. The League again proved toothless and Italian forces stationed in Eritrea moved on Ethiopia and invaded it, much to the dismay of the other European powers.

Britain feared Italian plans in the Mediterranean and the Red Sea and its potential threats to attack Egypt. Any danger to Egypt threatened the Suez Canal and the passageway to India, the crown jewel of the British Empire. After 1935, the British army further increased its presence in Egypt, with its navy using Alexandria as the main Mediterranean base instead of Malta. To British war strategists, Egypt would become more important than ever. As more British troops arrived, the similarities to the 1914 military build-up became ever clearer to Egyptians. It was becoming evident that any potential war would have grave and far-reaching domestic consequences.

In light of international events and the British domestic military build-up the Egyptian public became increasingly restless, fearing that a potential war would impact negatively on all segments of Egyptian society. From November 1935 to January 1936, a massive wave of demonstrations occurred, with secondary and university students forming the core. To quell the violence, the British had to show more flexibility, and the 1936 Anglo-Egyptian treaty was arguably an attempt by the British to pacify a restless Egyptian population. The impact of World War II and its aftermath on domestic nationalist movements was by no means unique to Egypt. In their study of the Mau Mau uprising in Kenya, McAdam *et al.* argue that:

> the postwar trend towards decolonization and the wave of nationalist movements it helped spawn was viewed as a serious threat to Kenya's sizable white settler population, and to a lesser extent, by the colonial authorities. This sense of threat was heightened by the onset in 1948–1949 of a vigorous pro-Communist rebellion in the British colony of Malaya.... For their part,

Kenyan nationalists viewed these events as evidence that an unprecedented *opportunity* for independence lay at hand. The result was increased popular mobilization in Kenya and elsewhere in Africa.[99]

Availability of a master frame: the nationalist movement

The concept of political opportunity needs to be elastic enough to encompass socio-cultural factors, not simply depend on state institutional actors. Gamson and Meyer argue that "opportunity has a strong cultural component and we miss something important when we limit our attention to variance in political institutions and the relationship amongst political actors."[100] Indigenous cultural factors play a strong role in mobilization, especially the existence of a powerful 'master frame' that several movements can utilize as part of their individual and collective struggle.

Such processes can be observed in early twentieth-century Egypt, where various political actors utilized the nationalist frame. Wealthy landowners and industrialists used it to protect their financial interests, seeking to build an indigenous capitalist class that was not subordinate to foreign influence. The student movement, while demanding employment and better wages, framed their activism within the broader nationalist struggle. Likewise, the labor movement's economic demands were increasingly framed within the nationalist movement. The anti-colonial frame became a powerful 'master frame' that encompassed several social groups and movements. McAdam defines this master frame as one of four types of "expanding cultural opportunities" that increase the likelihood of mobilization, the fourth type (most relevant to this case) being "the availability of an innovative 'master frame' within which subsequent challengers can map their own grievances and demands."[101]

The anti-colonial master frame, in this analysis, becomes important not only for mobilization but also for the development of a national identity. Nationalism can be construed as one of the most potent sources for such identification, the construction of a national identity representing a powerful means to unite citizens within a territorially bounded community to resist the onslaught of colonialism.

Hall argues that identification "turns out to be one of the least well-understood concepts. It is drawing meanings from both the discursive and the psychoanalytic repertoire, without being limited to either."[102] Identification relies on the recognition and belief in a 'common origin'[103] or as Anderson explains, a belief in the imagined community of the nation. For Anderson, it is the construction of these imagined communities that has provided nations with the cohesive materials necessary to form a state.[104] Arguably, the anti-colonial master frame helped the development of an Egyptian identity and contributed to mobilization in the pre-1952 period. Moreover, nationalist politicians harnessed that frame to attract students and workers to their parties, and use them for their own protests and mobilizations. The lack of viable organizations for students and workers over the following decades would always put them at risk of co-optation by more organized forces.

Assessing the threat environment

As previously outlined, the other part of the political process model focuses on specific threats in a movement's environment that encourages the movement to respond, such as state-attributed economic problems, erosion of rights and state repression.[105] It could be construed that a combination of these factors restricts a movement and increase the cost of collective action. On the other hand, these threats could provide incentives to mobilize and challenge the state. Several of these threats can be observed in the pre-1952 period.

State-attributed economic problems

The combination of factors such as external borrowing, increased economic influence of foreigners, population growth and urbanization, created harsher economic conditions for a majority of Egyptians. The existence of economic grievances against the state impacts mobilizations by social movements.[106] Two state-attributed economic problems will be investigated here: land access and price increases.

Land access

Starting in the nineteenth century, large landowners had been able to further increase their holdings. Some then moved to the cities and acted as absentee landlords who managed and consolidated their estates through agents.[107] Modern irrigation methods employed since the time of Muhammad Ali continued to increase farmable land, and these large landowners continued to increase their ownership of reclaimed lands through their access to credit and patronage networks. By converting their property to a *waqf* (religious endowment), such landowners were able to take advantage of low tax rates and increase their ownership at the continued expense of the *fellahin*.[108] Some of these landowners grew very wealthy and were able to court the king and his entourage to gain the title of Pasha. This wealthy class inadvertently joined the nationalist struggle, mostly supporting and occasionally joining the Wafd.[109] In the years before the 1952 coup, the inequalities in landownership were glaring. Out of six million arable *feddan*s of land, 34 percent was held by only 0.5 percent of land owners, while 70 percent of owners had holdings of one or less *feddan*s.

Estimates of the landless rural population ranged from 44 percent[110] to 60 percent[111] of rural families, further highlighting massive inequalities in Egyptian society. These landless families worked as laborers on the estates of absentee landlords, and usually entered into sharecropping agreements structured so that the tenants would repay their debts for land by handing over their entire cotton crops and part of their wheat to the landlord while keeping corn and fodder for the livestock.[112] However, as rents skyrocketed from LE5 per *feddan* in 1896 to an average of LE25 to LE50 per *feddan* in 1952, the average income per *feddan* remained stagnant, ranging from LE25[113] to LE17.[114]

Tenants tried to supplement their income by looking for side agricultural work, by sending relations to find work in the cities, or through land reclamation. But wages were meager, and many tenants were left in perpetual debt to local moneylenders often associated with the landlord.[115] Land access became an increasingly state-attributed problem because of the government's failed attempts to face down the large landowners increasing their holdings at the expense of the *fellah*. This increased the grievances of the rural population against the British, as well as the successive governments of the pre-1952 era.

Price increases

Another factor contributing to state-attributed economic problems was price increases. World War I had increased pressure on the Egyptian treasury, and, under advice from British advisors, more banknotes were printed to feed the local population and support the war effort, yielding severe inflation.[116] The higher inflation was also not only the result of government policies, but also as a result of the war itself. The combination of land access and price increases affected the rural and urban populations, further exasperating their grievances and arguably provided the student and labor movements with increased impetus for protests.

The 1946 uprising

Social movements are not static, stand-alone entities operating in a vacuum; rather, they internally change or shift according to the environment, and interact with one another through processes of spillover and diffusion.[117] Such processes occurred between the labor and student movements, beginning in 1919. Relational diffusion, the mode of this interaction, occurred through the spread ideas, tactics and practices from one movement to the other through direct interpersonal contact. A key vehicle of this contact was the Egyptian left, which provided a space for workers and students to meet and organize. In 1942, two Marxist discussion and study groups were founded: the Egyptian Movement for National Liberation (EMNL) and Iskra (Arabic: *al-sharara*, the spark).[118] Abdalla argues that toward the end of World War II the growing communist movement increasingly influenced the student movement.[119]

Both EMNL and Iskra would gain traction among the student population. EMNL in particular had a large body of student membership and was able to increase its membership at Cairo University, Alexandria University and even Al-Azhar.[120] EMNL had a broad base, while Iskra was more elitist and focused on the dissemination of Marxist theory (via study groups) to segments of the left-wing intelligentsia.[121] The organization established a study center called *Dār al-Abḥāth al-ʻIlmiyya* (House of Scientific Research) which published literature and gave classes on communist thought.[122] Many of these groups would provide a meeting point for labor and student activists to connect, communicate and debate the issues of the day within a socialist framework.

al-Lajna al-Ṭullābiyya wa al-ʿUmmāliyya

The period between the world wars saw key transformations in the Wafd Party. Originally the most popular vehicle for the nationalist cause, it had begun to lose its support base, thus opening up space for new political actors. The Wafd of the 1930s and 1940s was not the same as the Wafd of 1919. Slowly but surely, large landowners and industrialists began to fill its leadership ranks, increasingly shaping it as a party with the goal of protecting elite interests.[123] While the 1936 treaty supposedly granted Egypt nominal independence, it was nonetheless viewed by large segments of the population as a capitulation to the British and highlighted the inability of the Wafd to negotiate complete independence. The Wafd's shunning of any militant actions (whether strikes, factory occupations, or armed resistance) had alienated segments of the Egyptian population, particularly students and workers, who were looking for more radical action to oppose the British. By the 1940s, the Wafd had lost some of its support and mobilization abilities.[124]

The 1940s saw old and new political actors enter the fray and compete for the leadership of the nationalist movement. The first was the Wafd and its offshoots, like the Liberal Constitutionalists and the far-right Egyptian Green Shirts. The second was the Muslim Brotherhood, which increased its popularity through a powerful discourse that combined traditionalism with anti-colonial sentiment. The third was the initially weak Egyptian left, comprised of several groups that only occasionally cooperated, whose main success was to recognize, highlight and advocate for the economic dimension of the nationalist movement, as opposed to focusing only on the political aspects of it.[125]

During and after World War II, the Egyptian left was able to grow for several reasons. First, confidence was shattered in political parties such as the Wafd, especially after what became known as the '2nd of February Incident' in 1942 when the party accepted British military assistance in a successful bid to return to government.[126] Second, the left began to be viewed more favorably as a consequence of the Soviet victory over Germany, and in particular the Soviet achievements on the eastern front during the war.[127] Having said that, the left was not able to fully capitalize on these factors as it remained fragmented.

The postwar aspirations of Egyptians had exponentially increased as they sought independence and more economic opportunities. It was now clear that the traditional political leadership was not be able to meet these aspirations, and people sought other nationalist leaders and groups. Having taken some time to coalesce and become more independent from entrenched political elites, the student and labor movements were increasingly at the forefront of the nationalist struggle. As noted in the passage above, the power of the working class had increased during the war years due to the rise in industrial production and the thousands of workers who were used to support the Allied efforts. In 1945, a group of workers formed *Lajnat al-ʿumaʾal lil-taharur al-watani* (The Workers Committee for National Liberation), which included student members and openly communist union leaders and workers. At the height of its popularity, its numbers included 18,000 workers, mostly drawn from the factories of Shubra al-Khiemah.[128]

The student movement solidified and organized itself accordingly in 1945–1946. Leftist students organized a national student congress on October 7, 1945 on the campus of Fouad 1st University.[129] Attended by school, college and university students from across Egypt, the congress concluded by adopting three main resolutions:

1 The struggle for national independence is not only a struggle against military occupation, but is also a struggle against colonial domination of economic, political and cultural aspects of Egyptian society.
2 Local oligarchs are the local partners of the colonial power and should accordingly be treated as enemies of Egypt.
3 The only way to fight colonialism is a unified front between all anti-colonial powers.[130]

The last point is particularly pertinent, calling for a unified front between the student and worker movements.[131] One of the first official meetings to occur between the movements happened in the office of the Cairo union of tram workers, and was attended by not only by tram workers, but also workers from Shubra al-Khiemah factories and students from various schools and faculties.[132] The relationship between the workers continued to develop further over the following months and led to the development of a formal organization, *al-Lajna al-Ṭullābiyya wa al-ʿUmmāliyya* (The Committee for Students and Workers, NCWS), which included Marxist students, Wafdist students unhappy with the Wafd leadership, al-Azhar students and unionized workers from various factories.[133]

1946 would prove to be high point for resistance against the British. The Wafd was no longer the sole spokesman for the nationalist movement, as more radical groups began to take center stage. In January and February 1946, thousands of students and workers demonstrated against the British. Botman describes what happened on February 9, 1946:

> On February 9 [1946] students called a massive strike. They marched by the thousands … from the university grounds in Giza toward Abdin Palace, chanting: "Evacuation! No negotiation except after evacuation!" When they reached the Abbas Bridge, which they needed to cross to reach the palace, they clashed with the police. The police opened the bridge while students were crossing it, causing the deaths of over 20 students by drowning and 84 serious casualties. In protest against the police's behavior, demonstrations erupted in parts of Mansura, Zagazig, Aswan, Shabin al-Kom, Alexandria and Cairo.[134]

In response to the loss of life, NCWS called for a general strike on February 21, 1946, a call heeded by thousands of students and workers across Egypt.[135] This can be construed as the first mass mobilization coordinated by workers and students. They were each representing their interests but also united under the main cause of national liberation. Not only were the actions coordinated, but the chants were unified, and protestors sang a song written and composed by the NCWS:

> O People, cross the seas of blood and do not weep, for now is the time of sacrifice
> Let's break the shackles of submission, for together, we can gain independence
> The people of the north, the people of the south, one hand and one heart
> To attack the colonialist's heart, for unification is the power of the people
> Whoever is scared in our ranks will be shamed, and whoever betrays us will be destroyed
> We will not respond to the voice of reason, struggle is the only way to victory.[136]

As is apparent from the highly emotive poem, the workers and students effectively viewed themselves as the vanguard of the Egyptian liberation movement, presenting a much more radical and militant position than the Wafd and other groups. The NCWS was also able to gain ground: as Botman argues, "the Egyptians were responding to the new leadership."[137] Even though the NCWS was short-lived, it nonetheless:

> contributed to the Egyptian political arena a new formula for the collaboration between various leftist and nationalist political groups. It demonstrated that the lead in the struggle for national liberation had been taken from the hands of the "old" nationalist parties, mainly the Wafd, by new radical forces. It also reflected the ideological struggle within the Wafd between the "old guard," represented by the right wing, and the "new left," which represented an utterly different socio-political agenda, and which was in many ways, closer to the "nationalist-communists".[138]

The importance of the NCWS is that it is the first case in contemporary Egyptian history of direct collaboration between workers and students, however such collaboration was not sustained. The failure of the NCWS, as well as individual student groups and workers unions to form viable and independent organizations of their own negatively affected their ability to mobilize and make claims on the state. In the absence of organizational structures, social movements find it increasingly difficult to sustain their collection action.[139]

The period from 1946 to 1952 would see further radicalization of the nationalist movement. Public pressure mounted on successive governments and the king's ability to influence events from behind the curtain decreased. The 1948 defeat of the Egyptian army in Palestine further involved the military in the nationalist movement through what would become known as the 'Free Officers,' who capitalized on the increasing restlessness of the population and nationalist radicalization. The Free Officers were themselves not ideologically unified, with currents of nationalism, Islamism and communism spread within them. They were initially allied with the Muslim Brotherhood and the left, but soon the alliance came to an end.

This chapter critically discussed the development of the student and labor movements in the pre-1952 era, highlighting the opportunities and threats faced by both movements, and how they responded. It also showed how both movements framed their goals within the broader nationalist struggle, and highlighted spillover and diffusional processes as demonstrated by the events of 1946. The next chapter will investigate the political economy of the new Free Officers regime and under the presidency of Gamal Abdel Nasser. It will highlight the opportunities and threats that both movements would face, and how the movements responded.

Notes

1 Alexis de Tocqueville, *The Old Regime and the Revolution* (New York: Random House, 1955 [1856]), 177.
2 Henry Dodwell, *The Founder of Modern Egypt: A Study of Muhammad Ali* (Cambridge: Cambridge University Press, 1931).
3 For an elaboration of these brutal methods, especially within the context of building the army, see Khaled Fahmy, *All the Pasha's Men: Mehmed Ali, His Army and the Making of Modern Egypt* (Cambridge: Cambridge University Press, 1997).
4 For more on agriculture during that era, see Helen Anne B. Rivlin, *Agricultural Policy of Muhammad 'Ali in Egypt* (Cambridge, MA: Harvard University Press, 1961).
5 Mourad Wahba, *The Role of the State in the Egyptian Economy, 1945–1981* (London: Garnet Publishing, 1994), 18.
6 Galal Amin, *Qiṣṣat al-iqtiṣād al-maṣri: min ʿahd Muhammad Ali ilā ʿahd Mubārak* (The Story of the Egyptian Economy: From The Era of Muhammad Ali to The Era of Mubarak) (Cairo: Dār al-Shurūq, 2012), 12.
7 Ibid., 13.
8 Richards and Waterbury, *Political Economy of the Middle East*, 21.
9 Roger Owen, *Cotton and the Egyptian Economy, 1820–1914: A Study in Trade and Development* (Oxford: Clarendon Press, 1969), 29.
10 Rivlin, *Agricultural Policy*, 143.
11 Arthur Edwin Crouchley, *The Economic Development of Modern Egypt* (London: Longmans and Green, 1938), 92.
12 Richards and Waterbury, *Political Economy of the Middle East*, 21.
13 Ibid., 105.
14 John Marlowe, *Spoiling the Egyptians* (London: Andre Deutsch, 1974), 96.
15 Ibid., 96–97.
16 For more on Said's wasteful spending, see David Landes, *Bankers and Pashas: International Finance and Economic Imperialism in Egypt* (Cambridge, MA: Harvard University Press, 1981).
17 Crouchley, *Economic Development*, 134.
18 Marlowe, *Spoiling*, 224.
19 Charles Issawi, *Egypt in Revolution* (London: Oxford University Press, 1963).
20 Robert Mabro, *The Egyptian Economy, 1952–72* (Oxford: Oxford University Press, 1974), 18–24.
21 For more details of foreign control of the Egyptian economy from the time of

Khedive Ismail onwards, see John Marlowe, *A History of Modern Egypt and Anglo-Egyptian Relations, 1800–1953*, 2nd edn (Hamden: Archon Books, 1965) and Maḥmūd Mitwallī, *al-Uṣūl al-tārīkhiyya lil-rasmaliya al-miṣriyya wa-tata'wurihā* (The Historical Roots of Egyptian Capitalism and Its Development) (Cairo: GEBO, 1973).

22 Marius Deeb, "The Socioeconomic Role of the Local Foreign Minorities in Modern Egypt, 1805–1961," *International Journal of Middle East Studies* 9, no. 1 (February 1978): 11–22.

23 Cited in Charles Issawi, "Egypt Since 1800: A Study in Lop-Sided Development," *The Journal of Economic History* 21, no. 1 (March 1961): 12.

24 Afaf Lutfi al-Sayyid-Marsot, *The History of Egypt: From the Arab Conquest to the Present* (Cambridge: Cambridge University Press, 2007), 107.

25 See Robert Vitalis, "On the Theory and Practice of Compradors: The Role of Abbud Pasha in the Egyptian Political Economy," *International Journal of Middle East Studies* 22, no. 3 (August 1990): 291–315.

26 See Robert L. Tignor, "The Egyptian Revolution of 1919: New Directions in the Egyptian Economy," *Middle Eastern Studies* 12, no. 3 (October 1976): 41–67.

27 John Waterbury, *The Egypt of Nasser and Sadat: The Political Economy of Two Regimes* (Princeton: Princeton University Press, 1983), 59.

28 Taha Abdel Alim, *Bināyat al-tabaqa al-'amila al-sina'iya al-miṣriyya* (The Composition of the Egyptian Industrial Working Class) (Cairo: NP, 1987), 76–77.

29 Ibid.

30 See Juan Ricardo Cole, *Colonialism and Revolution in the Middle East: Social and Cultural Origins of Egypt's Urabi Movement* (Cairo: American University in Cairo Press, 1999).

31 Abdel Monem al-Ghazali, *21 Febrayer: Youm al-nidal ḍidd al-isti'mar* (21 February: The Day of Resistance against Colonialism) (Cairo: NP, 1958), 9–10.

32 L. James, "The Population Problem in Egypt," *Economic Geography* 23, no. 2 (April 1947): 99.

33 Ibid.

34 Saad Eddin Ibrahim, "Over-Urbanization and Under-Urbanism: The Case of the Arab World," *International Journal of Middle East Studies* 1 (1975): 39.

35 Ibid., 39.

36 Table cited in Janet L. Abu-Lughod, "Urbanization in Egypt: Present State and Future Prospects," *Economic Development and Cultural Change* 13, no. 3 (April 1965): 318–319.

37 Jack A. Goldstone and Charles Tilly, "Threat (and Opportunity): Popular Action and State Response in the Dynamics of Contentious Action," in Ronald R. Aminzade, Jack Goldstone, Doug McAdam, Elizabeth Perry, William Sewell, Sidney Tarrow and Charles Tilly (eds.), *Silence and Voice in the Study of Contentious Politics* (Cambridge: Cambridge University Press, 2001), 149.

38 Abu-Lughod, "Urbanization in Egypt," 320.

39 Robin Cohen, Peter Gutkind and Phyllis Brazier (eds.), *Peasants and Proletarians: The Struggle of Third World Workers* (London: Hutchinson and Co., 1979), 11.

40 See Amin Ezz el-Din, *Tārikh al-tabaqa al 'amilah al-misriyya mundh nash'atiha hattā thawrat 1919* (The History of the Egyptian Working Class since its Beginnings Until the 1919 Revolution) (Cairo: Dār al-Kitāb al-'Arabī, 1967).

41 Abdel Aziz Ramadan, *Taṭāwur al-ḥarakat al-waṭaniyya fi misr, 1918–1936* (The Development of the Egyptian Nationalist Movement, 1918–1936) (Cairo: Dār al-Kitāb al-'Arabī, 1968), 82.

42 Amin Ezz el-Din, *Tārikh al-tabaqa al 'amilah al-misriyya mundh nash' atiha hattā thawrat 1919* (The History of the Egyptian Working Class since its Beginnings Until the 1919 Revolution) (Cairo: Dār al-Kitāb al-'Arabī, 1967), 57–56.

43 al-Ghazali, *21 Febrayer*, 20.

44 Muḥammad Khālid, *al-Ḥarakah al-niqābiya bayn al-māḍī wal-ḥāḍir* (The Union Movement Between the Past and the Present) (Cairo: Dār al-Ta'āwun, 1975), 24.

45 Ezz el-Din, *Tarikh*, 178–188.

46 Robert L. Tignor, "The Egyptian Revolution of 1919: New Directions in the Egyptian Economy," *Middle Eastern Studies* 12, no. 3 (October 1976): 43.

47 Magdi Fahmy, "Dawr al-tabāqa al-'amila fī-l-ḥarakat al-waṭaniya" (The Role of the Working Class in the Nationalist Movement), *al-Tali'a*, 39–40.

48 Mohamed Said Idris, *Hizb al-wafd wal-tabaqa al-'amilah fi misr 1924–1952* (The Wafd Party and the Working Class in Egypt 1924–1952) (Cairo: Dar al-Thaqafa, 1989), 174–175.

49 Abdel Salam Abdel Halim Amer, *Thawrat ulio wal-tabāqa al-'amila* (The July Revolution and the Working Class) (Cairo: al-Hay'a al-'Amma lil-Kitāb, 1987), 34–35.

50 Gamal el-Banna, *Nasha' at al-ḥarakat al-niqābiyya wa taṭāwurihā* (The Birth of the Union Movement and its Development) (Cairo: al-Mu'assasat al-Thaqāfiya al-Umaliya, 1962), 106.

51 Ezz el-Din, *Tarikh*, 169–170.

52 Rami Ginat, "The Egyptian Left and the Roots of Neutralism in the Pre-Nasserite Era," *British Journal of Middle Eastern Studies* 30, no. 1 (2003): 7.

53 Gamal Magdi Hassanin, *al-Mumizāt al-'amah lil-tarkīb al-ṭabāq fī masr a'ashiya thawra 23 Yunio* (The General Indicators of Class Structure Before the Revolution of the 23rd of June) (Cairo: NP, 1971), 24.

54 Ibrahim Amer, *Thawrat masr al-qawmiya* (Egypt's National Revolution) (Cairo: NP, 1956), 81.

55 William J. Handley, "The Labor Movement in Egypt," *Middle East Journal* 3, no. 3 (July 1949): 283.

56 Rifa'a al-Tahtawi, an Imam sent to lead an educational mission to France in 1826, proved quite influential in the development of Egypt's educational system. An Azharite scholar, he was nominated by his mentor as a religious guide to a group of Egyptian students that Muhammad Ali was sending on an educational mission to France in 1826. According to Tahtawi's memoir *Riḥla* (Journey), during his time in France he read works by Condillac, Voltaire, Rousseau, Montesquieu and Bézout, among others. In 1831, Tahtawi returned home to Egypt to undertake a career in journalism, education and translation. He was appointed head of the School of Languages in 1835, which had a great impact on the emerging Egyptian intellectual milieu. Three of Tahtawi's published volumes are works of political and moral philosophy in which he introduces his Egyptian audience to aspects of the European Enlightenment, including ideas such as secular authority and political rights and liberty; ideas regarding how a modern civilized society ought to be and what constituted by extension a civilized or 'good Egyptian'; and ideas on public interest and public good. Tahtawi praised the concepts of equality and democracy that he observed in France, and diagnosed a 'lack of participation' as one of the maladies of Egypt. He suggested an open system where ideas could be debated freely for the good of the people. He heavily criticized Muslim thinkers of the time who refused to learn from the West, arguing that

> such people are deluded, for civilizations are turns and phases. These sciences were once Islamic when we were at the apex of our civilization. Europe took them from us and developed them further. It is now our duty to learn from them as they learned from our ancestors.

See P.J. Vatikiotis, *The History of Modern Egypt*, 4th edn (Baltimore: Johns Hopkins University Press, 1991), 113–116 and Azzam Tamimi, "Democracy in Islamic Political Thought," *Encounters: Journal of Inter-Cultural Perspectives* 3 (1997): 1–35.

57 Mansoor Moaddel, "Discursive Pluralism and Islamic Modernism in Egypt," *Arab Studies Quarterly* 24, no. 1 (Winter 2002): 14.

58 Donald Malcolm Reid, "Cairo University and the Orientalists," *International Journal of Middle East Studies* 19, no. 1 (February 1987): 52.
59 Donald Malcolm Reid, *Cairo University and the Making of Modern Egypt* (Cambridge: Cambridge University Press, 2002).
60 FO 141, 1223 (1947), "British Propaganda: Effendi Class" (C.W. Austin to Sir Ronald Campbell), cited in Abdalla, *Student Movement and National Politics*, 21.
61 For statistics on employment figures in the early 20th century, see J. Dunne, *An Introduction to the History of Education in Egypt* (London: Luzac and Co., 1938).
62 Anwar Abdel Malik, *Dirāsāt fi-l-thaqāfa al-wataniya* (Studies in the National Culture) (Beirut: Dar al-Tāliya, 1967), 259–261.
63 A.J.M. Craig, "Egyptian Students," *Middle East Journal* 7, no. 3 (Summer 1953): 295.
64 Marius Deeb, *Party Politics in Egypt: the Wafd and its Rivals, 1919–1939* (London: Ithaca Press for the Middle East Centre, St Antony's College, Oxford, 1979), 13.
65 Abdalla, *Student Movement and National Politics*, 33.
66 Foreign Office Cable Number 141, 892 (1943), "Education and Student Employment."
67 Abdalla, *Student Movement and National Politics*, 47.
68 Ibid., 48.
69 Ibid., 75.
70 The first university *fedayeen* battalion left for the Canal Zone on November 9, 1951. See Abdalla, *Student Movement and National Politics*, 86.
71 Ibid., 36.
72 See Jordi Tejel Gorgas, "The Limits of the State: Student Protest in Egypt, Iraq and Turkey, 1948–63," *British Journal of Middle Eastern Studies* 40, no. 4 (2013): 364 and H. Erlich, *Students and University in 20th Century Egyptian Politics* (London: Frank Cass, 1989), 57–58.
73 Abdalla, *Student Movement and National Politics*, 43.
74 Charles Issawi, *Egypt at Mid-Century: An Economic Survey* (London: Oxford University Press, 1954), 67.
75 Tareq Y. Ismael and Rif'at el-Sa'īd, *The Communist Movement in Egypt, 1920–1988* (Syracuse: Syracuse University Press, 1990), 21.
76 Ibid., 21–22.
77 Rif'at el-Sa'īd, *al-Yasar al-Misri, 1925–1940* (The Egyptian Left, 1925–1940) (Beirut: NP, 1972), 261.
78 Ibid., 362–368.
79 Ibid., 353–354.
80 Abdel Azim Ramadan, *Taṭāwur al-ḥarakat al-waṭaniya fī masr, 1918–1936* (The Development of the Nationalist Movement in Egypt, 1937–1948) (Cairo: Dār al-Kitāb al-'Arabi, 1968), 733.
81 Ahmad Farid, *al-'Allāqat al-maṣriya al-britāniya wa atharahā fī taṭāwur al-harakat al-wataniya fī masr* (Egyptian British Relations and its Impact on the Nationalist Movement in Egypt 1914–1952) (Ph.D. dissertation, Faculty of Arts, Cairo University, 1960), cited in Assem Abdel Moteleb, *al-Talaba wal-ḥarakat al-waṭaniya fī maṣr 1922–1952* (The Students and the Nationalist Movement in Egypt 1922–1952) (Cairo: Dār al-Kutub wal-Wathā'iq al-Qawmiya, 2007), 135.
82 Ibid., 136–137.
83 Gorgas, "Limits of the State," 365.
84 Handley, "Labor Movement in Egypt," 279.
85 Ibid.
86 Ibid.
87 Cited in Abdalla, *Student Movement and National Politics*, 297.
88 Ibid.
89 See Richard Berk, *Collective Behavior* (Dubuque: W.C. Brown, 1974) and Max Hierich, *The Spiral of Conflict: Berkeley 1964* (New York: Columbia University Press, 1971).

90 See Misagh Parsa, *States, Ideologies, and Social Revolutions: A Comparative Analysis of Iran, Nicaragua, and the Philippines* (Cambridge: Cambridge University Press, 2000).
91 See Samuel D. Kassow, *Students, Professors, and the State in Tsarist Russia* (Berkeley: University of California Press, 1989).
92 See Craig J. Calhoun, *Neither Gods Nor Emperors: Students and the Struggle for Democracy in China* (Berkeley: University of California Press, 1997).
93 Ecology here denotes the impact of the campus physical environment on students and the reaction of students toward the environment.
94 Dingxin Zhao, "Ecologies of Social Movements: Student Mobilization during the 1989 Prodemocracy Movement in Beijing," *American Journal of Sociology* 103, no. 6 (May 1998): 1495.
95 Ibid., 1495–1496.
96 See Anthony Oberschall, "Oppurtunities and Framing in the Eastern European Revolts of 1989," in Doug McAdam, John D. McCarthy and Mayer N. Zald (eds.), *Comparative Prespectives on Social Movements* (Cambridge: Cambridge University Press, 1996), 93–121.
97 Zayid Mahmud, *Egypt's Struggle for Independence* (Beirut: NP, 1965), 148.
98 See John H. Spencer, "The Italian-Ethiopian Dispute and the League of Nations," *The American Journal of International Law* 31, no. 4 (October 1937).
99 Douglas McAdam, Sidney Tarrow and Charles Tilly, *Dynamics of Contention* (Cambridge: Cambridge University Press, 2004), 96.
100 See William Gamson and David Meyer, "Framing Political Opportunity," in D. McAdam, J. McCarthy and M.N. Zald (eds.), *Comparative Perspectives on Social Movements* (Cambridge: Cambridge University Press, 1996), 25.
101 Doug McAdam, "Conceptual Origins, Current Problems and Future Directions," in D. McAdam, J. McCarthy and M.N. Zald (eds.), *Comparative Perspectives on Social Movements* (Cambridge: Cambridge University Press, 1996).
102 Stuart Hall and Paul Du Gay, *Questions of Cultural Identity* (London: Sage, 1996), 2.
103 Ibid.
104 Benedict Anderson, *Imagined Communities: Reflections on the Origin and Spread of Nationalism* (London: Verso, 1983).
105 Paul Almeida, "Opportunity Organizations and Threat-Induced Contention: Protest Waves in Authoritarian Settings," *American Journal of Sociology* 109, no. 2 (September 2003): 345–400.
106 See Charles Tilly, *From Mobilization to Revolution* (Reading: Addison Wesley, 1978), 99 and John D. McCarthy and Mayer N. Zald, "Resource Mobilization and Social Movements: A Partial Theory," *American Journal of Sociology* 82, no. 6 (1977): 1212–1241.
107 Doreen Warriner, *Land Reform and Development in the Middle East* (Oxford: Oxford University Press, 1962), 30.
108 Hamied Ansari, *Egypt: The Stalled Society* (New York: SUNY Press, 1986), 59.
109 In the 1950 Wafd-majority parliament, 119 of 317 MPs owned more than 50 *feddans*. Ibid., 71.
110 Mahmoud Abdel-Fadil, *Development, Income Distribution and Social Change in Rural Egypt* (London: Cambridge University Press, 1975), 44.
111 Warriner, *Land Reform and Development in the Middle East*, 20.
112 Kyle Anderson, "Land Reform: The Invented Tradition of Social Revolution in Egypt" (unpublished honors thesis, University of Michigan, 2009), 25.
113 Ibid.
114 Ansari, *Egypt*, 75.
115 Anderson, *Land Reform*, 26.
116 Tignor observes that the inflation was a result of government policies and had further inflamed nationalist sentiment. He argues:

> The most serious economic problem Egypt faced in the latter war years was rampaging inflation. This inflation was related to many governmental economic policies, for the state had increased the amount of currency in circulation at times when, because of a reduction in imports, the quantity of goods available for purchase was severely limited. Prices for all commodities was on the ascent, causing the state to set up a control board in March 1918, with the duty of fixing maximum prices on cereals, meats and other necessary items and seeing that the cities and the British troops were properly supplied.... Spiralling inflation however, afforded golden opportunities for powerful business firms controlling the manufacture and distribution of necessities to reap unanticipated profits. The huge gains of these companies, coming, as they did, at the expense of the rank and file of the population, caused Egyptian nationalist critics to scrutinize and attack the behaviour of these firms, all of which were dominated by foreign capital and foreign administrators.
>
> (Tignor, "Egyptian Revolution of 1919," 44)

117 David S. Meyer and Nancy Whittier, "Social Movement Spillover," *Social Problems* 41, no. 2 (May 1994): 277.
118 Abd el Moteleb, *al-Ṭalaba wal-ḥarakat al-waṭaniya fī maṣr 1922–1952*, 211.
119 Abdalla, *Student Movement and National Politics*, 49.
120 Ibid., 50.
121 Anthony Gorman, *Historians, State, and Politics in Twentieth Century Egypt: Contesting the Nation* (London: Routledge, 2003), 90.
122 Ibid.
123 Shohdi Attia, *Taṭāwur al-ḥaraka al-waṭaniya al-miṣriya 1882–1956* (The Development of the Egyptian Nationalist Movement 1882–1956) (Cairo: al-Dār al-Maṣriya lil-Kutub, 1957), 94.
124 Mohammad Anis and Ragab Haraz, *al-Taṭāwur al-siyāsi lil-mujtamaʿa al-masri al-hadith* (The Political Development of Contemporary Egyptian Society) (Cairo: Dar Al Nahda Al Arabia, 1972), 218–219.
125 Ibid., 219–320.
126 For an analysis of the incident, see for example Charles D. Smith, "4 February 1942: Its Causes and Its Influence on Egyptian Politics and on the Future of Anglo-Egyptian Relations, 1937–1945," *International Journal of Middle East Studies* 10, no. 04 (1979): 453–479.
127 Ginat, "Egyptian Left," 7–8.
128 Abdel Aziz al-Mahdi, *al-Ḥarakah al-ʿumaliya wa atharahā fī taṭāwur maṣr al-siyāsī, 1930–1945* (The Labor Movement and its Impact on the Development of Egyptian Politics, 1930–1945) (Ph.D. dissertation, Faculty of Politics and Economics, Cairo University, 1976), 261.
129 al-Ghazali, *21 Febrayer*, 12–13.
130 Cited in Selma Botman, *The Rise of Egyptian Communism, 1939–1970* (Syracuse: Syracuse University Press, 1988), 60.
131 It is noteworthy to mention that the Muslim Brotherhood students attended this congress and attempted to disrupt it as they felt that they were not in charge of the student movement at that time as the leftist and more radical elements took a larger role in organizing the student movement. They had submitted their own resolutions to be included in the final communication which were not accepted, so they withdrew from the congress. See Richard Mitchell, *The Society of the Muslim Brothers* (Oxford: Oxford University Press, 1969), 44.
132 Abdel Aziz al-Rifaʿi, *al-ʿUmal wal-ḥarakat al-qawmiya fī maṣr al-ḥāditha* (Workers and the Egyptian Nationalist Movement in Modern Egypt) (Cairo: NP, 1968), 156.
133 Ibid., 19–20.
134 Selma Botman, *From Independence to Revolution: Egypt, 1922–1952* (New York: Syracuse University Press, 1991).

135 February 21 is since then commemorated as National Students Day. A plaque installed at Cairo University recognized the students who lost their lives that day. For further details on the February 1946 protests, see also Mohamed Hassanin Heikal, *Sphinx and Commissar: The Rise and Fall of Soviet Influence in the Arab World* (New York: Collins, 1978), 47–48; Botman, *Rise of Egyptian Communism*, 58–62; and Joel Beinin and Zachary Lockman, *Workers on the Nile: Nationalism, Communism, Islam, and the Egyptian Working Class, 1882–1954* (Cairo: American University in Cairo Press, 1998), 340–342.

136 Reprinted in the *al-Tali'a* newspaper, February 1966.

137 Botman, *Rise of Egyptian Communism*, 63.

138 Ginat, "Egyptian Left," 12.

139 For an elaboration on that argument, see Anthony Oberschall, *Social Conflict and Social Movements* (Englewood Cliffs: Prentice Hall, 1973).

3 The Nasser era

Economy is always political to some extent.

M.M. Knight[1]

Introduction

After approximately a century and a half of ruling Egypt, the Muhammad Ali dynasty saw the demise of its rule in 1952. As the Egyptian navy fired off its final 21-gun salute for the deposed King Farouk as he headed to exile on the royal yacht *al-Mahrousa*, the Egyptian people were beginning to familiarize themselves with their new rulers. Mohammed Naguib was the figurehead of the Free Officers movement, but the true power lay within an inner core of the Officers, and particularly one man, Gamal Abdel Nasser.

This chapter critically discusses the political economy of this new regime, its impact on the labor and student movements, and how these movements responded. It investigates how the movements were corporatized into the state structure and provided with benefits, in exchange for loyalty to the regime. It uses the 1968 protests against the regime as a case study to highlight the spill-over and diffusional process between the movements and critically assesses how successful they were able to challenge the regime.

The political economy of the new regime

Background

Even though the Officers' movement against King Farouk was a *coup d'état*, their actions enjoyed widespread support amongst the Egyptian people, especially in the early years. The Free Officers' stated aims were to end the British occupation of Egypt and eliminate all aspects of imperialism, build economic independence and create a more just society through implementing social and economic reforms. Arguably, there was a definite need for such a movement, as Egypt under the Muhammad Ali dynasty and especially under King Farouk was suffering economically and socially, as highlighted in the previous chapter. The stage was ripe for the deep changes brought by the Free Officers and Gamal

Abdel Nasser. Under Nasser and in due course, a large bureaucracy was created, industries were nationalized and land was confiscated and redistributed. After 1952, Egyptian society was slowly transformed through these reforms, as well as land reform, income distribution, education, employment, social security and health care policies. Even though there was progress on several fronts, some of the factors highlighted in the previous chapter such as urbanization, population growth, limits of the one-crop economy and influence of foreign interests over economic matters continued to affect the economy.

The Free Officers inherited an economy that was still dominated by the colonial powers. Not only were there thousands of British troops stationed in Cairo and the Canal Zone, but also almost the entire banking system from Al Ahly Bank to the smallest lenders was under foreign control. The insurance sector was also under foreign control, meaning that the colonial powers controlled the core of the economic and financial system.[2] To re-establish Egyptian control over the economy, sound economic policies would have to be formulated and implemented, something that took some time to develop. In the initial period of their rule, the Free Officers had no specific idea of how exactly they were to govern and lacked a vision of economic development to gain back control of the economy. Waterbury argues there is no evidence that the Free Officers initially gave much thought to the economic policies of the Egyptian state,[3] and it showed in their haphazard approach to economics. Indeed, it was clear that with regards to policy-making in general, the Free Officers "made it up as they went along."[4] Baker concurs and argues that the Free Officers "had no action program that would have provided some conception of the society their revolution aimed at creating."[5] Their haphazard policy platform can clearly be seen in their program of reform, which consisted of six general and vague guidelines around which economic policy came to be framed: ending feudalism; destroying imperialism; ending monopolies and the domination of capital over government; establishing social justice; building a strong national army; and creating a sound democratic system.[6]

The regime's economic policy was at times disjointed and confused, it had started branding itself 'socialist' from the late 1950s on, but in effect their policies were inherently state capitalist. Nasser himself seemed unclear about what socialism actually meant. In 1958, he stated: "I cannot therefore say that our present economic regime is cooperative, or socialist-cooperative in the way that regimes are practiced elsewhere … it is a system that emanates from the needs of the country."[7] This lack of economic theory was matched by a lack of an overall ideology, something Nasser seem to make up as he became more popular. He himself was not an ideologue; his book *Falsafat Al-Thawra* (The Philosophy of the Revolution) contains general tenets of what has come to be known as Nasserism, which were by no means well developed or articulated.[8] When asked once about his specific view on economic theory, he replied with this ambiguous response:

> Many people say we have no theory: "we would like you to give us a theory." What is the theory we are following? We answer, a socialist, democratic cooperative society. But they persist in asking for a clearly defined

> theory. I ask them, what is the object of a theory? I say that I was not asked on the 23 July to stage the revolution with a printed book, which included my theory. This is impossible ... those who ask for a theory are greatly complicating matters. This is torture.... Our circumstances were that the revolutionary application, our revolutionary application, may be prior to the theory. Then what is the theory? The theory is the evidence of the action.[9]

However, after Nasser consolidated his power in and after 1954, some coherent economic planning began to take place. It had a decidedly ISI thrust to it, and five-year plans were conceived as the main strategic blueprint for economic development and management. Within the context of Richards and Waterbury's political economy framework, ISI is the second state strategy to be deployed by Egypt and was an attempt to move away from the agro-export led growth. The first Five-Year Plan (1959–1964) was successful as it generated GDP growth rates of 6–7 percent per annum and helped created approximately one million jobs in non-agricultural sectors.[10] The growth in the economy and the improvements in people's livelihoods in the decade between 1955 and 1965 is an example of how the state policy and structure variable have a positive impact on the other two variables, economic growth and social actors. This positive impact is not only through job creation, but also in terms of social welfare. Prior to the revolution, there were scarcely any state-run social welfare or health care programs in Egypt, and education was mostly restricted to a small segment of society. Nasser initially began by lowering university fees and eventually made university education free of charge. Large segments of the Egyptian people previously denied university education were able to join universities, earn degrees, and join the growing middle class. After their education was complete, graduates were guaranteed jobs in the expanding public sector.

Industrial development and the expanding public sector

In the early years of Abdel Nasser's rule even though there was political change with the ouster of King Farouk nonetheless there was continuity in terms of economic policy of the war years. This was evident in the traditional character of the economic goals, mainly the focus on investment in agriculture: irrigation, drainage and land reclamation. It could also been seen in the reliance on the private sector, both foreign and domestic, for investment. At the time the major debate was not the choice between public and private investment, but rather the role of foreign capital and how much it should be allowed to invest.[11] The nature of the debate would change drastically in the following years as the emphasis on public investment grew. By the mid-1950s, the regime decided to steer the economy toward heavy industrialization. Industries were created, factories were built and workers were trained. Cooper described the regime's mantra as a "form of semi-populist, state capitalist, developmental nationalism."[12] While the growth in the public sector had greatly benefited the economy of Egypt during Nasser's time, by the time of Mubarak it would have a negative effect in terms of an oversized and inefficient public sector.

Nazih Ayubi argues that the Egyptian economy and bureaucracy went through some remarkable changes after the reforms implemented by Nasser sunk in:

> from 1962/63 to 1969/70, the national income of Egypt increased by 68 percent resting on an increase in the labor force of no more than 20 percent, yet at the same time posts in the public bureaucracy had increased by 70 percent and salaries by 123 percent. The rate of bureaucratic growth has thus far exceeded the rate of growth in population, employment and/or production.[13]

When King Farouk's reign ended, it is estimated that the public sector only accounted for 13 percent of GDP.[14] Over the coming decades, the size of the public sector would increase exponentially.

Agricultural policy

Right after 1952, a key element of the Free Officers' public discourse was the abolition of 'feudalism' and the implementation of land reform. The first land reform law was proclaimed as law by decree in September 1952, despite desperate attempts to derail it by large landowners who knew that it would be disastrous for the wealthy landed elite.[15] The land reform law accomplished just what it set out to do: it reduced the traditional power base of the landed elite and set about creating conditions for a broader distribution of wealth. Before the Free Officers' coup, the number of people who owned 50 acres of land or more numbered 11,800 and they owned 38 percent of arable land, with an average of 200 acres per person. At the pinnacle of this category were 60 people who owned more than 1,000 acres, with average ownership of 4,800 acres.[16]

Through various nationalizations of foreign interests, a huge transfer of resources from the private sector to the public sector was undertaken in the belief that the government would be able to redistribute the wealth equally to all citizens. As the 1950s ended, it was clear from the economic policies that the state was viewed as the engine of growth for the economy, rather than the private sector. There was an attempt to jumpstart the economy through revolutionary means, not just to create economic independence, but also to attempt to re-engineer society in a socialist fashion.[17] Agricultural policy was not only geared for a redistribution of wealth in rural areas, but also designed in the long term to speed up the process of industrialization itself by transferring agricultural surpluses away from rural areas to finance urban growth.[18] The land reform aimed also to expand the market for industrial Egyptian products, as it was assumed the *fellahin* who would receive more land would have more income to spend on consumer goods.[19] These points were articulated by Nasser himself in a 1954 speech on the anniversary of the Officers' movement:

> If you wish to call it a government of businessmen and financiers, you are right again. Agrarian Reform, which has served the farmer, has also rendered a service to Egyptian capital, which was buried beneath the ground. This government has opened new fields of activities through its projects for industry and agriculture. It has guaranteed profits in some cases and has granted many facilities to capitalists willing to start new industries. What is the truth then? The truth is that this is a government for the whole nation, the government of farmers and workers, of officials and students, of financiers and businessmen; of the rich and the poor; of the weak and the strong; of beginners and those who have attained success. It is the government that looks on all Egyptians as one big family and is working for the common good.[20]

Retreating role of the private sector

Even though Nasser had publicly called for Egyptian industrialists to be part of the development process, the role of the private sector was questioned as the 1950s came to a close. Egyptian industrialists in the pre-1952 era had attempted to set up a manufacturing base to attempt to diversify Egypt's economy away from agriculture. However, the new regime viewed the old capitalist class with suspicion, and many of the richest families in Egypt found their assets nationalized by the regime: not only their land, but sometimes their residential properties and personal belongings were also confiscated. By the end of the 1950s, the new economic paradigm shifted the focus of development away from a public–private partnership, to make the state the center and engine of economic development. The political gains Nasser made after the 1956 Suez Canal War raised his stature incredibly amongst Egyptians and across the region. This unified a large segment of Egyptians behind him as he fought off the interference of the former colonial powers. Nasser's popularity after 1956 through to 1967 and even arguably until his death in 1970 would provide him and the regime with a singular opportunity to re-engineer the domestic political and economic arena. After an initial attempt to rely on private capital, nationalization was perceived as the way forward to transfer wealth from the private sector, both foreign and local, to finance the state's expansion.

The industrialization program was successful in its initial stages. Financed partially by foreign donors, from 1957 to 1960 EGP 330 million was invested in the chemicals, building, engineering and mining sectors, which reflected in higher employment.[21] However this level of investment was unsustainable, in part because the regime had calculated that foreign aid would be matched by private sector financing, which didn't occur. Also the regime had quickly depleted the sterling balances from the pre-1952 era.[22] The only choice available was nationalization of banks, land and factories controlled by foreigners and ultra-wealthy Egyptians. Wahba writes, "Military order No. 5 for 1956 sequestered societies, foundations and associations, whether foreign or Egyptian, which the Minister of Economy and Finance considered as operating under British or French control or representing British or French interests."[23] The Ahly Bank and Misr Bank were both nationalized in February 1960, followed by a large number of factories in 1961.[24] This occurred in conjunction with the introduction of five-year plans to guide economic development,[25] the phase labeled by Bush as "directed capitalism"[26] and by Cooper as "state capitalism."[27] By the end of 1961, the greater part of all large and medium sized financial and industrial enterprises were nationalized.[28]

In 1952, 72 percent of gross capital formation was in the private sector; by 1960, the state was responsible for 74 percent of gross capital formation;[29] and by 1965, that figure would reach 90 percent.[30] The nationalization decrees were in effect the culmination of Nasser's attempt to establish full state control over the direction of the economy and therefore the political environment. Waterbury argues that:

> The decrees were improvised is undeniable; equally so is the fact that they were not motivated by economic factors ... Nasser was a leader acutely conscious of potential threats to his regime and control. Whenever possible he anticipated these threats (real or imaginary) and tried to pre-empt them.... Dismantling the upper reaches of the private sector therefore contributed directly and commensurately to the regime strength by placing the levers of economic control in its hands.[31]

Socio-economic gains and 'Nasser's bargain'

The 1952 Officers' movement made significant socio-economic gains, and indeed a variety of indicators show that the people's livelihoods had improved in terms of access to education, health care and jobs. At a macroeconomic level, it is undeniable that certain aspects of the economy were improving in the late 1950s and early 1960s. Cook argues:

> Overall gross domestic product increased dramatically in the early 1960s before declining sharply in 1966. Income per capita also improved modestly and steadily throughout the decade before declining in 1966, though it rebounded in 1968 and 1969. The plight of the Egyptian worker was markedly improved—at least for those who were gainfully employed.[32]

The first Five-Year Plan (1959–1964) was able to generate high rates of growth for the economy through public investments and production, and these were beginning to reflect positively on the livelihood of the Egyptian people. The first decade of the regime's policies (1955–1965) provided the economy with an enviable growth rate for a developing economy, on average 7 percent per annum, which slowed down to 3 percent over the following decade.[33] Cooper aptly describes the economy as follows:

> It was a form of semipopulist, state capitalist, developmental nationalism. It was an economic halfway house, aiming to distribute gains to all groups, save a handful of "exploitative" capitalists. Investment policy was aggressively

> developmental, aiming at a rapid and broad-based industrialization. Consumption policy was aggressively populist, guaranteeing rapidly expanding living standards all around. All this was channeled through the state, with the state becoming not only the super capitalist, but the provider of first resort.[34]

The higher growth rate achieved through direct state intervention and a minimal role for the private sector allowed the state to substantially increase its role in the production and manufacturing sector as well as establish a broad system of price and cost controls. This reflected positively on people's livelihoods, as the regime was able to implement social welfare policies (free education, health care) as well as rent controls for the ever-growing population.

An unwritten social contract began to develop between Nasser and the people, what Shehata termed "Nasser's bargain," that is, his pledge to provide social services, employment, subsidies, education and health care in exchange for exercising total control of the economic and political environment.[35] The stability of the state rested upon that bargain, and Nasser, as well as successive Egyptian presidents after him, would face challenges to their authority when attempts by the state to renege on the bargain occurred.

In the Nasser era, this populist developmental nationalism showed its limits by the mid-1960s, as the "investment demands of developmentalism clashed with the consumption demands of populism."[36] The Achilles' heel of ISI is the economy's ability to generate foreign currency.[37] At various junctures Iraq, Iran and Algeria had followed an ISI strategy reasonably comfortably as they were able to earn foreign currency through the export of petro-chemicals. This is not the case for Egypt where ISI was not augmented by the export of petro-chemicals. Richards and Waterbury argue that:

> Egypt's new industries were designed to market their products in Egypt. They did not have the economies of scale and basic operating efficiency that would have allowed them to export to other markets. Thus although they needed imports to function, they could not generate the foreign exchange to generate them.[38]

The foreign currency issue would exacerbate after 1965 and the economy would be in crisis after the disastrous defeat in the 1967 War. The defeat would have political and economic consequences, which will be discussed later in the chapter.

The labor movement

The Free Officers were able to harness the discontent against the king and the British to their advantage, and initially thousands of workers came out to support the 1952 coup. However, as the months passed and the new regime attempted to consolidate its power, it began to view labor activism with suspicion. The government began to crack down on unauthorized worker activism, as highlighted by the Kafr el Dawar incident in 1952.

Only months after the Officers assumed power, union leaders in the Kafr el Dawar Textile Factory led the workers in a strike for better conditions. The workers were demanding free union elections and parity in benefits and holidays with the desk-based employees of the factory, as well as an end to involuntary redundancies. The strike attracted more than 10,000 workers[39] who were ironically emboldened by the pro-working class slogans and speeches of the Free Officers.[40] Fearing instability and subversive communist influence, the new military regime moved quickly against the workers, arresting 545 and charging 29 with a list of offences that included arson, destruction of property, theft of police weapons, resisting arrest and murder.[41]

In a swift trial by a military tribunal, ten workers received lengthy jail sentences, and two of the union leaders, Mustafa Khamis and Muhammad al-Baqari, were sentenced to death. Allegedly, the 19-year-old Khamis appeared before Mohammed Naguib himself, 12 days before his execution, and refused a more lenient sentence in exchange for informing on others behind the workers' protests.[42] Khamis and Baqari were both executed on September 7, 1952,[43] and became martyrdom symbols of the Egyptian labor movement in the decades following. While the executions were swift and ruthless, new pro-labor laws were gradually implemented to preempt further unrest, with the unspoken rule that favorable laws would be implemented in exchange for workers not protesting and not being involved in political activities. Arguing against a Marxist view of Egyptian labor, Kassem postulates that:

> The workers accepted such rules, while overlooking the September executions, indicated a weakening of class-consciousness in Egypt. The assumption is reinforced in the words of one veteran activist who noted the lack of protests against the executions of their colleagues stemmed from the workers belief that "the executions were a regime stand against the communists not the workers." This weak class-consciousness on the part of the workers eventually assisted in the facilitating their cooptation by the new regime.[44]

Despite the swift executions, the Free Officers had made some overtures to certain union leaders in an attempt to co-opt them, and there was no general union agreement on a collective response. Beinin and Lockman argue that the labor movement had a historic choice, either to

> press its independent demands in opposition to the limits imposed by the state and risk becoming isolated from the nationalist movement that had provided the overall context for working class political activity throughout the twentieth century, or to accommodate itself to the new conditions.[45]

The difficulty of this choice was not made easier for having no united leadership. The Free Officers' Stalinist slogan "Unity, Order, and Labor" was just one other indication of the new regime's carrot or stick approach to social movements that it could not fully control. Ironically, the workers' mobilizations, which were viewed as heroic during the pre-1952 era, were now perceived as a threat.[46]

Nasser's bargain: the labor version

Strong efforts were directed by the Nasser regime toward building a populist coalition with workers and the union movement, as the regime understood that labor was a powerful social force that could drastically affect stability. Bianchi argues that "Nasser had good reason to regard labor as a key factor in either consolidation or loss of power."[47] The union movement eventually reached a historic compromise with the regime, by which favorable labor legislation was enacted but the unions were co-opted into the state structure in a corporatist model.[48]

Union leaders in effect became state employees, who theoretically were placed to collectively bargain with the state but whose power and influence was in reality drastically reduced. This is achieved through the cultivation of a union culture that relies on patronage and clientelism between the union leaders and the state apparatus on one hand, and between the co-opted union leaders and the workers on the other. The leaders of official unions ensure the workers' loyalty to the state and maintain industrial peace, in exchange for socio-economic gains and rights. Nonetheless, even though in this corporatist model the state effectively controls the union apparatus, workers are still able to influence economy policy and obtain state concessions in a limited fashion.[49]

Laws 317, 318 and 319 of December 1952 and further labor laws culminating in the landmark 1959 Labor Code all granted long-standing demands of the labor movement.[50] They included doubling the minimum wage, reducing the work day, and guaranteeing an annual raise, bonuses for satisfactory performance, health and social insurance, and subsidies on basic goods.[51] However, one of the foremost gains by workers was limiting the capacity of employers to dismiss employees arbitrarily (*al-faṣl al-taʿassufiī*). Arbitrary dismissal had been a key issue during the pre-1952 era, when employers were able to dismiss workers "not for misbehavior on the job, but solely because of production cutbacks or other market considerations."[52] This was a key gain for the workers, who now for the first time enjoyed some degree of job security. The cumulative impact of all these rights, according to Ibrahim, "had the effect of empowering Egypt's working class as never before."[53]

In return for these rights, Nasser required the allegiance of the labor movement, which he was able to harness early on in 1954 in his confrontation with Naguib. In what later became known as the March 30th Crisis, Nasser was able to exploit the labor movement and thousands of workers came to the streets to support him.[54] The strike of transport workers in Cairo on March 27–28 in support of Nasser's call for the "continuation of the revolution" as opposed to Naguib's emphasis on civilian rule,[55] gridlocked the city for days and showed Nasser's mass popularity.[56] The showdown was won by Nasser. It would not be the last time workers and unions would support him and the regime. Beinin writes:

> During the Suez Crisis and the 1956 War, trade unions mobilized support for the nationalization of the Suez Canal and actively participated in the national defense. Trade union leaders called a general strike on August 16, 1956, at the time of the London Conference, to demonstrate support for the nationalization of the canal. Many unions collected financial contributions from their members to assist in the war effort. The textile federation urged its union to set aside labor disputes during the war, and production in some mills increased.[57]

One of the demands that were not met was the insistence of some trade union leaders in 1952 to form a general trade union, something that the regime resisted from early on as it feared subversive communist influence. In recognition of the importance of absorbing union activity into the state structure, in 1955 the regime established the Permanent Conference of Egyptian Trade Unions as a forum for union leaders to conduct a dialogue with the state.[58] The General Federation of Egyptian Trade Unions (GFETU) was formed by 1957, comprised predominantly of union leaders carefully selected by the regime. Beinin writes that

> the government did not take any chances on the political composition of the federation. The government submitted the names of the seventeen members of the executive board of the GFETU to the founding conference. There were no nominations from those attending the conference, and no election was held.[59]

Over the coming decades, the GFETU would continue its role as the officially sanctioned union. Its networks of patronage and clientelism would operate through the Nasser, Sadat and Mubarak eras.

In 1962, Nasser announced a new policy directive, the "Charter for National Action." Henceforth, Egypt would be governed by the principles of 'scientific socialism.' The vehicle for this next phase would be *al-ittiḥād al-ʿarabī al-ishtirākī* (Arab Socialist Union, ASU), the precursor for Mubarak's NDP (National Democratic Party).[60] This was in effect the formalization of one party rule. Nasser's vision of the ASU was a party formed of workers, peasants and students at the vanguard of Egyptian and pan-Arab socialist liberation. Yet none of these corporatized social movements were actually allowed to wield any real political power, and rather they were used as a façade to maintain authoritarian rule. Hinnebusch describes what Nasser was trying to build as "socialism without socialists," which effectively meant that—rather than an empowered working and middle class leading change—a new state capitalist bourgeois was created with a liberal and consumption-oriented ideology.[61]

The Nasser regime was acutely aware of the potential impact of labor unrest on regime stability, and sought to maneuver the gains made by workers to placate labor. The regime promoted the concept of reciprocity, which entailed that workers were expected to express their appreciation of these measures by showing more enthusiasm for their jobs and thus increasing productivity.[62] This was explicitly stated in the ASU Charter for National Action, which stated: "Every citizen should be aware of his defined responsibility in the whole plan, and should be fully conscious of the definite rights he will enjoy in the event of success."[63]

The corporatist structure allowed Nasser to centrally organize unions directly under the state. Workers were given certain rights and guarantees but several new prohibitions were also announced, including "a ban against inciting class antagonisms, organizing work stoppages, trying to overthrow the political system, and using force to recruit union members."[64] As part of this trade-off, the implementation of fairer labor laws almost eliminated the risk of job loss in factories, one of the main causes of collective action in the pre-1952 era. Goldberg argues that

> it was in the interests of the workers, managers and the state officials to introduce a "corporate" economic and political system. Relatively few workers—only some of the most highly skilled workers in a few key industrial sectors—benefited from maintaining completely open labor markets. Most workers preferred administered markets where wages were set by the state.[65]

While this bargain was maintained, the Nasser regime expected (and mostly received) the ongoing consent of workers and unions, even as their numbers grew. Table 3.1 shows the increase in the number of workers from the pre-1952 era to the first years after the coup.

The ensuing lull in collective action due to corporatizing the union movement was also aided by Nasser's rising stature locally, regionally and internationally. Nasser's pan-Arabism was at its peak during the late 1950s and early 1960s. He was able to convert Egypt's military defeat in the 1956 war into a political victory for himself, Egypt and the developing world. By championing the Non-Alignment Movement (NAM) and supporting decolonization in Arab, African, and Asian countries, Nasser raised his international profile to new heights. This anti-colonial Third-Worldist posture also worked to gain him further domestic legitimacy. Nasser's regional ambitions did not end there, as he pressed for the short-lived union with Syria from 1958 to 1961. Nasser continued his quite-successful foreign policy until he overplayed his hand against Israel in 1967. The

Table 3.1 Industrial employment (1937–1954)

Year	*Number of workers*
1937	139,600
1952	264,927
1954	263,863

Source: Ellis Goldberg, "The Foundations of State-Labor Relations in Contemporary Egypt," *Comparative Politics* 24, no. 2 (January 1992): 153.

Six Day War, as it became known, effectively put an end to Nasserism and pan-Arabism.[66] The war showed Egyptians that the Nasser regime was actually much weaker than it had portrayed itself to be.

The student movement

Government spending on education had expanded before 1952. However, the scope and breadth of education was not in line with the semi-populist developmentalist policies that Nasser would begin to implement which would require an army of engineers and doctors, amongst other graduates. The first few years of Free Officer rule saw further expansion in educational spending. The student-to-population ratio increased from 71 state school pupils per 1,000 inhabitants in 1952–1953 to 102 in 1958–1959, and from 1.95 to 3.07 university student per 1,000 inhabitants in the same period.[67]

Public investment in education rose from EGP2.5 million to EGP33.3 million over the same period.[68] As observed in Table 3.2, the next few decades would see a drop in illiteracy levels, which at the turn of the nineteenth century had been at 93 percent of the population. The table also highlights the discrepancy between male and female illiteracy, which continues to date.

The same pre-1952 tensions between traditionalist and modernist educational systems highlighted in Chapter 2 would continue in the Nasser era. Crecelius writes that

> the Young Officers inherited a nation deeply split over modernist and traditionalist orientation, an reformed Azhar, and a religious class which was desperately trying to defend its own crumbling position while refusing to participate in the modernization of Egyptian life and thought.[69]

A law passed in 1961 provided for the conversion of Al Azhar into a modern-style university offering degrees in a variety of science and humanities disciplines, in addition to the traditional disciplines of Islamic law and theology.[70] The conversion of Al Azhar to a modern university would have a lasting and profound impact. First, as it would help create generations of politicized students with Islamist leanings and, second, it would bring it under direct government control. Overall, the number of students across school, vocational and university programs would increase exponentially in the first decade of the new regime. Table 3.3 shows the increase in student numbers from the years 1953–1954 to 1965–1966.

Nasser's bargain: the student version

The regime understood well that university students, like the labor movement, were a potential source of threat or support. At that same time, the regime needed to expand education to match its populist developmental policies. The whole educational system was then restructured, with wide-ranging changes

Table 3.2 Number and percentages of illiterate people in the population of Egypt 15 years and older, by sex (1907–1995)

Years	*Total population*			*Male population*			*Female population*		
	# total	*# illiterate*	*% illiterate*	*# total*	*# illiterate*	*% illiterate*	*# total*	*# illiterate*	*% illiterate*
1907	6,653,301	6,174,315	92.8	3,281,642	2,841,642	86.8	3,371,659	3,326,116	98.6
1927	8,539,142	7,496,994	87.8	4,182,109	3,252,868	77.8	4,357,033	4,244,126	97.4
1937	9,551,419	8,366,389	87.6	4,736,485	3,718,580	78.5	4,814,934	4,647,809	96.5
1947	11,389,181	9,023,584	79.2	5,581,963	3,806,383	68.2	5,816,218	5,217,201	89.7
1960	14,705,584	10,817,276	73.6	7,251,668	4,285,862	59.1	7,453,880	6,531,414	87.6
1976	21,526,506	13,317,501	61.9	10,935,539	5,051,502	46.2	10,590,967	8,265,999	78.0
1986	28,715,309	16,000,050	55.7	14,615,632	6,229,046	42.6	14,099,677	9,771,004	69.3
1995	39,007,000	18,954,000	48.6	19,808,000	7,205,000	36.4	19,199,000	11,749,000	61.2

Source: Salah Abdel Tawab, *Patterns and Dynamics of the Pre-University Education in Egypt: A Developmental and Demographic Perspective* (unpublished M.Phil thesis, Cairo Demographic Center, 1997), 18.

Table 3.3 Student enrollment by education level from 1953/1954 to 1965/1966 (in 000s)

Level of education	*1953/1954*	*1965/1966*	*% increase*
Primary	1,393	3,418	145
General Preparatory	349	574	65
Vocational Preparatory	3	27	800
General Secondary	92	209	127
Vocational Secondary	19	101	432
Teacher Institutes	24	49	104
Universities	54	124	130
Total	1,934	4,502	132

Source: Mahmoud Faksh, "The Consequences of the Introduction and Spread of Modern Education: Education and National Integration in Egypt," *Middle Eastern Studies* 16, no. 2 (May 1980): 45.

including the institution of universal primary education and the abolition of school fees, nationalization of foreign schools, expansion of vocational training, emphasis on girls' primary education to minimize the illiteracy gap between sexes,[71] a massive reduction of university fees, the construction of new universities, and the expansion of faculties in existing universities. Between 1952 and 1965 the number of university students quadrupled, indicating the regime's emphasis on supporting the growing middle class (one of its key support bases). Abdallah correctly points out that "the expansion of higher education must be regarded as the prime educational achievement of the 1952 Revolution."[72]

There were several factors behind this massive expansion of higher education. First, university education and subsequent employment in the public sector continued to be the main vehicle of social mobility. Second, the regime, especially in the industrial expansion phase (from 1955 to 1965), needed trained specialists and thus promoted increased enrollment in science, engineering, agriculture and medicine. Third, university education had become effectively free, a far cry from the prohibitive costs in the pre-1952 era, which encouraged people from a disadvantaged socio-economic background to get their secondary school certificate and then enter university.[73] While the expansion of education was an achievement in itself, the regime's policies lacked a longer-term strategy regarding how to absorb the exponentially growing number of students into the workforce. By the mid-1960s, the regime's policies yielded the unintended consequences of a massive surplus of university-educated graduates.

Controlling the students

The Nasser regime had inherited a higher education sector that included highly politicized university campuses, as the student movement had been a key component of the nationalist struggle from 1919 onwards. To consolidate its power, a showdown with the universities was inevitable. Abdalla writes that "it's not surprising that the first major confrontations faced by the military regime were with workers of the industrial city of Kafr el Dawar in 1952 and with universities in 1954."[74]

In the immediate aftermath of the 1952 coup, the Revolutionary Command Council (RCC) enjoyed massive support of students and faculty members alike. However, in the 1954 crisis and Nasser's showdown with Naguib elements of the intelligentsia, including university professors, sided with Naguib in his call for a return to civilian rule. In March 1954, the teaching staff of Alexandria University called for an end to martial law and the dissolution of the RCC. Nasser ordered the arrest of a number of university professors, denouncing them as "opponents of the revolution."[75] This stifling of dissent in campuses across Egypt began a lull in student activism that would last until the 1968 uprising.

As with the labor movement, the Nasser regime moved to co-opt the student movement into the corporatist state structure. Until 1967, Nasser was successful in diverting student activism to state-sponsored activities. This was achieved through state-sponsored student unions that fell under the ASU structure. Nasser's security apparatus moved to control campuses across Egypt, as students and professors were recruited as informants to spy on other students and fellow staff members.[76] Some students were given nominal participatory avenues in national politics to placate them, while in reality the regime was controlling the levers. The Faculty of Engineering at Cairo University, which usually was home to some of the best and brightest minds from across Egypt,[77] and which had been a hotbed of student activism in the pre-1952 era, saw a lull in activism (especially during the early 1960s).

In a historical testimony, student leader Nabil Abdalla recalled that, when he entered that faculty in 1961, many students would conduct pro-regime activities so that the authorities would notice them, thus improving their career prospects.[78] When the dissolution of the union between Egypt and Syria occurred in September 1961, the authorities encouraged pro-regime protests on campus.[79] There were several Nasserite and Arab nationalist student groups operating on campus, whether under covert or overt control of police lieutenants.[80] The state's coercive apparatuses were manifesting themselves directly in universities across Egypt to stifle any anti-regime student activism. Even though increasing numbers of students were attending university, academic freedom and creativity were casualties of the period. Abdalla writes that:

> This demobilization and demoralization of what had been an autonomous political movement was engineered through a combination of coercion and socialization. Indirect political control of the student population through the university administration was made tighter and strengthened by direct political control.[81]

The socialization was a conscious effort on the part of the Nasser regime to adapt students to the regime's populist outlook. It manifested itself in the curriculum, starting from primary education through secondary and finally university programs. Faksh writes that students

> were repeatedly taught the various patriotic themes of Islam, nationalism, Arabism and socialism. Textbooks are full of stories about the glory of medieval Islamic heroes and the great Arab nationalist struggle against colonialism and other political and socio-economic injustices that culminated in the 1952 revolution.[82]

Faksh reflects on his own school experience:

> It would be safe to assume that the ceaseless efforts to bring about identification with the regime have been somewhat successful. My classmates and I developed a strong sense of identification and pride with Arabism, anti-colonialism, and nationalist leader of Nasser's caliber. On different occasions, as the government deemed necessary, we were able to express these feelings and attitudes by demonstrating in support of regime causes and against anti-regime causes, domestic or foreign.[83]

This socialization was also explicit on the part of the regime. The National Charter of 1961 stated that:

> the object of education is no longer to turn out employees who work in the government offices. Thus, the educational curricula in all subjects must be reconsidered according to the principles of the revolution. The curricula should aim at enabling the individual human being to reshape his life.[84]

The university experience itself trained the students to be acquainted with the mechanics of the state bureaucratic structure, where graduates take their places as cogs in the larger machine. Binder observes, regarding the workings of the Egyptian educational system of the 1960s:

> Imperfect a system though it may be, the university performs a very important socializing function for the administrative elite of the country. As they learned about the overt character of the political system and its ideal goals in grammar school, they learn about its internal workings, the flow of authority, prestige, and permitted deviations during their higher education.[85]

The Egyptian left: a disintegrating bridge between the labor and the student movements?

Despite these attempts at socialization and the stifling of critical debate, various leftist organizations continued to operate, first overtly, then covertly. The Egyptian communist movement had a complex relationship with the new regime. While initially some communist organizations such as the Democratic Movement for National Liberation (HADETU) had welcomed the Officers' movement against the king, the 1952 Kafr el Dawar incident and the execution of Khamis and Baqari, both of whom were suspected of communist organization membership, showed the regime's intent toward leftist organizations. From 1953 to 1955, the various currents of the Egyptian communist movement were united in their opposition to the new regime, and were able to gain more followers, especially amongst students and the intelligentsia. The communist movement did have working-class supporters during its earlier opposition to the king, but its composition was changing by the mid-1950s. On this, Beinin has noted:

> The social base of the post-World War Two Egyptian communist movement was primarily the Western-educated urban intelligentsia—the *effendiyya* and secondarily a small but rapidly growing industrial working class. The *effendiyya* has been the political class of modern Egypt, and the country's political currents have drawn their active cadres from this stratum. While the communists did have significant working class support 1942–1954, by the mid 1950s the university educated *intelligentsia* was the most important component of the movement, especially at a leadership level.[86]

By 1955, Nasser had begun reorienting his foreign policy toward the Eastern Bloc, while maintaining his non-aligned stance. The agreement to purchase weapons from Czechoslovakia as well as other overtures forced a reassessment within the communist movement, with some communists now calling for cooperation with the regime.[87] Beinin writes that this rapprochement with the regime

> is consistent with the historic general orientation of the three tendencies in the Egyptian communist movement, which placed the Egyptian national liberation struggle at the top of their political agenda and sought the integration of the communist movement with the nationalist movement as the primary strategic task of Egyptian communists.[88]

The 1956 Suez War would reaffirm the communists' position, as they supported the regime against the aggression of the old colonial powers (Britain and France) and Israel. However, as Nasser's stature rose even further, he was able to consolidate his power and move against the communists. By the late 1950s and early 1960s, even though the state's ostensible goal was 'socialism,' Nasser arrested a large number of communists from among the unions, the students and the intelligentsia. Many communist activists would be tortured in the regime's prisons, and some died while incarcerated.[89]

This repression of the communist movement drove many activists underground. After Nasser's further orientation toward the Eastern Bloc, many communists were released from prison in 1964. Nasser recognized that the leftist students and youth would continue to be a thorn in the side of the regime if not co-opted into the state structure. The regime then sought to channel the students' energies and activism through formal channels, such as the Socialist Youth Organization (*munāẓamāt al-shabāb al-ishtirākī*), which was formed in 1964. Khaled Mohyideen, the only RCC member with communist sympathies, was tasked with forming the organization. A wide range of activists from a range of currents became the nucleus of the organization: Marxists, Baathists, Arab nationalists, Nasserists, and progressive elements from the Muslim Brotherhood all joined. The organization would prove to be a fruitful training ground for students and youth, some of whom would reach positions of leadership over the coming decades.[90] While the Socialist Youth Organization was part of the co-opted left in Egypt, contacts between students and workers continued in underground organizations as well. Hani Shukrallah, a leftist student leader from the 1970s era and a well-known journalist and public intellectual in Egypt, highlights some of the links between the labor and student movements:

> There were also underground communist organizations that had a presence here and there, which subsequently leads to the formation of The Egyptian Communist Labor Party. There were a group of Marxist from the 1960s, but basically the new cadres were comprised of students and textile workers from Alexandria. Until 1973, you will find more workers than students and intellectuals in the communist organizations, which is uncharacteristic of the left at that time.... The leaders of the coal strike were members of this small leftist organization. There was a link between the students and workers at the time; both were coming to the same consciousness. Both groups were learning from each other. For example, wall magazines, which are a student invention, spread among the workers movement. The chants and the tools of resistance were being shared between both movements.[91]

Assessing the opportunity environment

While the Nasser era was characterized by a general closing of the political system, nonetheless some political opportunities did present themselves. The first was access to labor and educational sectors, continuing on from the previous era. The second was regime weakness, which manifested itself in spectacular fashion through the defeat in 1967.

Labor and educational sector access

As discussed in the previous chapter, increased labor and educational sector access occurred in the pre-1952 era. However, due to the co-optation strategies pursued by the Nasser regime, both labor and student movements would see a lull in their activism. Union activity would see a decrease as well, reflected in the smaller number of unions which were consolidated and finally came together under the umbrella of the GFETU. The increased number of workers was not met by an increase in union activity.

Meanwhile, student numbers in the higher education sector continued to expand massively, as noted in Table 3.3. As the number of graduates increased, there was a discrepancy between supply and demand for educated workers, even though the regime had promised university graduates jobs in the expanding public sector after their graduation. This led to a saturated public sector, which began giving menial, low-paying office jobs to graduates just to ensure their employment.[92] Having absorbed the lesson from the pre-1952 era that a growing number of unemployed educated youth may pose a challenge to the authorities, the regime's promise of guaranteed employment sought to quell potential social unrest. Like the workers, the students did not take advantage of their exponentially increasing numbers to challenge the regime in its early years. It would take a major crisis for the regime to show weakness that students and workers could take advantage of. Such as a crisis would manifest itself in the disastrous 1967 War.

Regime weakness

Regime weakness provides an opportunity for challengers to mobilize.[93] Nasser's co-optation of the labor and youth movement was indeed highly effective, for a period of time. However, the 1967 defeat unprecedentedly highlighted the regime's vulnerability and exposed it to its domestic challengers. The defeat in the 1967 War effectively ended Nasser's pan-Arabist vision and created a seismic shift in Arab politics itself.[94] Nasser had been able to ride a constant wave of popularity domestically, regionally and internationally since the 1956 Suez War, which was a military defeat but a moral victory for the regime. The 1967 defeat broke the aura of invincibility around Nasser, and thereafter wide segments of society, including the labor and student movements, would begin to show their discontent.

In theory, regimes in democratic settings are held accountable to their people through a variety of mechanisms including elections, independent state institutions and a free press. There is a wide range of models of democracy and their successful implementation differs greatly between one country and another. However, in general, a democratically elected government would be held responsible before its citizens, such accountability acting as a mechanism to regulate leaders' behavior (such as engaging in war or occupation). Such mechanisms generally do work, but they do not always work perfectly.[95]

However, in authoritarian settings, such routine accountability mechanisms are virtually non-existent. An autocratic ruler can use a victory in a risky war to solidify his rule at home. If a war is lost, however, it would have domestic consequences even in authoritarian settings. A variety of studies have looked at the impact of war on regime stability.[96] Among those, the studies conducted by Mesquita *et al.* have used statistical data from wars that unfolded from 1816 to 1975 to assess their impact on both authoritarian and democratic governments.[97] The study concluded that the results

> demonstrate quite clearly that the outcome of war has a dramatic effect on the fate of the regime involved.... Although broadly based in time and ranging across all types of political systems, the results are fully consistent with the claim that the political welfare of governmental regimes is directly tied to the performance of the nation in war.[98]

The impact of war on the stability of regimes can be drastic and even yield regime change, but it can also lead to instability that the regime can weather, given some concessions. The Nasser regime had attributed the 1948 Arab defeat and the establishment of Israel to the legacy of colonialism and cronyism under King Farouk. The regime framed its discourse as fiercely populist and anti-colonialist, and the 1956 political victory had helped it immensely. The 1967 defeat laid bare many of the propaganda claims of the regime, and indeed people in Egypt were now speaking openly against the regime. Halliday argues:

> Like all crises, 1967 appeared to present opportunities as well as setbacks. Out of this catastrophe, many people in the region came to believe that new political perspectives and possibilities had opened up. In Egypt itself, the military defeat coincided with heightened social tensions. Peasants, workers and students, in a movement that began with the Qamshish peasant uprising of 1965, challenged the social compromises of Arab socialism.[99]

Assessing the threat environment

As previously outlined, the other part of the political process model focuses on specific threats in a movement's environment. There are a variety of factors that can be construed as such threats, but generally the social movement theory literature highlights three categories: state-attributed economic problems, erosion of rights and state repression.[100] During the Nasser era, especially until 1966, large segments of society benefited economically and socially from the regime's policies, so there is no strong case for state-attributed economic problems then (this would manifest itself more under the Sadat regime).

The erosion of rights under Nasser is debatable, as the corporatist state structure led the labor and student movements to willingly surrender some of their rights in exchange for some benefits. Regardless, there is a strong case that increased state repression formed a threat to the social movements. State repression can act as a powerful incentive to instigate protests and instability. While this does not occur automatically, in the case of populist-authoritarian states like Egypt was during the Nasser era, regime challengers wait for the state to show signs of weakness to begin to translate their discontent against repressive measures into protests.

Repression of opposition

After consolidating his power internally, Nasser began to secure his rule by repressing opposition groups. Wickham writes that he

> banned all opposition groups and imposed state control over areas where they had formerly reached out to the mass public. At the same time, the regime robbed such groups of a key constituency through the co-optation of educated, lower middle class youth.[101]

These tactics were not opposed by the public in general, as Nasser maneuvered from a position of strength. Here was a leader who, for the first time in modern Egyptian history, led a revolution that put Egyptians in charge of Egypt. Nasser was a charismatic leader who, given his earlier successes after the 1952 coup, was considered very popular among most Egyptians and sought to transform Egypt into a modern secular society. The main groups which were a threat to Nasser's rule were the old landowning class and Islamists, and to a lesser extent the workers and the students.

Nasser moved not only against landowners, students and the workers but also against the Islamists. While thorough analysis of Islamism as a social movement is beyond the scope of this book, it is certainly relevant to the Islamist students. While Nasser suppressed the Islamists, it was Sadat who invited their students back to campus to act as a bulwark against the Nasserite and leftist students, a clear opportunity for a segment of the student movement that will be elaborated in the next chapter. However, Nasser's suppression of Islamism in all its forms initiated a classic cycle of repression–violence–repression that prevailed through Mubarak's era. In contrast to popularly accepted views that Islamists, as irrational actors, resort to unpredictable violence, Hafez and Wikarowitcz argue:

> Violence is only one of a myriad of possibilities in the repertoires of contention and becomes most likely where regimes attempt to crush Islamic activism through broad repressive measures that leave few alternatives. In Egypt, the cycle of violence began largely in response to a broad crackdown on the Islamic movement that ensnared moderates, radicals and a number of managerial bystanders. The crackdown included arrests, hostage taking, torture, executions and other forms of state violence.[102]

Islamists resorting to violence is an example of social movements seeking other avenues of contestation when denied legitimate ways to express themselves and participate in the political process. Nasser's authoritarianism and suppression of these movements would be one of the key inheritances he would leave his successors.

The 1968 uprising

The 1967 Arab–Israeli War shattered the relative peace between the regime and the student and labor movements, which had been in place since 1954. Immediately after the defeat, and as a clear sign of the continued co-optation of a large segment of the labor movement, the GFETU signaled its support of Nasser. In the evening of June 9, 1967, in a highly emotive broadcast address to the nation, Nasser took personal responsibility for the defeat and announced that he had submitted his resignation. The GFETU leadership immediately announced its support of the embattled president and went to the Maspero TV building to attempt to broadcast a statement that called on all workers to strike until Nasser rescinded his resignation.[103] The GFETU leadership also issued a statement proclaiming that the "struggle against Israel will not stop until Palestine is returned" and that Nasser would be the one to return it.[104] Nasser reassumed power after protests erupted across Egypt calling for his return. Such was his popularity and dominance of Egypt's political and social landscape that after the defeat, Umm Kulthum, the iconic Egyptian singer, would sing to him her song on 'behalf' of the people: "Stay! You are the hope" (*ibqa! fa anta al-amal*).

Even though Nasser returned to power, there were cracks in the façade of the regime as anger and discontent bubbled from various segments of society. This did not happen instantaneously. Gradually, over the course of the next year, protests began to occur in various Arab capitals. Anderson writes:

> A catalyst had to be added to the frustrations felt by the loss. By spring 1968, the shift occurred when students came to recognize that the leaders who had led the defeat were consolidating their positions around the new political realities. In Egypt, the spark was a strike called on February 21, 1968, by workers in Helwan, to oppose the lenient verdicts meted out to Egyptian Air Force leaders for their failures in June 1967. The action continued for the next week as students from all of Cairo's universities and many more workers joined the initial participants.[105]

The regime had loosened its grip on the students at Cairo University and other campuses across the country in the aftermath of 1967. Wall magazines (*mugalaʿat al-ḥāʾiṭ*), which had been previously banned by the regime, returned to university walls (especially Cairo University). In these magazines, students would now directly criticize the Nasser regime, as well as caricature it in a variety of drawings that ridiculed Nasser and his mouthpiece, Mohammed Hassanien Hiekal.[106] Even Nasser himself acknowledged the wall magazines at Cairo University and defamed the students responsible, saying in a speech that "sons of the landowner class which has been abolished have been attacking the revolution on campus."[107] As highlighted by Hani Shukrallah's previous testimony, the wall magazine was a tool invented by the students, but in a case of diffusion of tactics, began to be used also by workers in the factories.

Opposition to the regime had been quietly gaining pace across Egypt and on university campuses and on factory grounds. In February 1968, after the lenient sentencing of air force generals who were in command during the 1967 War, workers and students began a wave of protests that was of a size and scale unheard of since the pre-1952 era. The protests became increasingly politicized, as the students called for freedom of expression and the press, as well as laws that allowed political organizing—directly challenging the status quo in effect since 1954. Kerr argues that the split between the regime and the students was initiated by a generation of students who "had the achievements in their memory and lived the [1967] defeat in reality."[108] Shukrallah, who was a student during this period, observes:

> The 1967 defeat shook the regime. The working class was recreated under Nasser and expanded hugely. In a corporatist model, you and the regime are

> one thing; your leverage is your access to the regime. It's not that the workers were dormant, the regime did give them access. All the unions and syndicates were empowered to a certain extent. I have a problem with young people viewing this era as completely dim and oppressive; it was much more complex than that. There was a kind of implicit bargain between the regime and the working/poor class, which some people term "Nasser's bargain." There are two main outcomes of 1967. Firstly, the predominance of the corporate discourse and populist authoritarian discourse got shattered, resulting in liberating the workers and encouraging them to resist. Secondly, in the 1970s through the 1980s, they start resisting the gains they have made previously; it was a defensive era during the Sadat regime. Workers were looking for different instruments and tools to gain their rights.[109]

Contact between the workers and students was maintained through several communist organizations that had gone underground during the Nasser era. This is particularly true of the Helwan industrial area on the outskirts of Cairo, where some underground organizations continued to meet. The February 1968 protests took place across Cairo and its working-class suburbs, especially Helwan and Shubra al Khiema. The first outbreak of the protests occurred in Helwan, which housed the state military factories and a sizable population of workers. Nabil Ghany, one of the few remaining labor leaders of the era, spoke of his own personal experience of the events of 1968:

> In 1968, I was a member in an underground leftist youth organization in Helwan. On the day they announced the verdict against the war's aviation leaders, we had heard about the subsequent protests in the factories, we were in a meeting and we agreed that to call on the youth organizations in Helwan to come out in protest. We made those calls from the telephone of Helwan Youth Camp, calling several student organizations to go out in protest against the verdicts. We did some calls to young workers in factories, and they did join the protest the following morning and they were joined by several groups of workers. The demonstration gathered in front of the aviation factory in Helwan. Helmy El Bassiouny and Mahmoud El Nokrashy, members of the board of the socialist union in Helwan, tried to negotiate with the protestors telling that the verdicts will be reconsidered, to no avail. The demonstration continued.[110]

The proximity of the industrial working-class hub, Helwan, to Cairo meant that workers who congregated there could then march on the capital. When the workers in Helwan military factories heard about the lenient sentencing of the air force generals, they stopped work on their machines and started protesting. The factory management tried to dissuade the workers, but they insisted on marching toward the GFETU headquarters.[111] On their way to the capital, the workers attacked and occupied the Helwan police station, leading to clashes when the police sent in reinforcements. When news of the clashes reached Cairo

University, several student groups headed to the Cairo train station to welcome the Helwan workers to Cairo, forcing the Minister of Interior to cut the Helwan–Cairo train line to stop the workers from coming into the capital.[112] The Cairo university students announced that a march would head to the center of the capital and directly to parliament. As news of the protests reached them, thousands of workers in Shubra el Khiema and elsewhere went on strike and joined the protests in solidarity.[113]

The worker and student marches joined together and for the first time since 1946, both movements were engaged in combined protests against an incumbent regime. The combined student/worker march was able to reach parliament and demanded a retrial for the air force generals, freedom of the press, and transition to a more democratic and inclusive political system.[114] The regime tried to deal with the protests and militant sit-ins in various ways, initially through non-violent means by sending government delegations and state security forces to attempt to negotiate, then by violent means when those negotiations failed. A huge demonstration unfolded in Tahrir Square, and the police was no longer able to control the crowds. Foreshadowing what would occur several decades later in 2011, in the protests against Mubarak, the army was called in. However, the elite divisions that led the army to side with the protestors against Mubarak in 2011 were simply not there in 1968. Hussein writes that "the army first intervened inconspicuously with tear gas, but it was driven to opening fire, hitting large numbers of demonstrators and killing a tailor, for whom Cairo later held an elaborate funeral."[115] The protests dwindled in the face of direct repression from the army, but the regime knew it had to absorb this anger or risk further upheaval that would threaten its stability. Nasser responded with the March 30th Program (more on which shortly).

The regime was then faced with another round of protests in November 1968. An Israeli attack on Naga Hammadi again pointed toward the weakness of the regime in the face of external enemies, and rumors spread that there were secret capitulation negotiations with Israel. On November 20 and 21, massive student demonstrations across university campuses erupted comprised of various ideological currents (Wafdist liberals, communists, the Muslim Brotherhood) united against the regime. Some of the biggest protests occurred in the Nile Delta city of Mansoura, where workers and students, supported by a sizable part of the population, confronted the police, who opened fire, killing several people.[116] In Alexandria, the Polytechnic Institute was occupied and the governor was held hostage as the students demanded the release of all students arrested. Hussein describes the events of November 1968:

> The top leaders were seized with panic. They saw their margin for maneuver slipping away and decided to resort to massive and ruthless intervention by the army, to bloody repression. Before the end of the day they ordered all secondary schools and universities closed and massed army detachments (held in readiness for this purpose ever since the February revolt) in the capital and the surrounding region. Helicopters crisscrossed the sky over the

> city in search of gathering crowds. If the inhabitants of Cairo started to move in earnest, uprisings could spread throughout the country. On that Sunday demonstrations did in fact take place in the capital and many other cities, including the towns of Upper Egypt where the Naga Hammadi raid had created a state of extreme tension.... The forces of repression used machine guns against the crowds, leaving scores dead on the streets, and aroused a hatred which drew the unemployed, the workers and the students even more closely together.[117]

The regime recognized that cosmetic domestic reforms would not be enough to subdue the unrest. According to Hussein, only an escalation with Israel in the Canal Zone area could restore the regime and the army's prestige.[118] The regime initiated the 'War of Attrition' against Israel, which, while targeting an external enemy, would also help rally the people behind the regime against an outside aggressor. This kind of limited war was controlled in the sense that it could provide limited military gains while providing maximum domestic propaganda effects. While this might be a somewhat cynical analysis, nonetheless it is valid considering the grandstanding by Nasser in the lead up to the 1967 War, and the actual performance of the Egyptian army during the war. The conflict with Israel was used by Nasser to further his stature in Egypt and regionally, and it would also be used to attempt to restore his stature post-1967.

The Soviet Union had helped rearm the Egyptian army, and while it was not yet prepared to face the Israeli army in open combat, it would be able to engage it in limited skirmishes across the banks of the Suez Canal, by artillery bombardment of Israeli positions in Sinai, and through sabotage commando operations on a variety of Israeli targets. In classic Cold War posturing, the United States was heavily involved in arming the Israeli military, and on the other side Nasser was being supplied and armed by the Russians. In secret weapons deals, the regime was able to obtain Russian SAM 3 batteries, Russian technicians to service them, and Russian pilots to help train Egyptian pilots and fly bombing sorties with them. Enormous publicity was given to the smallest operations from the front, highlighting the heroism and spirit of sacrifice of the soldiers.[119] Israel retaliated through incursions and bombing raids on military and civilian targets, such as the factory in Abu Zaabal and the Bahr el Baqr school, further rallying the people behind Nasser. Arguably, this limited war served its purpose as various segments of society fell in line and closed ranks in the face of the external enemy.

The bombing of the Bahr el Baqar school in April 1970 and the subsequent death of 46 children in particular would enrage all segments of the population. After the bombing, the GFETU issued a statement denouncing the murder of the school children, declaring its support of the regime in its confrontation with Israel.[120] The student and labor movement's activism in 1968 would retreat during the Attrition War, and would pick up again after Nasser died and Sadat took over. The calculated escalation of the Attrition War would end with Nasser's acceptance in 1970 of the Rogers Plan.

Limitations of diffusion and spillover in 1968

While indeed processes of diffusion and spillover had been observed in 1968, the main difference between 1946 and 1968 was that the protests of 1968 were more organic, uncoordinated and spontaneous in nature. In 1946 student and labor activists were able to coordinate their protests through the NCWS, which was able to organize and coordinate protests and articulate collective demands. However, even then the coordination did not sustain momentum. The organic and haphazard nature of the 1968 protests was a reflection of the stifling of dissent in the Nasser era, as well as the corporatization of both the student and labor movements into the state structure. Workers and students were not allowed to build organizations that were fully independent of the state. As previously argued, the absence of organizational structures makes it increasingly difficult for social movements to sustain collective action.[121]

The main gains of 1968 were the loosening of regime control on the political environment and again empowering the labor and student movements through a new generation that would carry on its activism well into the Sadat era. These are tangible gains for movements that had been repressed since 1954, forcing the state to retreat. Hussein writes:

> Even before the end of the demonstrations, it (the regime) decided to overturn the sentences against the military chiefs which, by its clemency, had triggered the Helwan demonstration and to try them before a new court. This gesture, which the leaders made in order to appease the popular feelings, nevertheless revealed a basically new objective situation: the masses challenged the regime's authority (since obviously the sentence had been a political decision taken by it) and expressed this challenge in a totally illegal way.[122]

International context

The international context of the student protests must also be highlighted, as student and workers' protests were occurring across the globe. In 1968, from Berlin, Rome, Paris, Prague and London, to Cairo, Shanghai, Mexico and Karachi, a wave of protests unfolded in several countries. The protests were responses to local situations, but gathered momentum as news of this singular challenge to authorities gathered pace.

There are many examples of such protests across the globe: against the war in Vietnam and the anti-war movement in the United States; the civil rights movement, militant workers' and student protests in Europe; and upheaval in the Middle East all combined to make 1968 a revolutionary year. Hussein argues that the global protests in 1968 "reflected the specific conditions which determined the concrete situation in each country. However, an awareness of the revolt's character as a worldwide phenomenon with worldwide implications bringing into question a worldwide structure was inescapable."[123] Owen concurs, writing:

> I viewed what was going on in Egypt's universities between 1968 and 1973 very much through the lens of the world-wide student movement of those years, in Paris, increasingly in America beginning with the anti-Vietnam War demonstrations at the University of Wisconsin at Madison, and then later, more tragically at Kent State, and then at many British universities including Oxford when I was then teaching—in which, as always, national and more specifically student issues were combined.[124]

Outcomes

The February and November 1968 protests were the first of their kind to occur against the Nasser regime, which was already under immense strain from the 1967 defeat. Nasser had no choice but to respond to public pressure and liberalize the system, at least nominally, to placate an increasingly restless population. He responded to the February 1968 protests by issuing the March 30th Program, which offered relative liberalization of the political system.[125] In effect, this was a classic attempt by the regime to absorb the shock of 1967 and avoid its repercussions.[126] Nasser "positioned himself as a reformer and sought to meet the demands emerging from Egyptian society without ever risking the core authoritarian institutions of the political order."[127] He admitted there were centers of power operating in the country, and vowed to reform the ASU, which he declared was ineffective in representing the people. Nasser's declaration undermined the very institution he had created to combat the continuing fragmentation of social control. From 1968 onwards, he subverted the ability of the ASU to mobilize or control various segments of the population. He dissolved the ASU Secretariat, halted the activities of its youth organization, purged its left-leaning members, and finally arrested its Secretary General, Ali Sabri.[128] In a highly controlled and directed general referendum, the March 30th Manifesto was ostensibly approved by 99 percent of the population, with some polling booths in the countryside reporting 100 percent turnout.[129]

Part of the March 30th Program was a signal of the state modifying its development model through the promise of economic reform. The initial five-year plans had yielded some benefits to the economy, but almost all gains were lost after 1967 as the Egyptian state began to direct even more resources away from developing the economy toward rebuilding the army. Nasser knew that the next period would need the involvement and financing of the private sector, as the Egyptian deficit could no longer be financed by external loans from friendly neutral and Eastern Bloc states. Through the March 30th Program, the regime signaled to the frozen private sector that it would again be able to play a role in the economy as it faced this fiscal crisis.[130] The program could be considered the true beginning of the *infitah* policy that Sadat would formalize and launch six years later, given the implicit acknowledgment that the economy would move from the state-led development (SLD) model to a more open economy—something for which Egyptian industry and manufacturing was unprepared.

Even though the 1968 uprising was effectively repressed, it was a significant historical precedent demonstrating how the student and the labor movement can challenge the authoritarian state. Nasser's policies had given great hopes to the majority of the people, yet such populist polices became untenable over time. Under the so-called Arab Socialism, the Egyptian state had been induced into a state of artificial expansion that proved unsustainable. The newly formed classes had great expectations. The increases in education and state guarantees of employment had strengthened the regime, while at the same time ultimately threatening its stability.

In addition to these tensions, there was another dilemma faced by the regime: the expansion of education and state services resulted in an influx of migrants from the rural areas of Egypt to urban centers such as Cairo. Cairo's infrastructure was ill-prepared for this rapid urbanization, especially given widespread unemployment, and the migrants were unable to adapt to city life. This multitude of problems, coupled with the disastrous 1967 War, signaled a retreat of the state. Not only had Egypt lost the Six Day War, but the regime was spending nearly 25 percent of the national income on defense, which only served to further exacerbate the economic problems already faced by Egypt.[131] Waterbury observes that at the end of the Nasser era:

> A new kind of capitalism, state capitalism as some call it, had taken over the power structure of the country and instituted monopolies in the name of the people in several domains. The distribution of income remained sharply skewed, absolute poverty probably continued to involve most of Egypt's population, and disease and illiteracy were only marginally eroded.[132]

Even though there were several socio-economic gains made by wide segments of society, when Nasser passed away he would leave a heavy inheritance for his successor, Anwar Sadat. The combination of population growth and urbanization, observed in the pre-1952 era and which continued through the Nasser years, would explode in the Sadat era. Further, Sadat faced a restless student movement that would continue to protest in the early 1970s, calling for war with Israel to regain the Sinai. Sadat would also inherit a bloated public sector and a generation that grew up under 'Nasser's bargain,' whose conditions and promises they expected to continue. The multitude of internal and external challenges facing the new regime would require a realignment of Egypt's economic and foreign policy over the 1970s, something Sadat would aim to achieve.

Notes

1 Qouted in Issawi, "Egypt Since 1900," 1.

2 ʿAbd al-Majīd Muḥammad Rashid, *al-Kartha wal-wahm: mustaqbal siyāsat al-iṣlāḥ al-iqtiṣādi bi-Miṣr fi ẓill niẓām al-awlamaʾah* (Catastrophe and Delusion: The Future of Economic Reform Policy in Egypt in Light of Globalisation) (Cairo: Al-Shurta, 2007), 47.

3 Ibid., 49.

4 Steven Cook, *The Struggle for Egypt: From Nasser to Tahrir Square* (Oxford: Oxford University Press, 2011), 57.
5 Raymond William Baker, *Egypt's Uncertain Revolution under Nasser and Sadat* (Cambridge, MA: Harvard University Press, 1978), 101.
6 See Gamal Abdel Nasser, *Falsafat al-thawra* (The Philosophy of the Revolution) (Cairo: Bayt al-ʿArab, 1996) for Nasser's own articulation of the aims of the revolution. The book is fascinating by its own accord and shows Nasser's generalist, non-ideological, and sometimes vague discourse.
7 Nasser's Speeches, January 27, 1958, *Biblioteca Alexandria*, Nasser digital repository, http://nasser.bibalex.org/home/main.aspx?lang=ar (accessed October 1, 2014).
8 Nasser, *Falsafat al-thawra*.
9 Mourad Wahba, *The Role of the State in the Egyptian Economy, 1945–1981* (London: Ithaca Press, 1994), 79.
10 Richards and Waterbury, *Political Economy of the Middle East*, 189.
11 Galal Amin, "The Egyptian Economy and the Revolution," in P.J. Vatakotis (ed.), *Egypt since the Revolution* (London: George Allen & Unwin, 1968), 40.
12 Mark Cooper, "Egyptian State Capitalism in Crisis: Economic Policies and Political Interests," *Middle East Studies Journal* 10 (1979): 482.
13 Nazih Ayubi, *Bureaucracy and Politics in Contemporary Egypt* (London: Ithaca Press, 1980), 252.
14 Donald Mead, *Growth and Structural Change in the Egyptian Economy* (Homewood: R.D. Erwin, 1967), 272–273.
15 Wahba, *Role of the State*, 50.
16 Ismail Abdallah, "Thawrat yulio wal-tanmiya al-mustaqilla" (The July Revolution and Independent Development), in *Thawrat thalātha wa ʿashrīn ulio: qaḍāyā al-ḥaḍr wa tahdiyat al-mustaqbal* (The 23rd of July Revolution: Current Cases and the Challenges of the Future) (Cairo: Dār al-Mustaqbal al-ʿArabī, 1987), 214.
17 Ibid., 273.
18 Ray Bush, *Economic Crisis and Political Reform in Egypt* (Boulder: Westview Press, 1999), 11.
19 Joel Beinin, "Labor, Capital, and the State in Nasserist Egypt, 1952–1961," *International Journal of Middle East Studies* 21, no. 1 (February 1989): 72.
20 Quoted in "Goals of the Egyptian Revolution," in Wahba, *Role of the State*, 59.
21 Abdallah, "Thawrat yulio wal-tanmiya al-mustaqilla," 272.
22 John Waterbury, *The Egypt of Nasser and Sadat: The Political Economy of Two Regimes* (Princeton: Princeton University Press, 1983), 31.
23 Wahba, *Role of the State*, 56.
24 Abdallah, "Thawrat yulio wal-tanmiya al-mustaqilla," 273.
25 Robert Tignor, *Capitalism and Nationalism at the End of Empire: State and Business in Decolonizing Egypt, Nigeria and Kenya, 1945–1963* (Princeton: Princeton University Press, 1998), 114–42.
26 Bush, *Economic Crisis and Political Reform in Egypt*, 13.
27 Mark Cooper, *The Transformation of Egypt* (Baltimore: Johns Hopkins University Press, 1982), 18.
28 Khaled Ikram, *The Egyptian Economy, 1952–2000: Performance, Policies, Issues* (London: Routledge, 2006), 6.
29 Patrick O'Brien, *The Revolution in Egypt's Economic System: From Private Enterprise to Socialism, 1952–1965* (London: Oxford University Press, 1966), 100.
30 Waterbury, *The Egypt of Nasser and Sadat*, 81.
31 Ibid., 78.
32 Cook, *Struggle for Egypt*, 88.
33 Ikram, *Egyptian Economy*, 65.
34 Mark Cooper, "Egyptian State Capitalism in Crisis: Economic Policies and Political Interests," *Middle East Studies Journal* 10 (1979): 482.

35 Dina Shehata, "The Fall of the Pharaoh," *Foreign Affairs*, May/June 2011, 26.
36 Cooper, "Egyptian State Capitalism in Crisis," 483.
37 Richards and Waterbury, *Political Economy of the Middle East*, 189.
38 Ibid.
39 P.J. Vatikiotis, *The History of Modern Egypt From Muhammad Ali to Sadat* (London: Weidenfeld & Nicolson, 1980), 377.
40 Aḥmad Sharaf el Din, *Asrār jadīdah ḥawl mazbhat Kạfr al-dawwār wa istishhād Khamis wal-Baqari* (New Secrets of the Kafr al-dawwar Massacre and the Martyrdom of Khamis and al-Baqari) (Cairo: Hisham Mubarak Centre, 2007), 28–35.
41 Ibid.
42 Ibid., 42.
43 Joel Beinin and Zachary Lockman, *Workers on the Nile: Nationalism, Communism, Islam, and the Egyptian Working Class, 1882–1954* (Princeton: Princeton University Press, 1987), 423.
44 Maye Kassem, *Egyptian Politics: The Dynamics of Authoritarian Rule* (Boulder: Lynne Rienner, 2004), 90.
45 Ibid.
46 Beinin, "Labor, Capital and the State," 71.
47 Robert Bianchi, *Unruly Corporatism: Associational Life in Twentieth Century Egypt* (Oxford: Oxford University Press, 1989), 78.
48 For detailed analysis of corporatism in Egypt, see ibid.
49 See Marsha Pripsein Posusney, *Labor and the State in Egypt: Workers, Unions, and Economic Restructuring* (New York: Columbia University Press, 1997).
50 Marsha Pripsein Posusney, "Irrational Workers: The Moral Economy of Labor Protest in Egypt," *World Politics* 46, no. 1 (October 1993): 83–120.
51 Ibid.
52 Beinin, "Labor, Capital, and the State," 74.
53 Saad Eddin Ibrahim, "Egypt's Landed Bourgeoisie," in Ayse Oncu, Caglar Keyder and Saad Eddin Ibrahim (eds.), *Developmentalism and Beyond: Society and Politics in Egypt and Turkey* (Cairo: American University of Cairo Press, 1994), 31.
54 Beinin and Lockman argue that even though most unions supported Nasser, there were some minority radicalized left-wing unions who supported Naguib. See Beinin and Lockman, *Workers on the Nile*, 437.
55 According to Vatikiotos:

> although not an original or active member of the Free Officer movement, (Naguib's) eighteen months in office as Prime Minister had earned him wide popularity in the country. Older than his RCC colleagues and a member of a military family he was by temperament more inclined to favour a return to constitutional government.
>
> (*History of Modern Egypt*, 384)

56 Kassem, *Egyptian Politics*, 91.
57 Beinin, "Labor, Capital and the State," 82.
58 Ibid., 75.
59 Ibid.
60 Wahba, *Role of the State*, 117.
61 Raymond A. Hinnebusch Jr., *Egyptian Politics Under Sadat: The Post-Populist Development of an Authoritarian-Modernizing State* (Cambridge: Cambridge University Press, 1988), 31–33.
62 Posusney, "Irrational Workers," 91.
63 Cited in Hrair Dekmejian, *Egypt Under Nasser: A Study in Political Dynamics* (Albany: SUNY Press, 1971), 140.

64 Robert Bianchi, "The Corporatization of the Egyptian Labor Movement," *Middle East Journal* 40, no. 3 (Summer 1986): 432.
65 Ellis Goldberg, "The Foundations of State-Labor Relations in Contemporary Egypt," *Comparative Politics* 24, no. 2 (January 1992): 154.
66 The defeat in the 1967 war effectively ended Nasser's pan-Arab vision and created a seismic shift in Arab politics itself. See Fouad Ajami, *The Arab Predicament: Arab Political Thought and Practice since 1967*, 2nd edn (Cambridge: Cambridge University Press, 1992) and Abdallah Laroui, *The Crisis of the Arab Intellectual: Traditionalism or Historicism?* (Berkeley: University of California Press, 1976).
67 Cited in Ahmad Abdalla, *The Student Movement and National Politics in Egypt, 1923–1973* (London: Al Saqi Books, 1985), 101.
68 Ibid.
69 Daniel Crecelius, "Al-Azhar in the Revolution," *Middle East Journal* 20, no. 1 (Winter 1966): 34.
70 Mahmoud Faksh, "The Consequences of the Introduction and Spread of Modern Education: Education and National Integration in Egypt," *Middle Eastern Studies* 16, no. 2 (May 1980): 44.
71 Abdalla, *Student Movement and National Politics*, 104.
72 Ibid., 105.
73 For an elaboration on the three factors, see Faksh, "Consequences," 46.
74 Abdallah, *Student Movement and National Politics*, 120.
75 Ibid., 120.
76 Ibid., 125.
77 To gain entry to the university, the grades obtained during the *thanawiya ʿammah* (high school certificate) were a key indicator. The hardest faculties to get into were usually engineering and medicine as they required scoring in the top percentile of grades. Students in their applications could preference certain universities also and usually Cairo University would be the highest in Egypt, therefore the Faculty of Medicine and Engineering at Cairo University would require the highest grades to enter. This system continues to this very day.
78 See Aḥmad Hishām, ed., *Min tārīkh al-ḥarakah al-ṭullābiya al-maṣriyah, kulliyat al-handasah Jāmiʿat al-Qāhira, October 1961–October 1972* (From the History of the Egyptian Student Movement, Faculty of Engineering, Cairo University, October 1961–October 1972) (Cairo: Eeeon Publishing, 2012), 27.
79 Ibid., 26.
80 Ibid., 29.
81 Abdallah, *Student Movement and National Politics*, 124.
82 Faksh, "Consequences," 52.
83 Ibid., 42.
84 Abdalla, *Student Movement and National Politics*, 116.
85 Leonard Binder, "Egypt: The Integrative Revolution," in Lucian Pye and Sidney Verba (eds.), *Political Culture and Political Development* (Princeton: Princeton University Press, 1969), 415.
86 Joel Beinin, "The Communist Movement and Nationalist Political Discourse in Nasirist Egypt," *Middle East Journal* 41, no. 4 (Autumn 1977): 569.
87 Ibid., 575.
88 Ibid., 576.
89 See Gennaro Gervasio, *al-Ḥaraka al-markisiyya fi Maṣr 1967–1981* (The Marxist Movement in Egypt, 1967–1981) (Cairo: al-Markaz al-Qawmi lil-Tarjama, 2010), 210.
90 See Abdel Ghaffar Shukr, *Munāẓamat al-shabāb al-ishtirāki: tajrubah maṣriyyah fi iʿdaʾad al-qaḍah 1963–1976* (The Organisation for Socialist Youth: An Egyptian Experiment in Leader Formation) (Lebanon: Centre for Arab Unity Studies, 2004).
91 Personal interview, Cairo, March 7, 2013.

92 Elaborating on the long-term impact of the massive increase in university graduates and attempts by the government to absorb them in the public sector, Kerr observes:

> The university graduates constitute a growing force of unusables whose social and economic expectations have been raised to unrealistic levels by their education. The result of mass higher education has been to redistribute poverty in the name of social equality, in a manner that threatens to simply to replace an illiterate class of unemployed proletarians with a literate and more sharply alienated one.... The disappointments are sharp as thousands of not-so-bright young men in their soiled collars and cheap suits eke out a shabby and insecure but desperately respectable existence on ten pounds a month as minor clerks, book keepers, school teachers and journalists. They are assured from time to time in the press and in the president's speeches that as educated men they are the vanguard of the nation's progress, but they are impotent to fashion even their own progress.
>
> (Malcolm Kerr, "Egypt," in James Coleman (ed.), *Education and Political Development* (Princeton: Princeton University Press, 1965), 169, 187)

93 Goldstone and Tilly, "Threat (and Opportunity)," 185.

94 See Ajami, *Arab Predicament* and Laroui, *Crisis of the Arab Intellectual*.

95 An example of how accountability mechanisms do not always work perfectly could be seen in the 2003 Iraq War when democracies such as the United States, the United Kingdom and Australia invaded a sovereign country under dubious pretexts, despite massive public opposition of their populations.

96 See, for example, Jack Goldstone, "Theories of Revolution: The Third Generation," *World Politics* 32 (1980): 425–453, James DeNardo, *Power in Numbers: The Political Strategy of Protest and Rebellion* (Princeton: Princeton University Press, 1985) and Alan Lamborn, *The Price of Power: Risk and Foreign Policy in Britain, France and Germany* (Boston: Unwin Hyman, 1991).

97 Bruce Bueno de Mesquita, Randolph Siverson and Gary Woller, "War and the Fate of Regimes: A Comparative Analysis," *The American Political Science Review* 86, no. 3 (September 1992): 638–646.

98 Ibid., 644.

99 Fred Halliday, "1967 and the Consequences of Catastrophe," *MERIP*, www.merip.org/mer/mer146/1967-consequences-catastrophe (accessed October 1, 2014).

100 See Charles Tilly, *From Mobilization to Revolution* (Reading: Addison Wesley, 1978); and Goldstone and Tilly, "Threat (and Opportunity)."

101 Carrie Wickham, *Mobilizing Islam: Religion, Activism and Political Change in Egypt* (New York: Columbia University Press, 2002), 21.

102 Mohammed M. Hafez and Quintan Wiktorowicz, "Violence as Contention in the Egyptian Islamic Movement," in Quintan Wiktorowicz (ed.), *Islamic Activism: A Social Movement Theory Approach* (Bloomington: Indiana University Press, 2004), 61.

103 Muḥammad Khālid, *al-Ḥarakah al-niqābiyah bayn al-māḍī wal-ḥāḍir* (The Union Movement Between the Past and the Present) (Cairo: Dār al-Ta'āwun, 1975), 138.

104 *Al Umaal Newspaper*, June 1967, 3.

105 Betty Anderson, "The Student Movement in 1968," *Jadaliyya*, March 9, 2011, www.jadaliyya.com/pages/index/838/the-student-movement-in-1968 (accessed October 1, 2014).

106 Hishām, *Min tārīkh al-ḥarakah al-ṭullābiya al-maṣriyah*, 56.

107 Ibid., 57.

108 Cited in Abdalla, *Student Movement and National Politics*, 137.

109 Personal interview, Cairo, March 7, 2013.

110 Personal interview, Cairo, March 24, 2013.

111 Mahmoud Hussein, *Class Conflict in Egypt: 1945–1970* (New York: Monthly Review Press, 1973), 293.

112 Ibid.
113 Ibid., 293–294.
114 Ibid., 294–295.
115 Ibid., 297.
116 Ibid., 313.
117 Ibid., 315.
118 Ibid., 343.
119 Ibid., 323.
120 *Al Umaal Newspaper*, February 19, 1970, 1.
121 See Anthony Oberschall, *Social Conflict and Social Movements* (Englewood Cliffs: Prentice Hall, 1973).
122 Hussein, *Class Conflict in Egypt*, 299.
123 Ibid., 275.
124 Roger Owen, "Remembering Ahmad Abdalla," *Al Ahram Online*, June 6, 2011, http://english.ahram.org.eg/t/NewsContentP/4/13783/Opinion/Remembering-Ahmed-Abdalla.aspx (accessed October 1, 2014).
125 For the full March 30th Program, see *Al Ahram*, March 31, 1968, 1–3.
126 Abdalla, *Student Movement and National Politics*, 145.
127 Cook, *Struggle for Egypt*, 104.
128 Joel S. Migdal, *Strong Societies and Weak States: State-Society Relations and State Capabilities in the Third World* (Princeton: Princeton University Press, 1988), 200.
129 Hussein, *Class Conflict in Egypt*, 310.
130 Cooper, *Transformation of Egypt*, 18.
131 P.J. Vatikiotis, *The History of Egypt*, 4th edn (Baltimore: Johns Hopkins University Press, 1991), 386–387.
132 Waterbury, *Egypt of Nasser and Sadat*, 48.

4 The Sadat era

> He who wants to inflame the political situation in Egypt, will find the incendiary device in the students or the workers.
>
> Anwar Sadat, commenting after the 1977 Bread Uprising[1]

Introduction

As highlighted by the March 30th Program, Gamal Abdel Nasser in his final years came to the conclusion that the all-encompassing statist approach to the economy was not sustainable. Upon Nasser's death in 1970, Sadat inherited a state with a myriad of social and economic problems, including high unemployment, disenfranchised workers and students, a corrupt and bloated bureaucracy—in short, a state capitalist system that was increasingly unable to meet the needs of Egyptians.

In addition to these internal problems, Egypt was at war with Israel and the Sinai Peninsula remained occupied. Sadat was in a precarious position as factions vied for power after Nasser's death. This chapter will investigate the political economy of the Sadat regime and its impact on the labor and student movements, and how the movements responded. It uses the 1977 Bread Intifada as the case study to investigate social movement mobilization and assess diffusional and spillover processes between the movements.

The political economy of the Sadat regime

Consolidation of power

When Sadat came to power he initially "seemed content to rule in the shadow of Nasser, as was symbolized by the placement of his picture in public places and government offices alongside of, not in the place of Nasser's."[2] During the early days of Sadat's presidency, Nasserites in the government were still in positions of influence in the armed forces, police and in the presidential office itself. Sadat first moved to neutralize them to end any internal threats to his power. Sadat had felt that the Nasserites were treating him with disdain,[3] did not respect his leadership, and that they would ultimately challenge his authority.

In a move that surprised many observers who had assumed that he would rule from Nasser's shadow, Sadat carried out his 'Corrective Revolution' (*al-thawra al-tasḥīḥiyya*) on May 15, 1971.[4] Over 100 Nasserites, including Sadat's former vice president Aly Sabry, were arrested and charged with plotting to overthrow Sadat's government. The Nasserites had erroneously assumed that they would be able to control Sadat. He had been one of the few remaining Free Officers in the political arena who was not sidelined by Nasser. They had approved his candidacy due to his resonance with the people, especially given his role as the radio announcer of the 1952 Officers' movement. Little did they know that it would take Sadat only one year to turn on them and remove them from power. The ouster of Sharawy Gomaa and Ali Sabri, both considered pro-Moscow, and the removal of Soviet advisors in the summer of 1972 indicated the new direction toward the West that Sadat would be taking. However, Sadat acutely understood that he was not a leader in the mold of Nasser, and that he would have to allow the elites more say in the rule of Egypt.[5]

Even though Sadat had purged Nasserites from the upper echelons of power, he understood Nasser's enduring mass popularity. Early in his rule, he felt obliged to frame his economic policy within a Nasserite angle so as not to alienate large segments of the population who continued to adore Nasser. In a telling 1974 interview with *Time Magazine*, Sadat stated, "I can assure you that if Abdel Nasser had lived until this moment, he would not have done other than what I have done. What is happening now is a continuation of what was in existence then."[6] Despite this claim, there would be a political tilt toward the right at the expense of the left and Nasserite tendencies.[7] It was after Sadat was able to establish his own legitimacy in the eyes of the people after the 1973 October War that he began to be openly critical of some aspects of the Nasser era, including Nasser himself. In his 1979 biography, Sadat would describe him as a great leader but prone to making decisions based on emotions.[8] The 1973 War finally allowed Sadat to dismantle Nasser's legacy and discredit Egypt's socialist experiment.[9]

Al-infitāḥ

The dismantling of Nasser's legacy would strongly manifest itself in Egypt's economic policy. Even though *al-infitāḥ* (the 'opening up' of the economy) was officially ushered in by Sadat, it was Nasser's March 30th Program in 1968 which can be considered to be the first official state directive regarding the policy change away from the economic policy of the earlier years of the Nasser regime. After the 1967 defeat Nasser was under pressure from various segments of society and the March 30th Program was an attempt to absorb some of that pressure, signaling the return of private capital to the economy after its earlier ostracization by the statist Nasser regime.

At the twilight of his rule, Nasser slowly ushered the private sector back in, but it would be Sadat who would swing the door wide open to both the domestic and the international private sector. While free trade and integration in the global economy were likely to have a positive impact on the Egyptian economy in the long run, the way *infitāḥ* was organized and implemented had negative consequences for the economy and socio-economically disadvantaged segments of the population.

The policy was first publicly announced in the October Paper of 1974, where the case was made for a major reorientation of Egypt's economic direction based on the consideration that the country was now in the midst of a 'construction battle'[10] to modernize the country by the year 2000. Explaining his rationale, Sadat wrote:

> Whatever the state of resources that we can mobilize locally, we are still in the most urgent need of external sources. The circumstances of the world today render it possible that we obtain these resources in a manner that strengthens our economy and hastens growth. On this basis we have called for an economic opening (*Infitah*), and it is a call founded upon the calculation of our economic needs on one hand, and available external funding on the other.[11]

To ensure the policy received some form of public legitimacy, the paper was put to a popular referendum and was overwhelmingly approved by the electorate. Sadat could then claim a popular mandate to implement *infitāḥ*.[12] After the 'Corrective Revolution' and then the 1973 October War, the *infitāḥ* policy was the final piece of the puzzle needed for Sadat to move beyond the shadow of Nasser. The regime began to undertake reforms of the public sector, as well as liberalization of the private sector, and took the first steps toward encouraging foreign direct investment (FDI) and establishing free trade zones. A new set of laws was promulgated in 1971 aiming at encouraging FDI, including guarantees against nationalization and confiscation, exemption from income tax for the initial five years, exemption of custom duties on imported machinery and equipment, the right to deal in foreign currencies with no state fiscal and monetary control, and the exemption of foreign capital financed projects from labor and economic state laws and regulations.[13]

Law 43, passed in 1974, is considered to be the official start of *infitāḥ*, as it opened the economy to Arab and foreign capital for investments in all sectors.[14] This was followed by Law 118, passed in 1975, which stipulated that the import and export of goods was now open to the private sector—effectively meaning the end of the state's monopoly on foreign trade. In terms of fiscal policy, Law 97, passed in 1976, lifted heavy restrictions in order for banks and individuals to trade freely in foreign currency.[15] Several banks with mixed Egyptian and foreign capital were established. In the trade sector, the government eased many restrictions on the import of highly profitable luxury consumer goods and reduced custom duties on many important items. After over a decade of a relatively closed and protected economy, Egypt was now open for business, leading the country head of Mobil Oil to exclaim in 1974, "There is a smell of money around this place."[16]

Despite the renewed emphasis on private sector investment, the high international capital inflows that Sadat anticipated did not materialize. Law 43 had provided generous incentives for foreign investment, but not to local capital. After the realization that FDI would not be attracted at the levels that were predicted, the barriers against local capital were removed,[17] but only for large enterprises.[18] The domestic private sector responded positively and increased its share of industrial production.[19] Despite this shift, the public sector still remained the dominant sector in the economy, being responsible until 1990 for 70 percent of investment, 80 percent of foreign trade, 90 percent of the banking sector and 95 percent of the insurance sector.[20] After more than a decade of SLD, the Egyptian state continued to loom large in the economy. Sadat was initially able to maintain this role as the re-opening of the Suez Canal increased revenues, oil production resumed, tourism increased, and higher remittances were received from expatriate workers in the Gulf.[21] This increase in revenues would diminish; by the end of the 1970s, despite the liberalizing efforts taken, the economy would be in crisis.

Despite the enduring major economic role of the state, *infitāḥ* indicated the end of Nasser's socialist and state capitalist direction and set the starting point for Sadat's economic policy. It would be a monumental change in state policy, and less so of state structure. This change would also have consequences for economic growth and structural change, as well as for social actors, which will be discussed throughout this chapter.

The October War in 1973 and Egypt's symbolic victory further strengthened Sadat, and allowed him to deal the final blow to Nasser's legacy and inaugurate the open door policy the next year. Lachine argues that

> while the October War ended in a military stalemate, it proved the Arab soldier capable of fighting effectively, shattering the idea of the invincibility of the Israeli Army that had reached mythical proportions after 1967. The war definitely ended in a political defeat for Israel.[22]

This political defeat would be used by Sadat both domestically and internationally.

Reorientation of foreign policy

After being strained during the Nasser era, the war strengthened the relationships between Egypt and the conservative and wealthy Gulf States. Waterbury writes: "by choosing war, Sadat forced the Arab oil rich states to come to the aid of brother Egypt (and Syria) against the number one enemy, Israel."[23] The use of oil as a weapon had also created massive profits for the Gulf States, as oil prices skyrocketed. As Sadat navigated Egyptian foreign policy objectives regarding Israel, he had made himself valuable to the West by maintaining and consolidating the peace. After decades of conflict in the Middle East, he was the first Arab leader to deal directly with Israel to seek some form of accommodation. He also moved away from Nasser's position of hostility toward the two major regional oil exporters, Saudi Arabia and Iran (the latter at least until the Shah was overthrown). In return, Sadat expected to gain some benefits for Egypt. Waterbury argues:

> Sadat, as always and not unreasonably, assumed that in return for the geopolitical advantages he offered the West, he could expect financial support, including the encouragement of foreign private investment. In other words, Egypt was a good investment in its own right with substantial nonfinancial dividends for its benefactors. When Richard Nixon visited Cairo in June 1974 the official joint communiqué talked of $2 billion in investment projects under serious consideration.[24]

Besides rapprochement with the Arab monarchies of the Gulf, Sadat engineered a realignment of Egyptian foreign policy away from the Eastern Bloc toward the West and particularly the United States. He had come to the conclusion that it was the United States, not the USSR, which would be able to influence Israel toward his stated goal of peace, as well as provide him with the financial and technical assistance Egypt needed. Due to his outspokenness against 'imperialist powers' during the Nasser era, the Nixon administration was uncertain of the new Egyptian president's intentions toward the United States. Egypt and the United States had maintained minimal formal diplomatic contact as official diplomatic relations were severed after 1967. This uncertainty began to dissipate as informal meetings between the United States and Sadat were held starting in 1970: Donald Bergus, the US *chargé d'affaires* (then working out of the Spanish embassy in Cairo) met Sadat on October 3 that year and cabled back to the State Department the following:

> Personally, I was much more impressed by Sadat's performance than I had expected to be. I found it hard to believe that this was the same man who had indulged in so much plain anti-American rabble-rousing in public meetings throughout Egypt during the first six months of this year. Perhaps his new responsibilities have made some change. Throughout the conversation Sadat stressed his and UAR's feelings of friendship towards America. We can talk about very difficult matters and as friends, and that the Israel problem (is the) only real obstacle to close relations between the two governments.[25]

In February 1974, diplomatic relations with the United States resumed, and Nixon made a historic visit to Egypt that June. To US policy-makers and business leaders, the conflict with Israel was directly related to supporting the Egyptian economy. The view from the United States was that in return for de-escalating tensions with Israel, Egypt would be rewarded with further investments. This would have weighed heavily on Sadat's foreign policy decisions and ultimately his visit to Jerusalem and the Camp David Accords. Starting in 1974,

Cairo would receive a steady stream of US private and public sector leaders. That year alone, Cairo received David Rockefeller (Chairman of the Chase Manhattan Bank), Robert McNamara (President of the World Bank), and William Simon (United States Secretary of Treasury) for talks with Sadat and Egyptian officials.[26] The Chairman of Chase Manhattan Bank, David Rockefeller, who was on a tour of the Middle East, commented:

> I think that Egypt has come to realize that socialism and extreme Arab nationalism have not helped the lot of the 37 million people they have in Egypt. And if President Sadat wants to help them, he has got to look for private enterprise and assistance. I discussed this to a considerable extent with some of the Israeli leaders, and they agree with us. They feel that the position of President Sadat *vis-à-vis* his own country is a constructive one, and they feel there is a better chance of ending the war if help is given to him to build his own country in a sound economic way.[27]

Controlled political liberalization

In addition to the economic liberalization and reorientation of Egypt's foreign policy, the regime began to implement a process of controlled political liberalization. Sadat had released many of the political prisoners who were imprisoned under Nasser. He also began to move away from the one-party system of the ASU toward a controlled multi-party system in which four parties (right, left, Nasserite, center) were allowed to compete, albeit to a limited degree.[28] In March 1976, for the first time in a generation, Sadat authorized parliamentary elections, which were considered to be the freest the country had seen since the 1940s. Despite the attempt at plurality, the center was "for all intents and purposes Sadat's platform," and its party, known as the "Egypt Party," won 280 out of 352 parliamentary seats.[29]

The democratic moment was short-lived; the events of 1977 would show the president that liberalizing the system could have dire consequences for his rule. The controlled experiment with democracy could well be construed as Sadat attempting to liberalize the political system. However, it should also be seen within the international context of Sadat's rising stature as a Middle East leader wanting to be *perceived* as a democratizing leader rather than an autocrat. The elections were an effort by the regime to improve its global image and ensure that critical loans and aid continued to flow. Sadat would not attempt such an experiment again.

A new capitalist class

Politically, *infitāḥ* had a positive effect for Sadat as it helped create a new social base of support. In the pre-1952 era, the landowners had been the dominant political class who furthered their interests through patronage networks with the Palace and the British, as well as their participation in parliamentary life. Nasser was able to dislodge the landowner class and create a hybrid bureaucratic-military elite, supported by a growing middle class that would serve as his power base. During the Sadat era, socio-economic conditions would slowly yield the formation of a socially cohesive elite comprised of the bureaucratic elite, some old landowning families, and those newly enriched through *infitāḥ* policies.

Infitāḥ led to social changes unseen since the Nasser era. A new class of officers, bureaucrats, technocrats and managers emerged after two decades of state-directed modernization. This new class signaled the development of a "larger and more differentiated bourgeoisie spanning the private and public sector."[30] The recruitment of civilians into the new elite answered the imperatives of the new policy orientations and allowed Sadat to broaden the leadership team to embrace private sector elites.[31] Nasser has been duly criticized on a range of fronts; however, during his time as president and by virtue of his SLD policies, monopolistic activities almost ceased in comparison with the situation before 1952. Economic corruption would return during the Sadat era.

Foreign currency speculators were amongst the first to gain after 1975's Law 115 lowered capital controls and allowed individuals and local and foreign businesses to open foreign currency accounts and freely transfer abroad to international banks. This created a thriving black market in US dollars, almost single-handedly weakening the economy and increasing public debt. The state's anemic efforts at stopping these activities led to a general perception that the state only responded to challenges of its political authority, not its economic one. The gains of *infitāḥ* were not shared with wider society. Hinnebusch argues:

> Contractors, real-estate speculators and merchants flourished on the economic boom: importers, partners and agents of foreign firms, tourist operators, lawyers and middlemen who helped investors negotiate bureaucratic tangles, thrived on the cuts they took from the resource inflow.... Officials reaped commissions on state contracts and engaged in widespread corrupt practices. Together, these groups were forming a "parasitic bourgeoisie" living off *infitāḥ*.[32]

It was during the Sadat era that a new class of businessmen and oligarchs became very powerful. Business lobbies were established with wide state influence. An informal alliance was established between bureaucrats, technocrats and businessmen, which provided the main engine for the implementation of *infitāḥ*.[33] The new economic policies had encouraged a widening wealth gap, and by the end of 1975 there were nearly 500 new millionaires. *Al-Quṭat al-Simān* (the Fat Cats), as they became known in the Egyptian press, grew on the back of the speculative and non-developmental part of the economy.[34] The protest songs and poems of Ahmad Negm and Shiek Imam gained wide resonance, and after 1967 their work became increasingly anti-regime. By the time Sadat was in power, they would ridicule state policies with Israel in such timeless works as *la ṣawt ya ʿlu fawq ṣawt al-ma ʿraka* ("no voice rises above the din of battle"). By the mid-1970s, after the war ended, they would direct their attention toward the 'Fat Cats.'[35]

Accusations of corruption began to swirl around people close to Sadat and his inner circle, including members of his own family. Indeed, Sadat's own brother, Esmat, who went from being a truck driver to a wealthy smuggler of contraband, was convicted of corruption.[36] The *nouveau riche* and segments of the old land-owning class were able to increase their land ownership, effectively overturning parts of Nasser's land reform. Ayubi argues, "Corruption had to a large extent been 'institutionalized' in the 1970s, partly as a safety valve for the badly paid bureaucracy, and partly as an accompanying symptom of the laissez-faire policy."[37]

The *infitāḥ* economic policies were unsuccessful in creating a productive economy that strengthened the manufacturing base. It was the non-productive, speculative aspects of the economy that gained most, while the most marginalized parts of society became worse off.[38] Sadat's economic policy, pertinently described by Springborg as a policy of "privatizing profits and socializing losses,"[39] would have an adverse impact on society. The *infitāḥ* policies tended to focus on specific sectors (tourism, construction, housing) which provided limited long-term development impact.[40] Osama writes:

> Most of the projects are in tourism and construction: new Sheratons, Hiltons, and Holiday Inns, along with Xerox and Coca-Cola assembly lines. Some of the investment capital was directed to urban housing and real estate speculations, causing the land values to rise and making the housing problem of the average Egyptian even worse.[41]

Role of the IMF and the World Bank in the Egyptian economy

Egypt's first dealings with the World Bank go back to the early 1960s under Nasser's presidency. There was a balance of payments deficit as well as a foreign currency crisis due to a bad cotton crop in 1961 as well as a decline in rice exports in 1962. Egypt at the time was burdened with foreign financial obligations, notably for paying back Suez Canal shareholders after the 1956 nationalization, compensating the Sudanese government for the effects of the Aswan high dam, and compensating Great Britain for some of its nationalized assets.[42] In its first deal with the World Bank (1962), the Egyptian government agreed to accept a loan of 20 million GBP in exchange for the following four conditions:

1. A 20 percent devaluation of the Egyptian pound.
2. Raising the interest rate to 6 percent.
3. Ensuring commercial banks hold government bonds in its assets.
4. Implementing a credit ceiling at the Central Bank for lending banks to be able to lend to other non-governmental cotton-manufacturing producers.[43]

Egypt's relationship with the World Bank was closely tied to its relationship with the Western world and particularly the United States.[44] The 1962 deal constituted the first direct World Bank involvement in the Egyptian economy, and it would not be the last. After a lull following Nasser's reorientation toward the Eastern Bloc, in 1975 the World Bank dispatched an advisor to Egypt to recommend a development strategy. His recommendation entailed firm support to a totally liberalized economy, and was enthusiastically picked up by the Sadat regime until Sadat's assassination in 1981. While on paper the *infitāḥ* policy might have appeared sound, in effect it yielded massively negative consequences in its hasty implementation, for the economy was not prepared for the shock it received. By 1975, the balance of payments deficit had quadrupled.[45] Sadat began to slowly roll back some of the distributive policies of his predecessor as they were beginning to prove unsustainable. Waterbury argues that under Nasser:

> There was a major effort at redistribution of wealth that, ultimately, derailed the process of accumulation. In picking up the pieces, Sadat was no more willing to exploit the working class, but he put aside programs of income redistribution in favor of satisfying middle-class consumerism. Under Nasser accumulation took place primarily through nationalization; under Sadat it took place primarily through deficit financing and external borrowing.[46]

The IMF and the World Bank agreed to lend Egypt money under stringent conditions to attempt to structurally reform the economy and remove subsidies in place.[47] The second and third points of the IMF executive board decision regarding Egypt (adopted September 1975) stated:

> 2. The Egyptian authorities have reaffirmed their commitment to the "open door" policy. The Fund believes that in order for this policy to be successfully implemented, fundamental changes in economic policies are required. Domestically, subsidization needs to be sharply reduced to ease the budget deficit and release resources for investment.
> 3. The structural imbalances in the Egyptian economy are particularly severe in the external sector. To correct these imbalances, it is essential to make appropriate adjustments in exchange rate policies. It is also desirable to continue the present trend toward greater decentralization of foreign trade decisions and, in particular, to eliminate gradually the requirement of prior approval for imports.[48]

While the economic rationale to balance the budget might have seemed sound, it would be the poorest segments of society who paid the price for these policies. The attempt to remove subsidies would implode in the face of the regime during 1977. Due to changes in the international geo-strategic environment, Sadat was no longer able to obtain rents at the levels that Nasser had. Sadat's ability to use the Cold War to his advantage to extract rents was greatly diminished by the superpower *détente*, which further compounded the deficit.[49] At the time, however, Sadat was able to exploit the 1973 October War to his advantage (much as Nasser had with the 1956 Suez War) through an increase of foreign aid as well as obtaining credit under favorable conditions from the World Bank.

Despite the regime's effort to control the economy, Egypt's debt during the Sadat era would ultimately explode to unprecedented proportions. This was due to two factors: first, by allowing the import of non-essential and luxury goods after 1973, massive amounts of foreign currency would leave the country and were not matched by exports of industrial goods. Second, Sadat would increasingly use expensive, short-term borrowing to finance the deficit. The worsening economic conditions would have an adverse impact on society. Society responded, sometimes violently, to *infitāḥ* and its economic, political and social manifestations.

The student movement during the Sadat era

Further expansion of higher education

Even though there were fewer public sector jobs, nonetheless the numbers of students going to university increased exponentially, as Table 4.1 shows. The composition of the students themselves was changing. Erlich writes: "Sadat in contrast (to Nasser) conceived of higher education in populist Egyptian rather than elitist pan-Arabist terms, and initiated its opening to urban lower classes and to the rural and provincial population."[50] This had the effect of widening the Egyptian student base, ensuring that segments of society previously denied access to higher education (especially the rural youth) had a chance at social mobility. While that in itself is an admirable achievement, the way it was achieved was in no way admirable. Beattie writes:

> In early 1971, Sadat ordered the lowering of admission criteria, permitting practically all secondary school graduates to benefit from higher education.

Table 4.1 Expansion in university student enrollment (1970/1971 to 1980/1981)

Year	*Men*	*Women*	*Total*
1970/1971	131,890	46,065	177,955
1971/1972	146,124	52,950	199,074
1972/1973	164,620	64,114	22,8734
1973/1974	195,637	80,426	276,063
1974/1975	224,799	95,301	32,0100
1975/1976	29,6650	12,4934	421,584
1976/1977	317,519	136,131	453,650
1977/1978	334,701	141,835	476,536
1978/1979	336,707	149,071	485,778
1979/1980	350,683	159,576	5102,59
1980/1981	384,218	174,309	558,527

Source: Kirk Beattie, *Egypt During the Sadat Years* (New York: Palgrave, 2000), 94.

> This new generation of students carried with them their families' hopes and dreams that they might achieve a measure of upward social mobility. Poor peasants and destitute urban dwellers notwithstanding, university students now represented much more of a microcosm of Egyptian society.[51]

The impact of lowered admission standards would be twofold: first, the quality of the graduates continued to deteriorate. Second, the increased numbers of rural students meant more conservative cohorts, as arguably rural areas tended to be more conservative. This would provide the Islamist current with a generation of students sympathetic to their message. The majority of Islamist student leaders in the 1970s and 1980s came from rural areas, rather than urban city centers like Cairo and Alexandria. Beattie writes: "the rapid expansion of universities in provincial areas, as well as the increased attendance of urban universities by provincial students, all produced a huge increase in the number of students feeling 'uprooted' and disoriented."[52] Many of these uprooted students would find solace within familiar religious points of reference provided by the Islamist student group. The major ideological shift of students from left-wing politics to Islamism would occur from 1975 onwards, although early in the decade the leftist students were still in control of campus politics who had historically rallied around a pro-Palestine/anti-Israel platform.

Student activism

Despite the deteriorating economic conditions, it was the students, not the industrial working class or the *fellahin*, who would be first to challenge the Sadat regime.[53] The occupied Sinai continued to be the major issue that students and the general population rallied around. 1972 saw huge student protests against Sadat's inability to keep his promise to make 1971 *'ām al-hasm* (the decisive year)[54] in gaining back the Sinai from Israel.

Sadat gave a landmark-televised speech on January 13, 1972. In it, he blamed the preoccupation of Egypt's ally, the USSR, with the outbreak of the 1971 Indian-Pakistani War for preventing them from providing assistance, infamously labeling the lull in Egypt–USSR relations a "fog."[55] Students ridiculed this claim, saying that *'ām al-hasm* had become *'ām al-dabāb* (the year of fog). Hirst and Beeson write, "The 'fog' speech may have lulled, confused or even convinced the naive. But for the country's ardent youth, the students and the political activists, it was a red rag to a bull."[56]

Abdalla writes that student activism during the Sadat era began to take three main mediums.[57] The first was through wall papers (a continuation of the 1960s tradition), which were critical of Sadat and supported the Palestinian cause. The second was the formation of a variety of university societies or clubs, which allowed students a platform to discuss and debate ideas. The third was public meetings and forums, whether spontaneous or organized by the various societies.[58] Through these three mediums, students would directly challenge the authority of the president.

A student sit-in started at Cairo University spread across other university campuses to protest Sadat's 'fog' speech. The regime initially sought to engage the students, but ultimately resorted to arrests and violence. Even though the uprising was initiated by students, calls of solidarity and support came from the unions. Abdalla notes:

> The student movement had galvanized the Egyptian intelligentsia, and the professional unions came to the support of the uprising on the very day the students demonstrated in Cairo. Four of the most influential of these unions—the teachers, the lawyers, the engineers and the journalists—issued declarations which were published in the press.[59]

Indeed, the January 1972 protests that reached Tahrir Square were a clear precursor to the events that would unfold decades later, in the same square in January 2011. Hussein's description of the events in Tahrir Square on January 25, 1972, evoke what happened 39 years later on the same exact date:

> Liberation Square, principal crossroads of the capital, was the scene of a great school of democracy and fraternity, through the night from the 25th to the 26th of January. The students, who had decided to stay until the next morning, were joined by thousands of workers, unemployed, housewives, intellectuals, officials, all hurrying there, young and old, men and women, because that night they felt something new was being born in Egypt. The police forces received the order to surround the Square; and battles broke out between them and the thousands of demonstrators who had been there throughout the day.
>
> For the first time in many long years, Cairo relived urban guerilla warfare; each time the youth saw they were about to be surrounded, they broke up into neighboring streets, then regrouped in the same square or a near by one, to keep speaking out until the police arrived. And when the mass concentration became impossible, little groups formed and left for all parts of town, starting discussions on sidewalks, in cafes, at the doors of homes. And the ideas spread out in the midst of the explosion of tear gas canisters.[60]

Even after the student protests were effectively crushed early in 1972, by November the students had regrouped and during a nationwide student congress decided to form "committees for the defense of democracy" which factory workers were asked to join.[61] The student leaders were later arrested, and further protests erupted across campuses. Unable to contain the movement, Sadat moved to shut down the universities altogether in January 1973.[62] To justify and defend the repressive measures against students, Sadat compared himself to De Gaulle in 1968, saying:

> What was the outcome of the student uprising in France in 1968?—The collapse of the French economy. In France—and you all know and speak about

> the freedom of expression in France—what did De Gaulle do when he became certain that the student movement would ruin the French economy and it was organized by the Zionists and the Americans? He stormed the university. In Egypt there was not a single injury and the police intervened only after seven days.[63]

Most students had supported the Nasser regime until the 1967 War, which had highlighted the regime's inability to match its fiery rhetoric with actions. Sadat had inherited a student population that was already restless and anti-regime. Parts of the student population made the shift from Nasserism to actual left-wing politics. Hani Shukrallah recalls:

> It is well known that the transition that we witnessed at the time has roots that started before 1967 but became drastic after June 1967. We saw an entire generation that was brought up in Nasserism but starts rebelling against it by going to its left. It was spontaneous. People from very different backgrounds, whether socially or geographically, seem to reach the same conclusion at the same time: that Nasserism wasn't really socialism and that anti-imperialist struggle could have been carried out by an authoritarian regime. Thus, you are holding up the banner for both national struggle and social justice, carrying forward in rebellion to the previous times.[64]

The 1972 protests would usher in almost a decade of student activism against Sadat. It would be the first student challenge to the regime, but it would not be the last. Sadat recognized that the campuses were a challenge to his rule, and began to form and support a new current that would be loyal to him. The ideological composition of the 1972 student protests was a clear signal that Sadat needed allies to offset the influence of the leftist current on university campuses. Abdalla writes:

> The leaders of the January 1972 uprising formed the most politically conscious group of activists since the dispersal of the student movement in 1954. Its allegiance was generally to the left, though not exclusively "communist" as both the government and the right wing of the student movement claimed. The underground communist movement in Egypt at the time was still embryonic and in search of a power base within the student movement.... While the Communist movement provided the uprising with a number of activists who had some ideological influence on the larger core of student activists, the uprising itself formed a turning point in the development of the communist movement through the recruits which it brought to Communist organizations.[65]

In conjunction with his corrective revolution, Sadat began to buttress the Islamists to act as a bulwark against the Nasserites and the socialists. The regime also began to purposely conflate Marxism with Nasserism in its public discourse, as it knew that Marxism had negative pubic connotations due to the perception that it was an atheist ideology.[66] Sadat concluded that the Islamist current could become his ally in stifling left-wing and Nasserite activism on campus and broader public life. The increased opportunities for Islamist students this provided will be further elaborated later in the chapter.

The 1973 October War would provide some respite to Sadat, as the country rallied behind its leader in his political and military efforts to take back the Sinai. However, despite the positive outcome and the increase in Sadat's standing after 1973, student activism would return later in the decade. Sadat's effort to neutralize the student movement reflects an understanding of the importance of student activism and the threat it presented to his rule. Nasser had also recognized this as he attempted to co-opt the movement into the corporatist system. In a similar vein, the workers presented a challenge to the state.

The labor movement during the Sadat era

There was a slowing down of labor activism early in the Sadat era, which was to be expected given the contemporaneous Israeli occupation of the Sinai. Workers, like other segments of society, were waiting for a military offensive to regain the occupied land. For a year after the 1973 War workers remained quiet, but then protested cutbacks to their benefits in both the public and private sectors. Posusney gives an example:

> A 1974 strike at the private sector Tanta Tobacco company occurred when the owner suddenly switched workers from a monthly to a daily pay rate, resulting in about a 30 percent decline in wages. Workers sat in at a public sector plant that year after being denied their annual production reward when the production plan was not met the company had in fact acknowledged that the shortfall was not the workers' fault.[67]

The Sadat era saw the beginning of the dismantling of many of the economic rights bestowed on the workers by Nasser, and this had not been reciprocated with increased political rights. The corporatist union structure organized by Nasser continued during the Sadat era, becoming even more centralized, with the top echelon of the union leadership "increasingly self-recruiting, rendering it even more insulated than before from the threat of rank and file protests."[68] Union leadership became increasingly disconnected from the working class and unable to defend workers' rights.

Early in his rule, Sadat was focused on consolidating his power, as seen in the 1971 'Corrective Revolution' that removed key Nasserites who were ardent defenders of the status quo from power. Sadat sought to move away from socialist rhetoric, the USSR and the Eastern Bloc toward the free market and better relations with the US and Western powers. To pursue this new direction, Sadat would allow limited multi-party politics and apply free market rules to open the economy. Yet he continued to publicly refuse union participation in the political arena, arguing that their political role ended with colonialism.[69] To Sadat, unions were to be tolerated insofar as they served their members, without having a say in the political process.

The legislative framework for unions during the Sadat era

The 1971 constitution was similar to the one under Nasser in the sense that each gave more power to the executive at the expense of the legislative branch, a tradition that continues. The constitution specified unions' legislative framework, Article 56 stating that the right of workers to form unions on a democratic basis is protected by laws which regulate its operations and support the 'socialist path' of its members.[70] In that regard, the regime's approach to workers was not very different to its predecessors'. The main difference was that Sadat tended not to make speeches directed at workers while standing among them, as Nasser had done. He lacked the charisma and popularity that Nasser enjoyed.

Sadat tended to manage his relationship with the workers by attracting and enlisting leaders of official unions to act as intermediaries with the workers. Despite the partial liberalization of the political system, Sadat, fearful of workers and students, did not extend this liberalization to the union movement. The state continued to interfere in unions and sought to further cement its control of its management. As part of the 'Corrective Revolution,' Sadat's Presidential Edict Number 10 (1971) declared the dissolution of all union organizations. This was followed by ASU Edict Number 107 (1971) to form a temporary union management structure to oversee union business. The point of this restructure was to replace all Nasserite loyalist union leaders with pro-Sadat loyalists.[71]

Law 35 (1976) is considered to be the legislative backbone for organized labor unionism. This law would not change much over the following years and would live on into the Mubarak era. Its first edict stated that the Minister for Employment is tasked with 'overseeing' unions, while union leadership would lead and develop union strategy. This officially brought unions fully under the aegis of the government, much as al-Azhar was brought under the Ministry of Endowment during the Nasser era. These moves were designed to cement control over segments of society, labor and the religious establishment.

The union structure that developed in the 1960s formed a centralized, pyramid-like management with the minister at its apex, followed by the union leadership, then the various national branches, and then the members. Even though this pyramid structure ensured that union activity across Egypt was centralized (albeit under the watchful eye of the government), nonetheless it was weak in the sense that rank and file members could not effectively communicate their issues and grievances to union leadership.

Unable to communicate through official channels, the workers launched a series of strikes in the 1970s to draw attention to their demands. Most notable of those were the workers of Miṣr Ḥilwān Textiles in 1971, who called for a 5 percent wage increase, and the private sector Shubra al-Khīma Textile workers in 1972.[72] The Helwan metro workers and the Maṣr al-Mahalla workers protested in 1975, calling for improvements to their working conditions. Government cable workers went on strike the same year, calling for meals to be served during the working week, or at least an allowance for a meal. The call for a meal allowance also led to protests in 1976 at the 45 Military Factory, whose workers made similar demands.[73] Sadat tended to blame all labor-related activism on communist subversives, using the term very loosely to encompass anyone on the political left, from the socialists to the Nasserites, amongst others.[74]

Government control of unions

Even though the constitution specified that union organization was to occur through democratic elections, the government implemented a variety of mechanisms to ensure its control of the unions. The government organized the candidate lists for elections and ensured candidates would be pro-regime, or at least not against it. This was achieved by legislation that ensured that the candidate list had to be approved by the government. Second, the government controlled the electoral process itself by organizing the ballots to ensure that its preferred candidates won. Third, the GFETU was under the direct supervision of the Ministry. Fourth, union leaders preferred by the government were further co-opted into the state structure by allowing them to run for parliament.[75] Union leaders argued that the combination of a union position and a political role would ensure that workers were well represented—but in reality, these leaders came under further state control especially as they received immense personal gain. Leftist politician and a *Kefaya* founding member Aḥmad Bahā' al-Dīn Sha'bān, himself a student leader during the 1970s, describes unionism in the 1970s:

> At that time, all syndicates were under state control with heavy government and security presence. The professional syndicates (such as the engineers, doctors and lawyers) were better off than the workers syndicates. Workers syndicates were referred to as "yellow syndicates"; they suffered from major bureaucracy. The general syndicate (GFETU) is a big scam; its high level members receive a lot of benefits, cars, money, travel ... turning the supposed leader of the workers to a bourgeoisie figurehead who is dissociated from the reality on the ground. His main role was to silence street action in favor of maintaining security and obeying the regime.[76]

Worker activism would return despite government control of unions. Lachine writes:

> after the October War, in the face of widespread corruption and deteriorating living standards, labor unrest accelerated and the center of political opposition shifted from the university to the urban districts, factories and streets.... As Sadat's "social peace" disintegrated, the workers no longer waited for a spark from the universities to take to the streets.[77]

From 1975 on, workers protested worsening economic conditions across Egypt. In January that year, workers attacked stalled commuter trains in Cairo and stormed through the streets of the capital to protest against rising prices and corruption. They shouted, "O hero of the crossing, where is our breakfast?"[78]

Opportunities and threats

Opportunity for Islamist students and the Islamist movement

Tarrow defines political opportunity as "consistent—but not necessarily formal or permanent—dimensions of the political environment that provide incentives for collective action by affecting people's expectations for success or failure."[79] This means that opportunities do not need to be formal, and can be subtle enough to allow movements to perceive and take advantage of openings. According to Tarrow:

> Movements emerge because the conditions for mobilization have expanded in the polity in general, political opportunities may not be apparent all at once to all potential challengers. In fact, an advantage of the concept is that it helps us to understand how mobilization spreads from people with deep grievances and strong resources to those with fewer ones and less resources. By challenging elites and authorities, "early risers" reveal their opponents' vulnerability and open them to attacks by weaker players. By the same token, the latter groups more easily collapse when opportunities decline because they lack the internal resources to sustain contentions.[80]

These processes could be viewed early in the Sadat era, when Sadat unofficially encouraged Islamist activism, especially among students, to offset the Nasserite and leftist influences on campus. Thus, a major opportunity of this era was lifting the restrictions on Islamist students on campuses. He also freed some of the jailed Islamists, promoted the building of mosques, and supported the creation of Islamic student organizations to counter the influence of the Nasserites and other socialist organizations.[81] He supported these student groups by instructing the Egyptian government to "create an Islamic *tayyār* (current)," stating: "I want us to raise Muslim boys, and to spend money on them, so they can become our anchor in the university."[82]

Religion was used and manipulated by both the president and the Islamist groups. Sadat had used it as a tool to gain political legitimacy after the purge of the 'Corrective Revolution,' and the Islamist movement used it to continue on with its activities. Sadat used the media to enhance his image as a devout Muslim in an effort to contrast himself as more Muslim than his predecessor. Hassan Hanafi observed, early in Sadat's era:

> President Sadat has been given the title "the Believer President". He is always called by his first name Muhammad. He is shown in the mass media

> in his white *jallabiya* (traditional Egyptian garb), going to the mosque or coming out of it, with a rosary in one hand, Moses stick on the other, and with a prayer mark on his forehead.... He murmurs in prayer, closes his eyes and shows signs of humility and devotion. He begins his speeches with "In the name of God," and ends them with Quranic verses signifying modesty and asking for forgiveness.[83]

The Islamist student activists continued to gather support on campuses across Egypt. By undermining Nasser's political legacy, Sadat had encouraged a move away from socialism toward the ideas of the Islamists, and many students and professors made the ideological shift.[84] During the period from 1975 to 1977, the Islamist student movement (*al-Jamāʿat al-Islāmiyya*) gained wider traction on campuses across the country. Leftist students, who had controlled campus politics since the 1960s, were in retreat, and from 1974 on Islamist students would take control of student unions. These changes reflected the political changes at the elite level. Moreover, Sadat's political victory in 1973 further deprived the leftist current of one of their main critiques and rallying points against the regime: its failure to go to war.[85]

As the Islamist student *Jamāʿat* evolved, it began to splinter. Utvik writes that "two clearly distinct tendencies had emerged within that movement towards the end of that decade."[86] The first group decided to pursue their goals through narrow but legitimate avenues of participation. The second group, inspired by the writings of Qutb, considered the Brotherhood's position to be a capitulation to the authorities, and decided to pursue their agenda through violence. While it is beyond the present scope to discuss the violent strand that came out of the *Jamāʿat*, it is noteworthy to mention that the groups who did not pursue violence would join the political process through elections in various student unions, syndicates and eventually parliament.

The *Jamāʿat* members who decided to work through legitimate avenues dominated student political life in the 1970s and 1980s, with Islamist students winning eight out of 12 national student elections.[87] This generation of activists graduated to become journalists, doctors, lawyers and engineers. As they matured, they sought to join and ultimately control many of the professional syndicates and associations. The loosening state control over its political access provided this generation of Islamists with an opportunity for participation in the political process. Other Islamists chose not to participate in the process, rather preferring the path of violence and terrorism. Both would continue to operate during the Mubarak era.

It is ironic that early in his presidency Sadat had encouraged Islamist activism but toward its end he was combating it—and ultimately his presidency, and his life, ended at the hands of radical Islamists. After Sadat's visit to Jerusalem, the Islamists and the government were increasingly at odds. Some Islamist groups realized they could no longer support Sadat after the Camp David Accords with Israel and the rupture of relations with many Arab countries. Those who broke ranks, such as *Jamāʿat al-muslimīn* (popularly known as *al-Takfīr Wal-Hijra*, "the Group of Apostasy and Migration") and *al-Jihād al-Islāmī* (Islamic Jihad), chose to resort to violence.[88]

Threat: state-attributed economic problems

As previously outlined, state-attributed economic problems can be construed as a clear threat that mobilizes social movements. As Almieda succinctly points out:

> when organised groups convincingly attribute to specific agents the responsibility for decline in their economic conditions they may initiate campaigns to resist unwanted changes … the administrative expansion of the nation state makes it a common target for redress of economic problems.[89]

The period after the 1967 defeat, besides being emotionally devastating on the Egyptian people, was also economically harsh. Nasser and after him Sadat placed an emphasis on re-building Egypt's military at the expense of other public expenditures needed to maintain and develop the economy. Defense spending constituted approximately 15 percent of GNP, while economic investment fell to a record low of 9 percent during the same period.[90] Public sector financing would have an impact on the general population as more and more resources were directed to the war effort. After the war and despite all the rents, the budget deficit would continue to grow, as seen in Table 4.2.

Besides the worsening economic conditions, the Sadat regime would also have to deal with people's expectations from the legacy of 'Nasser's bargain.'

Table 4.2 Government revenues and expenditures 1974–1979 (in millions of EGP)

	1974	*1975*	*1976*	*1977*	*1978*	*1979*
Revenues:						
Indirect taxes	552	784	996	1,530	1,563	1,841
Direct taxes	197	256	345	460	613	743
Public economic sector surplus	338	364	574	652	1,012	1,351
Other	516	648	659	803	750	956
Total	**1,603**	**2,052**	**2,574**	**3,445**	**3,938**	**4,891**
Expenditures:						
Current	1,047	1,465	1,896	1,897	2,370	2,838
Consumer subsidies	410	622	434	650	900	1,370
Public investment	771	1,175	1,320	1,946	2,725	2,851
Total	**2,228**	**3,262**	**3,650**	**4,493**	**5,995**	**7,059**
Deficit:	**–625**	**–1,210**	**–1,076**	**–1,048**	**–2,057**	**–2,168**
Bank borrowing	219	731	857	471	809	1,149
Other	406	479	219	577	1,248	1,019

Source: Henry J. Bruton, "Egypt's Development in the Seventies," *Economic Development and Cultural Change* 31, no. 4 (July 1983): 695.

Students would continue to expect automatic employment in the public sector; workers would continue to expect the maintaining and increasing of their benefits. As Beattie writes:

> The harsh realities of postwar Egypt—the overcrowding of Cairo and Alexandria, severe housing shortages, and reduced prospects of gainful employment in the already bloated state bureaucracy—created an environment ripe with frustration.... The economy's weakness also translated into fewer funds for education. Despite significant expansion of higher education in the 1970s, Sadat's more liberal admission policy still meant more bodies crammed into university classrooms. Students often had to stand for lectures, and there were shortages of essential class material. The quality of education declined accordingly.[91]

Workers had made tremendous gains during the Nasser era, and would be the first to feel the impact of worsening economic conditions as the Sadat regime rolled back some of these gains. During the Nasser era workers had come to enjoy welfare benefits, including health care and subsidized accommodation, food and medicine, as well as fixed working hours, profit sharing and retirement entitlements. However, some of these benefits were unsustainable. Goldberg writes that the

> macro-economic price for the success of the Nasserist policies was the overstaffing of the public sector as well as the civil service and a constantly rising bill for subsidies. These led to lower output per employee, a reduction in factor productivity as well as decreased capacity of firm management to discipline the work force, and an increased drain on the state budget.[92]

Even though aspects of the regime's new approach were necessary to alleviate the budget strain and improve productivity, removing subsidies with no contingency planning would surely affect the poorest segments of society negatively. But Sadat was in a bind, and in order to continue to borrow from the World Bank and on the path of *infitāḥ*, he would have to cut subsidies. The workers, while not able to change the new direction of the government, were at least able to slow it down, through official union avenues and more importantly through protests and industrial actions. However, the changing international environment, as well as the changing local environment, would highlight a decrease in the opportunities of workers.

The students also began to feel the worsening economic conditions. As part of 'Nasser's bargain,' students were guaranteed employment upon graduation, something the Sadat regime could not honor as the 1970s moved on. The oil boom motivated millions of Egyptians to move to the Gulf in search for work and higher pay. This would actually work to Egypt's benefit, as the workers would send home remittances that boosted the Egyptian economy. However, with the lower oil prices after 1982, there were lower numbers of workers and a decrease in remittances, something that would deeply affect the political economy of the incoming Mubarak regime.

An increase in class antagonisms during the Sadat era, from the mid-1970s onwards was also observable. The middle class as well as the rural and urban poor would see an attack on their economic rights, even as the extravagant lives of the 'fat cats' and the bureaucratic-military elites became more visible. Despite the worsening economic conditions, Egypt in the 1970s earned the dubious distinction of being the world's largest importer of Mercedes Benz cars, as the luxurious new sedans competed with donkey-drawn carriages in the traffic-clogged streets of Cairo.[93] These class antagonisms would soon spill onto the streets. The 1977 'Bread Uprising' highlighted the effectiveness of the labor and student movements, who, despite operating in authoritarian settings, were able to defend certain economic rights against threats from the state.

The 1977 Bread Uprising

As the euphoria of the 1973 War subsided, the people were again aware of the multitude of economic, political and social problems still facing Egypt. The amount of money spent on the war had taken its toll on the budget, leading the finance minister at the time to conclude that 1975 had been the "worst economic year in the history of modern Egypt."[94] The government, under the guidance of the IMF and the World Bank, had begun to take austerity measures to attempt to balance the budget.

Resentment was building in various segments of society, and was reflected in popular discourse as read in Ahmed Fouad Negm and Sheikh Imam's poem *Shayyid quṣūrak*,[95] which accurately captures the mood of the people and their views on their rulers. The poem, written and sung in colloquial Egyptian, also provides a scathing socio-economic critique. The verse "Build your palaces on our fields" specifically addresses government policy, which had focused on real estate investments at the expense of agriculture, and demonstrates popular frustration with the regime's economic rationale and outlook. The verse "you can set up nightclubs near the factories" again speaks of the huge number of nightclubs and casinos that would spring up during the Sadat era and the popular discontent against them.[96]

As the fiscal situation worsened, and discontent brewed against the regime, in October 1976 the Cairo representative of the World Bank, Paul Dickey, sent a secret memorandum to Minister of Economy Zaki el Shafie. Dickey argued that Egypt was in need of some firm economic decisions, such as the devaluation of the Egyptian pound and the lowering and eventual removal of subsidies.[97] But there were no plans to offset the impacts of such measures. Dickey's suggestion worried the minister and his economic team, who tried to explain to him that Egypt had become a net importer—so a devaluation of the currency would exponentially increase the price of imports. Moreover, they feared the political impact of a removal of subsidies.[98] It soon became clear to the government that the suggestions in the memorandum were not suggestions but effectively orders.

The news of the proposed subsidy cuts leaked. Once the leaks became public, some independents in parliament attempted to oppose them, but to no avail. On the evening of January 17, 1977, the deputy prime minister, Abdel-Moneim el-Qaissouny, addressed parliament, signaling that the next five-year plan would include cuts in subsidies to major commodities and foodstuffs.[99] This would directly affect the lives of all Egyptians, and the next day's papers announced price increases for commodities such as bread, rice, pasta, gas, oil, sugar and even cigarettes.[100] News spread quickly, and the protests started the next morning. The workers in Helwan factories were the first to action, with thousands going on strike. Workers from the nearby military factories were quick to join, as well as those of Shubra al Khiemah, who occupied their factory. The protests spread to factories across Cairo and eventually across Egypt.[101] Baker writes:

> Angry crowds of students, workers, and the urban poor demonstrated in all the major cities, attacking symbols of state power, conspicuous consumption and Western influence. The targets reflected the widespread perception that the International Monetary Fund, backed by the United States, had instigated the regime's decision to cut back on government spending in ways that struck hardest the poor.[102]

In Alexandria, workers at the Naval Arsenal demonstrated and were quickly joined by workers from nearby factories. The demonstration headed toward Alexandria University and thousands of students joined the march.[103] The protests would take a violent turn, as protestors burned down the headquarters of the ASU in the Manshia district. Students at Ein Shams University held a conference to denounce the cuts, and started a demonstration that headed toward parliament. The demonstrators were joined by women, public servants and Cairo university students, and, together with other demonstrations from across Cairo, became a large mass of people heading towards Tahrir Square.[104] The demonstrations had developed into an uprising: cars were burnt and people battled the police across Cairo. In Giza Square, very close to the house of the president, bloody clashes occurred between the protestors and the police.[105] The socio-economic dimensions of the protests and the general anger toward the regime and the private sector elites were encapsulated in the chants that the protestors raised:

- *Yā sākinīn al-quṣūr, al-fuqarāʾ ʿayishīn fī al-qubūr!* (You who live in palaces we live in tombs!)
- *Sayyid Marʿī ya Sayyid bīh kīlu al-laḥma bāʿ b-gnīh* (Said Mariʾe, Said bey, a kilo of meat now costs a pound!)
- *ʿAbd al-Nāṣir yaʾmā qāl, khalī bālkum min al-ʿummāl* (Abdel Nasser always said it, take care of the workers!)
- *Hiyā bi talbis ākhir mudāʿa wa iḥnā bi naskun ʿashara bi ʿuda* (She [Sadat's wife Gihan] wears the latest fashions and we live ten in a room!)[106]

Sadat himself was on vacation at the presidential winter rest house in Aswan and preparing for the visit of Yugoslav president Tito. He was unaware of the protests and was giving an interview to a Lebanese journalist when he noticed smoke rising above the Aswan city center. Sadat asked, "What is this?" to which the reporter answered, "Maybe the protests in Cairo reached here?" Sadat allegedly replied, "What protests?"[107] The demonstrations had reached Aswan, and he saw with his own eyes protestors angrily approaching the rest house. He immediately "rushed out, leaving everything behind him, even official papers that needed his signature."[108]

Workers and students against the regime again

The 1977 uprising again shows the historic pattern by which the students join workers in protests. Whether originally about political grievances and then economic ones, or vice versa, this is a pattern that would carry through to the Mubarak era. Aḥmad Bahā' al-Dīn Sha'bān was arrested during the events of 1977. In a historical testimony he recalled:

> On the morning of the 18th of January, the students were discussing the shocking decisions and the anger that engulfed the people. Discussions were being held between the students and contact was established with other institutions and faculties and it was agreed that a march would head from Cairo University heading towards parliament.[109]

In clear historical pattern with 1946 and 1968, Sha'bān continues:

> As the march headed towards Qasr el Aini street, it was joined by another march organized by the workers of the Helwan industrial area. As both marches combined, bystanders joined and everyone was chanting *iḥnā al-sha'b ma' al-'ummāl ḍidd ḥukūma al-istighlāl!* (We are the people united with the workers, against the exploitative government!)[110]

Another student leader recounted:

> As we arrived on Kasr al-Aini street, the workers too were reaching the area on long rows of trucks from Helwan. The workers in their blue and khaki work clothes were waving their fists and shouting with enthusiasm. The traffic on Kast al-Aini street was paralyzed.[111]

As the number of protesters grew in Tahrir Square and around the parliament, the order was issued for the security services to attack the protestors and attempt to disperse them. The student leader recalls:

> The sound of light weapons fired in the air announced the arrival of the security police. Reflections in the parliament's dome from the heavy shooting

> gave the impression that the building was burning. The police closed in on the crowds from all sides at once.... Those coming from the direction of Kasr A-Eini street were especially heavily armed with rifles, tear gas, and clubs and shields. As they approached the people, the police charged in unison, eventually silence the crowd with their deafening roar. Tension spread through the silenced crowds. Then, strong voiced arose from the workers, shouting; "We will not fear, we will not fear for Citadel Prison". Student leaders then in turn called out: "Youth Youth! We are not afraid of terror."[112]

The 1977 uprising was spontaneous in nature: student and worker grievances against the regime had been building up over the decade, when the socio-economic conditions did not improve as Sadat had promised. Beattie writes that "most of the rioting was spontaneous, a profound expression of pent-up popular frustration, not premeditated acts by political organizations."[113] When worker and student protests erupted, they were joined by a mass of the urban poor whose own livelihoods were under threat by the subsidy removal. Shaʿbān recalls:

> Historically, you will find that the workers movement often inspired the student movement. For example, in the 1970s the High National Committee for Students was established, borrowing the name from the High National Committee for Workers and Students, which was formed in 1946. The student movement during the 1970s was mostly a leftist one. There was awareness about the importance of being tied to the working class, which happened organically.
>
> We tried to establish links in a more organized way, especially workers movements that were resisting, e.g., Nasr Motors factory, Textile factories.... Three Marxist organizations were born in university: Egyptian Communist Party, Egyptian Workers Communist Party and Egyptian Communist Party January 8. I was a member of the Egyptian Communist Party of January 8. with Kamal Khalil and many other students. It included students and workers. Because to the establishment of those three parties, an organic crossroad between workers and students was formed.... You will find that the leftist student movement was continuously supporting the workers' movement.[114]

These testimonies show that there was a certain degree of coordination between students and workers in 1977, but these links were not well developed. As previously highlighted, when the leftist students were leading the student movement in 1972, connections were developed with the labor movement, but no direct networking occurred as it had done in 1946 (and as would happen in 2011). Even though the protests were crushed by the regime, nonetheless the 1977 mobilization would be the final dress rehearsal for the events that would unfold in the same place, decades later.

Regime response

The regime had no option but to announce that it was revoking plans to cut the subsidies. On the evening of January 19, the government announced it was cancelling its decrees and the army was ordered to move onto the streets to maintain order and crush the protests. Sadat viewed the events of January 1977 as a direct threat to his power. Rather than formulating a policy response that would take popular demands into consideration, he again attempted to place blame for the uprising on a leftist–communist–Nasserite conspiracy, admitting that the government was not able to properly explain the necessity of the cuts. Speaking of the leftist current, he said: "They exploited it to the utmost. Why? To seize power! To seize it how? By destruction, sabotage, killing, robbing. That is what 18 and 19 of January was all about. It was the *intifada* of thieves."[115] Within days, hundreds of leftist and Nasserite activists, politicians, journalists, academics and students were rounded up by the security apparatus and incarcerated across Egypt.[116]

In the aftermath, and in line with Sadat's habitual approach of coating his policies with a popular mandate, an 11-point plebiscite was arranged to attempt to secure the public's perception of the events of January 1979 as a leftist plot. The plebiscite urged Egyptians to say yes to "peace, freedom and security" and no to "blood and destruction." Two of the plebiscite's provisions recognized the social injustices but simultaneously denounced the demonstrators.[117]

Highlighting its support of Sadat, the United States reacted quickly to the events. Wienbum argues that "to show support for the shaken regime following the food riots, the US acted immediately to shift $190 million in already committed capital development funds to commodities that would enter the economy quickly."[118] The government in the end had backtracked on the removal of subsidies. This is yet another example of how social movements in authoritarian settings are able to challenge a regime. Despite the closed political system, the labor and student movements, through their spontaneous but powerful protests, were able to roll back, at least in the interim, this threat to their economic wellbeing. However, the structural adjustment process would continue gradually and would be picked up enthusiastically by the Mubarak regime when it faced yet another fiscal crisis.[119]

Notes

1 *Al Akhbar*, January 31, 1977.
2 John Esposito, *Islam and Politics* (New York: Syracuse University Press, 1984), 212.
3 On one occasion, Aly Sabry, Sadat's Vice President and a staunch Nasserite who was often described as Moscow's man in Cairo, was having tea with the Soviet President Nikolai Podgorny during a visit to Egypt. When someone mentioned President Sadat, Sabry jokingly replied, "What president?" See Kirk Beattie, *Egypt During the Sadat Years* (New York: Palgrave, 2000), 45.
4 Gilles Kepel, *Jihad: The Trail of Political Islam* (Cambridge, MA: Harvard University Press, 2002), 65.

5 Raymond A. Hinnebusch, "Egypt under Sadat: Elites, Power Structure, and Political Change in a Post-Populist State," *Social Problems* 28, no. 4 (April 1981): 444.
6 *Time Magazine*, March 19, 1974.
7 The Sadat regime itself tended to intentionally confuse the left with the Nasserites, in order to discredit the Nasserites. Yet the left and the Nasserites differed substantially despite certain shared tendencies. Posusney aptly defines what is meant by 'left' during the 1960s and 1970s Egypt:

> The category of "leftist" is defined here in a specific historical and regional context, by the then standard dichotomies on economic and foreign policy issues. "Leftists" refer broadly to those who favored government intervention in the economy to support subaltern strata and promote national development intended to narrow the gap between Egypt and the advanced industrialist economies, combined with opposition to Western imperialism and Zionism. By this definition, the leftist camp compromised traditional Marxists, Nasirists and new Marxist groups which began to emerge in the late 1960's. Their programmatic unity should not mask important underlying differences ... Nasirism is not an atheistic ideology and is thus not, like Marxism, incompatible with Egypt's dominant religion, Islam. Nasirists also lack the philosophical commitment Marxists have to promoting labor militancy.... Finally, whereas Marxism advocates the abolition of capitalism and, ultimately, of the state itself, Nasirism promotes the state as the unifying core and driving engine of the nation.
>
> (Marsha Pripstein Posusney, *Labor and the State in Egypt: Workers, Unions, and Economic Restructuring* (New York: Columbia University Press, 1997), 102)

8 Anwar Sadat, *al-Baḥth ʿan al-dhāt* (The Search for the Self) (Cairo: Al Ahram, 1979), 224–225.
9 According to Baker after 1973

> The state mobilized its impressive resources to impose this official reading of history: in the seventies a flood of anti-Nasser publications appeared; standard school textbooks rewrote the record of the recent past to conform with the official line; and the government controlled media launched damning assessments of the Nasser years. By exposing the alleged failures of the Nasser regime, Sadat hoped to justify his own radical policy departures of economic and political liberalization, realignment with the West, and accommodation with Israel.
>
> (Baker, *Sadat and After*, 79)

10 Anwar Sadat, "The October Paper," April 1974 as cited in John Waterbury, *The Egypt of Nasser and Sadat: The Political Economy of Two Regimes* (Princeton: Princeton University Press, 1983), 123.
11 Ibid.
12 Waterbury, *Egypt of Nasser and Sadat*, 131.
13 Nadim Lachine, "The Open Door Policy of Anwar Sadat," *Association of Arab American University Graduates*, Information Paper 21 (1978), 13.
14 ʿAbd al-Qādir Shuhyib, *Muḥākamat al-infitāḥ al-iqtiṣādi fī maṣr* (The Trial of Economic *infitāḥ* in Egypt) (Cairo: Ibn Khaldūn, 1979), 16.
15 For a full listing of all the *infitāḥ* laws, see Gouda Abdel Khaleq, "*Aḥamm dalālat siyāsat al-infitāḥ al-iqtiṣādī*" (The Most Important Indicators of the Infitāḥ Economic Policy), in *al-Iqtiṣād al-miṣru fī rubʿa qarn 1952–1977* (The Egyptian Economy in the Quarter-Century 1952–1977) (Cairo: Egypt Institute for Books, 1978).
16 Cited in Osama Hamed, "Egypt's Open Door Economic Policy: An Attempt at Economic Integration in the Middle East," *International Journal of Middle East Studies* 13, no. 1 (February 1981): 1.
17 See Kate Gillespie, *The Tripatriate Relationship: Government, Foreign Investors and Local Investors During Egypt's Economic Opening* (New York: Praeger

Publishing, 1984) and Moheb Zaki, *Egyptian Business Elites: Their Visions and Investment Behavior* (Cairo: Dār al-Kutub, 1999).

18 Samer Soliman, "State and Industrial Capitalism in Egypt," *Cairo Papers in Social Science* 21, no. 2 (1999): 30.

19 Heba Handoussa, "Crisis and Challenge: Prospects for the 1990s", in *Employment and Structural Adjustment: Egypt in the 1990s*, ed. Heba Handoussa and Gillian Potter (Cairo: AUC Press, 1991), 3–21.

20 Illya Harik, *Economic Policy Reform in Egypt* (Gainesville: University Press of Florida, 1997), 20.

21 Ibid., 111.

22 Ibid., 16.

23 John Waterbury, *Egypt: Burdens of the Past, Options for the Future* (Bloomington: Indiana University Press, 1978), 206.

24 Waterbury, *Egypt of Nasser and Sadat*, 134.

25 Cited in Beattie, *Egypt During the Sadat Years*, 53.

26 Ali E. Hillal Dessouki, "Policy Making in Egypt: A Case Study of the Open Door Economic Policy," *Social Problems* 28, no. 4 (April 1981): 410–416.

27 Cited in Gouda Abdel Khaleq, "Looking Outside, or Turning Northwest? On the Meaning and External Dimension of Egypt's Infitah, 1971–1980," *Social Problems* 28, no. 4 (April 1981): 407.

28 Waterbury, *Egypt of Nasser and Sadat*, 366.

29 Ibid.

30 Raymond A. Hinnebusch Jr, "From Nasir to Sadat: Elite Transformation in Egypt," *Journal of South Asian and Middle Eastern Studies* 7, no. 1 (1983): 25–26.

31 Ibid., 42–43.

32 Ibid., 69–70.

33 Nahed Abdel Fatah, *al-ʿUmmāl wa rijāl al-aʿmāl: taḥawulāt al-furas al-siyāsiyya fi maṣr* (Workers and Businessmen: The Changes in Political Opportunities in Egypt) (Cairo: Al Ahram Center for Political and Strategic Studies, 2006), 349–350.

34 Beattie, *Egypt During the Sadat Years*, 151.

35 Translated in David Hirst and Irene Beeson, *Sadat* (London: Faber & Faber, 1981), 218.

36 Beattie, *Egypt During the Sadat Years*, 152.

37 Nazih Ayubi, *Overstating the Arab State: Politics and Society in the Middle East* (London: IB Tauris, 1995), 344.

38 The Egyptian economist Galal Amin, while noting the obvious differences, nonetheless made an interesting historical comparison of the similarities between the Sadat and Khedive Ismail eras. He argued that economic development under each was primarily characterized by investing in infrastructure and some public works, while neglecting the expansion of the industrial base. He also observed that a consumption culture was developed that relied heavily on imports. See Galal Amin, *Qiṣṣat al-iqtiṣād al-maṣri: min ʿahd Muhammad Ali ilā ʿahd Mubārak* (The Story of the Egyptian Economy: From The Era of Muhammad Ali to The Era of Mubarak) (Cairo: Dār al-Shurūq, 2012), 28–29.

39 Robert Springborg, *Mubarak's Egypt: Fragmentation of the Political Order* (Boulder: Westview Press, 1989), 11.

40 Raymond William Baker, *Egypt's Uncertain Revolution Under Nasser and Sadat* (Cambridge, MA: Harvard University Press, 1978), 145.

41 Hamed, "Egypt's Open Door Economic Policy," 4.

42 Gouda Abdel Khaleq, *al-Iqtiṣād al-dawlī min al-mazaʾiyya al-nisbiyya ilā al-tabādul al-lā-mutakāfiʾī* (The International Economy, from Relative Privileges to Asymmetrical Exchanges) (Cairo: Dār al-Naḥda al-ʿarabiyya, 1986), 195.

43 Amina Amin Helmy, "*Dawr ṣundūq al-naqd al-dawlī fī al-duwal al-namiʾa maʿa al-ishāra ilā al-tajriba al-maṣriya*" (The Role of the IMF in Developing Countries'

with a Focus on the Egyptian Experience) (M.A. thesis, Faculty of Economics and Political Science, Cairo University, 1988), 71–73.

44 According to Weinbaum US economic assistance through the Nasser era

> had been closely tied to the ups and downs of US-Egyptian relations. Following the post-war reconstruction of Western Europe, the Eisenhower Administration focused attention on assisting less developed but militarily allied countries. Egypt's failure to qualify did not preclude its receiving shipments on concessionary terms of US wheat. However, this aid was promptly suspended in 1956 after Nasser's nationalization of the Suez Canal. When relations improved during 1959 and 1960, Public Law (PL) 480 food shipments were renewed. In an agreement signed in March 1960, $32.5 million was also provided for economic development.
>
> (Marvin G. Weinbaum, "Egypt's 'Infitah' and the Politics of US Economic Assistance," *Middle Eastern Studies* 21, no. 2 (April 1985): 209)

45 Hinnebusch, Egyptian Politics Under Sadat, 57.

46 Waterbury, *Egypt of Nasser and Sadat*, 10.

47 For an overview of the involvement of the World Bank during those years, see The World Bank, "Arab Republic of Egypt, Report No 870" (Washington, DC: World Bank, 1976).

48 International Monetary Fund, *Arab Republic of Egypt*, Staff Report for the 1976 Article X IV Consultation (August 1976), 16–17.

49 See Craig Daigle, *The Limits of Detente: The United States, the Soviet Union, and the Arab-Israeli Conflict, 1969–1973* (New Haven: Yale University Press, 2012).

50 Haggai Erlich, *Students and University in 20th Century Egyptian Politics* (London: Frank Cass, 1989), 203.

51 Beattie, *Egypt During the Sadat Years*, 94.

52 Ibid., 204.

53 According to Hinnebusch:

> The students were a vanguard of political activism. Student opinion carried special weight because, as a broadly recruited group, students expressed the views of a wider public. While some students such as those from bourgeois families concentrated at the American university, were pro-government and many other were political apathetic, there was considerable student activism under Sadat and it usually took an anti-government form. Students were susceptible to dissidence because of their greater politicisatization and their high expectations at a time when career outlooks for many surplus graduates were bleak. As to make trouble for himself, Sadat continued the expansion of higher education, opening many regional campuses which spread student dissidence from the big cities to rural towns like Assiut and Minya.
>
> (Hinnebusch, *Egyptian Politics Under Sadat*, 243)

54 Abdalla, Student Movement and National Politics, 178.

55 Hirst and Beeson, *Sadat*, 126.

56 Ibid.

57 Abdalla, *Student Movement and National Politics*, 176–177.

58 Ibid.

59 Ibid., 186.

60 Mahmoud Hussein, "The Revolt of Egyptian Students," *MERIP* 11 (August 1972): 13.

61 Peter Johnson, "Retreat of the Revolution in Egypt," *MERIP* 17 (May 1973): 6.

62 Ibid.

63 Abdalla, *Student Movement and National Politics*, 185.

64 Personal interview, Cairo, March 7, 2013.

65 Abdalla, *Student Movement and National Politics*, 192–193.
66 Baker, *Sadat and After*, 107.
67 Posusney, "Irrational Workers," 100.
68 Bianchi, "Corporatization of the Egyptian Labor Movement," 432.
69 Anwar Sadat, Speech on the Occasion of National Doctors Day, March 18, 1980. *Bibliotheca Alexandria Sadat Digital Archive*, http://sadat.bibalex.org/speeches/browser.aspx?SID=924 (accessed October 1, 2014).
70 Constitution of the Arab Republic of Egypt, 1971, www.constitutionnet.org/files/Egypt%20Constitution.pdf (accessed October 1, 2014).
71 Khālid ʿAlī ʿUmar, *al-haqq fī-l-tanẓīm: al-huriyya al-niqābiya bayn al-utur al-tashrīʿiya wa mabadiʿī al-maḥkama al-dusturiyya wal-mumārasa al-ʿamaliyya* (The Right to Organize: Freedom to Unionize between the Legislative Framework, Principles of the Constitutional Court and Actual Practice) (Publication of the Hisham Mubarak Law Centre, 2008), 12, http://hmlc-egy.org/node/59 (accessed October 1, 2014).
72 Azza Khalīl, ed., *al-harakāt al-ijtimāʿiyya fī-l-ʿālam al-ʿarabī* (Social Movements in the Arab World) (Cairo: Matbouly, 2006), 332.
73 ʿUmar, *al-haqq fī-l-tanẓīm*, 12–13.
74 Beattie, *Egypt During the Sadat Years*, 160.
75 Abdel Fatah, *al-ʿummāl wa rijāl al-aʿmāl.*
76 Personal interview, Cairo, March 18, 2013.
77 Nadime Lachine, "Class Roots of the Sadat Regime: Reflections of an Egyptian Leftist," *MERIP* 56 (April 1977): 5.
78 Baker, *Sadat and After*, 128.
79 Tarrow, *Power in Movement*, 76–77.
80 Ibid., 71.
81 John Esposito and John Voll, *Islam and Democracy* (New York: Oxford University Press, 1996), 174.
82 Denis Sullivan and Sana Abed-Kotob, *Islam in Contemporary Egypt: Civil Society versus the State* (Boulder: Lynne Rienner, 1999), 73.
83 Ibid., 213.
84 Ibid., 116.
85 Beattie, *Egypt During the Sadat Years*, 201.
86 Bjørn Olav Utvik, "*Hizb Al Wasat* and the Potential for Change in Egyptian Islamism," *Critical Middle Eastern Studies* 14, no. 3 (Autumn 2005): 298.
87 Ibid., 296.
88 See Gilles Kepel, *The Prophet and the Pharaoh: Muslim Extremism in Egypt* (London: Al Saqi Books, 1985).
89 Paul Almeida, "Opportunity Organizations and Threat-Induced Contention: Protest Waves in Authoritarian Settings," *American Journal of Sociology* 109, no. 2 (September 2003): 352.
90 For a full macro and micro view of the Egyptian economy at the time see Heba Handoussa, "The Impact of Foreign Aid on Egypt's Economic Development, 1952–1986," in Uma Lele and Nabi Ijaz (eds.), *Transitions in Development: The Role of Aid and Commercial Flows* (San Francisco: International Center for Economic Growth Press, 1991) and Galal Amin, *Egypt's Economic Predicament: A Study in the Interaction of External Pressure, Political Folly and Social Tension in Egypt, 1960–1990* (Leiden: E.J. Brill, 1995), 7.
91 Beattie, *Egypt During the Sadat Years*, 95.
92 Goldberg, "Foundations of State-Labor Relations," 157.
93 Beattie, *Egypt During the Sadat Years*, 159.
94 Ghali Shoukri, "al-thawra wal-thawra al-muddadda fī Misr" (Revolution and Counterrevolution in Egypt), *Kitab el-Ahalli*, no. 15 (Cairo: El-Ahali, September 1987), 217.

95 Ahmad Fouad Negm and Shiekh Imam, *Shayyid quṣūrak* (Build Your Palaces), trans. in Lachine, "Class Roots of the Sadat Regime," 5.
96 There was a huge increase in the construction of nightclubs and casinos. Gulf Arabs and Libyans, rich from windfall oil profits, would come to Cairo to engage in activities prohibited by Islam such as gambling and drinking that were not allowed in their own countries. Even though the first casino contract for the Nile Hilton was approved in Nasser's time, the Casino's first operation started at the beginning of the Sadat era and was thus associated with the regime. See Beattie, *Egypt During the Sadat Years*, 162.
97 Moḥammad Hassanin Heikal, *kharīf al-ghadab* (The Autumn of Fury) (Cairo: Al-Ahram, 1988), 185.
98 Ibid., 186.
99 Ḥusayn ʿAbdel Rāziq, *miṣr fī-l-thāmin ʿashr wal-tāsiʿ ʿashr min yanayer: dirāsa siyāsiyya watha'iqiyya* (Egypt on 18 and 19 January: A Documentary Political Study) (Beirut: Dār al-Kalima, 1979), 70–71.
100 Ibid., 72.
101 Aḥmad Sādiq Saʿd, *dirasāt f-īl-ishtirākiyya al-Miṣriyya* (Studies in Egyptian Socialism) (Cairo: Dār al-Fikr al-Jadīd, 1990), 340.
102 Baker, *Sadat and After*, 18.
103 Aḥmad Sādiq Saʿd, *Dirasāt*, 341.
104 Ibid., 341–342.
105 Ahmad El-Massry, *48 Saʿāt ḥazzat Miṣr: Ri'yat shāhid aʿyān* (48 Hours that Shook Egypt: An Eyewitness Account) (Cairo: Maṭbuʿāt al-tadāmun, 1979), 30.
106 Riyad Moharam, *Dhikra intifādāt al-khubz 18–19 January 1977* (The Memory of the Bread Intifada, 18–19 January 1977), Al Hewar, www.ahewar.org/debat/show.art.asp?aid=241223 (accessed October 1, 2014).
107 Muḥammad Ḥassanin Hiekal, *Kharīf al-Ghadab* (The Autumn of Fury) (Cairo: Al-Ahram, 1988), 187.
108 Ibid.
109 *Al Wafd*, December 29, 2010.
110 Ibid.
111 Baker, *Sadat and After*, 129.
112 Ibid.
113 Beattie, *Egypt During the Sadat Years*, 209.
114 Personal interview, Cairo, March 18, 2013.
115 Cited in Baker, *Sadat and After*, 120.
116 Ibid., 122.
117 Ibid., 121.
118 Weinbaum, "Egypt's 'Infitah' and the Politics of US Economic Assistance," 214.
119 Ayubi, *Overstating the Arab State*, 346.

5 The Mubarak era (1981–2001)

> I will never accept corruption even from my closest relatives. Egypt is not the private estate of its ruler.
>
> Hosni Mubarak, October 1981[1]

Introduction

Upon Sadat's assassination in 1981, Hosni Mubarak assumed power and was initially regarded by many as an interim president. In his early years, he attempted to build consensus, tolerate opposition and promote partnership between the private and public sectors. Through extensive diplomatic efforts, he also led Egypt's reconciliation with other Arab countries after relations had been severed following Sadat's signing of the 1979 Camp David Accords. Yet it was during his presidency that the seeds for unprecedented popular mobilization would be sown, only to be reaped on February 12, 2011, when he was forced to step down. This chapter will investigate the political economy of the first two decades of the Mubarak regime. It will also explore the evolving relationship between the labor and student movement with the regime as it continued to roll back some of the socio-economic privileges of 'Nasser's bargain.'[2]

The political economy of the Mubarak regime

Consolidation of power

Mubarak began his presidency by releasing many political prisoners whom Sadat had jailed in his final years. In a publicity stunt designed to showcase his more inclusive approach *vis-à-vis* Sadat, high-profile prisoners such as Muḥammad Ḥassanin Hiekal were invited to an audience with the new president immediately following their release.[3] State control of the press was slightly relaxed to coincide with the equally slight opening of the political system after Sadat's final tumultuous months, which were famously described by Hiekal himself in his book as *Kharīf al-Ghadab* (The Autumn of Fury).[4] Yet although certain of the more repressive measures of Mubarak's predecessors were relaxed, the emergency laws remained in effect. This relaxation of the political environment ended in 1993, when the regime responded to the challenge posed by Islamist militants carrying out attacks on targets across the country.

Regionally, the new president made efforts to re-establish diplomatic relations with Arab states. Iraqi leader Saddam Hussein, fashioning himself as the leader of the Arabs, had led the charge against what he viewed as Sadat's betrayal. The Arab League Foreign Ministers had met in Baghdad in 1979 in an emergency summit called by Saddam, and had unanimously decided to move the headquarters of the Arab League from Cairo to Tunis. It would take almost a decade for normal relations to resume. After intensive Egyptian diplomatic efforts, an Arab League summit in Jordan in 1987 freed the Arab states from the collective prohibition of maintaining diplomatic ties with Egypt; in 1990, the Arab League states finally agreed to return the headquarters to Cairo.[5] Internationally, Mubarak maintained Egypt's realignment with the West and sought to further cement it with stronger economic relations with the United States, as well as more trade with Europe.

An economy in crisis

Mubarak inherited an increasingly disfigured economy described by Richards as "one of the many heavily indebted, middle-income countries, with gross macroeconomic imbalances and microeconomic distortions, both largely the creation of an earlier era of import-substituting industrialization."[6] At the core of Egypt's economic problems were two gaps: between investment and domestic savings and between imports and exports, both a legacy of *infitāḥ*.

In February 1982, the president invited prominent economists to a closed-door conference focused on the economy to attempt "to assess the state of the economy with an eye to formulate an action plan."[7] The meeting went on for days, and in its concluding communiqué stated that "the government would revert to central economic and social planning and steer the Open Door Policy towards production."[8] In the public sphere, and especially on the pages of *Al-Ahrām Al-Iqtiṣādī*, a vigorous debate unfolded, between neoliberal economists and advocates of *infitāḥ* against leftist economists and critics of *infitāḥ*. These critics argued that the Sadat years had been characterized by mass consumerism and a decrease in industrialization, with negative consequences for the poorer segments of society. Although the regime made a show of listening to the various positions, it continued toward the direction advocated by the more neoliberal economists, that is, toward more free market policies. At face value, attempting to liberalize the economy was the correct undertaking; however, again, the process and outcomes were problematic. Put simply, certain sectors of the economy were not ready for the structural adjustment program that was about to be inaugurated.

The regime was initially able to consolidate its power due to a combination of strategic rents extracted from the United States and other international donors. To achieve this, the government leveraged its importance as a regional US strategic regional partner after the Camp David Accords. The strategic importance of Egypt was a card Mubarak would play through to the very end of his presidency. International donors required Egypt to implement reforms, which the government accepted grudgingly, since Mubarak was very cautious not to shake the foundations of the political system he had just inherited. Some minimal reforms were successfully implemented, however the major ones needed were delayed by the government in a strategy described by Richards as a "successful disaster."[9] It was a successful strategy in the sense that it was able to alleviate the economic conditions and maintain stability for a period of time, but a disaster in that its efficacy lay in merely deferring the problem until it had become a much larger issue.

Despite the regime's ability to stabilize the economy by implementing some reforms and obtaining rents in the early 1980s, by the early 1990s, Egypt was facing a serious economic crisis. The crisis compromised of a combination of stagnation, negative economic growth and heavy indebtedness to international donors. Sadat had been able to leverage rents from the oil boom in the Gulf States, but the collapse of the oil boom in the mid-1980s signaled that Egypt could no longer depend primarily on Gulf rents. The collapse of the oil boom also meant the return of hundreds of thousands of Egyptian workers from the Gulf, which strongly reduced the inflow of remittances, as well as worsening the unemployment problem.

Perversely, Saddam's invasion of Kuwait provided Mubarak with a partial solution to many of Egypt's economic woes. In return for lending diplomatic and military support to the US-led coalition against the Iraqi strongman, Egypt received a "bonanza of economic rewards."[10] Some of Egypt's international debt was written off, and Egypt was given approximately $15 billion in emergency economic assistance. This aid partially helped revive Egypt's economy, but it also contained the seeds of Mubarak's downfall.

The Washington Consensus on the banks of the Nile

The late 1980s and early 1990s was a historic era described infamously (and prematurely) as "the end of history."[11] The 1991 collapse of the Soviet Union and the Eastern Bloc had proven to many the limitations of the socialist and state capitalist models. Murphy argues that the collapse of the Soviet Union "seemed to reinforce the case that there simply was no alternative if countries were to reverse the disastrous performances that had resulted from prolonged import substitution industrialization."[12] The new neoliberal economic mantra was strongly advocated by US President Ronald Reagan and British Prime Minister Margaret Thatcher. Keynesian economic orthodoxy retreated in the face of economists such as Milton Friedman and the Chicago school of economics.[13]

The new economic mantra with regards to state economic policy was theorized as a combination of cuts to government size and spending, deregulation, elimination of trade barriers, and the free flow of capital and privatization.[14] All these policies were designed to stimulate economic growth according to a more neoliberal model. The model, later termed by English economist John Williamson the

"Washington Consensus" for its prominent Washington-based advocates such as the IMF and the World Bank, would come to dominate global economic thinking. Some countries were better geared to gain benefits from it than others.

In lieu of the assistance received from the international community, Egypt was required to implement reforms along the lines of the Washington Consensus, which entailed the removal of state subsidies, devaluation of exchange rate, privatizing large segments of the public sector, and reforming foreign investment laws. Shehata argues that Mubarak would be the president to finally break 'Nasser's bargain.'[15] The regime was caught in a Catch-22: if it restricted the social and economic benefits bestowed by Nasser to the middle class and working class, it risked social upheaval that would threaten the regime's stability. If not, the economy risked being continuingly weakened, risking social upheaval further down the line. Mubarak chose a middle path, slowly rolling back certain economic benefits as well as undertaking structural reform as prescribed by the IMF and the World Bank. Mubarak sought to implement something he called a "productive *infitāḥ*," which "he promised would bring the benefits of liberal capitalism without the speculative excesses of the previous decade."[16]

Some of the Nasserite reforms that were rolled back included parts of the agrarian reform, which had been one of the focal points of the 1952 *coup d'état* that sought to redistribute land away from wealthy landowners to common farmers. On June 24, 1992, the Egyptian parliament reversed the agrarian relations law in which over one million families enjoyed partial property rights through secure tenancy at fixed rents.[17] Since early in the Sadat era, certain factions affected by the agrarian laws had been advocating an abolishment of some of these laws, which favored tenants over landlords. Sadat had complied, abolishing the agrarian reform dispute committees and allowing for the increase of rents.[18] The increased rent was an attempt by the landowners to extract more revenue, and ultimately push out the tenants in order to sell the land or rent it according to unregulated open market prices, or to raise livestock and hire laborers to farm the land on their behalf.[19] Such reform would indeed have the potential of inflicting severe hardships on millions of families who had enjoyed a modicum of protection since 1952. A tenant expressed himself bitterly to a newspaper:

> If I'm lucky enough to get out before the five year interval, I might get EGP6,000 or 12,000, but that would be spent in less than two years. Now there's talk of daily laborers getting EGP10 per day. But at my age who has the strength to work as a hand one day here, one day there? Where do I go, to the desert to reclaim lands? I'd die the next day. I've lived here all my life; I have nothing else.... When I'm gone, what will my wife do?[20]

This trend of reversing Nasser's agrarian reform laws continued under Mubarak, culminating in the June 1992 reversal of the agrarian relations law, despite heavy opposition from the leftist parties in parliament, who were too weak or too compromised to fight back on behalf of the tenants.

The initiation of Egypt's Economic Reform and Structural Adjustment Program (ERSAP)

The IMF and World Bank had been offering Egypt advice and assistance since Sadat's time in power, but it was not until the 1990s that both institutions really began to increasingly exert their influence over the Egyptian economy. Many public companies were being privatized to please international donors under the 1989 agreement with the IMF, albeit haphazardly. Momani argues that the government was so eager to please the IMF that it offered to sell "one company per week."[21]

The government began to implement the prescribed ERSAP. A prominent, privately funded think tank, the Egyptian Center for Economic Studies (ECES),[22] wrote that the "program was initiated in 1991 to rectify the imbalances between the demand and supply side of the economy."[23] It argued that the main symptoms of these imbalances were "the chronic deficits in the balance of payments and the government budget, and high inflation."[24] Remarkably, the previous executive director of the ECES, Ahmad Galal, who would later become Minister of Finance after the overthrow of Muhammad Morsi in 2013, would later criticize some of the economic reforms of the Mubarak regime.[25] He argued:

> The Nazif regime was a continuation of the previous regimes. The beginning was during the open door policy in the mid-1970s. We combined the worst of the two worlds: the mid-1970s and the late 1980s. The remaining of the welfare of the '70s along with the open policy in the 1980s allowed for a distortion to happen. Beginning of the '90s saw a change that continued to 2011. The agenda was a pro-growth agenda.
>
> ...I had many arguments with the World Bank about that and them calling Egypt "The Tiger on the Nile." I though all the while that they were wrong: you cannot measure development by how much growth you're making. You have to worry about who is getting it. And you must look at what kind of growth and where it is coming from: creative, productive, innovative, entrepreneurial type of activities? There is a good kind of growing and a bad kind of growing. Who is getting all the benefits? If it is a few and they are the same ones supporting you, then I am sorry this is not sustainable. Sooner or later something is going to go wrong.[26]

Indeed something would go wrong in spectacular fashion, but it took several more years (until 2011) for the failure to become clear. Under the guidance of the IMF and the World Bank and in agreement with Egypt's international donors and creditors after the debt relief following the first Gulf War, Egypt began its structural adjustment program in 1991. The program's stated aims were to rectify the imbalances between the economy's supply and demand, imbalances which had effected continuous deficits in the balance of payments and the government budget, as well as high inflation.

A variety of important privatizations were announced at a high profile symposium held in September 1990, sponsored by the Private Sector Commission in association with USAID, and attended by several high-level government officials.[27] At the symposium, the influential Deputy Prime Minister and Minister of Agriculture Youssef Wali expressed an admiration of the Soviet plan to transfer 80 percent of all large public sector companies to the private sector within 800 days, arguing that only defense, railways, postal services and energy production should be owned and managed by the state.[28] In hindsight, Wali could not have chosen a worse example of unregulated privatization than 1990s Russia.[29]

Deciding how to privatize

After the decision to privatize, the government had to decide how to go about it. According to the World Bank, there are three broad approaches to privatization: public offerings,[30] auctions[31] and negotiated sales.[32] In addition, governments can offer employees a stake through an ESOP (Employee Stock Ownership Plan). The Egyptian government employed a combination of all these approaches by July 1998,

> nine firms had been sold to strategic investors, and another thirty seven had a majority of shares floated on the stock market, while nineteen companies saw 30–40 percent stakes floated. Many of these cases had 5 to 10 percent of their sales reserved for employee purchases.[33]

Theoretically, ESOPs are designed to increase the workers' influence over managerial decisions, provide increased job security, as well as potentially increase their incomes via dividends.[34] However, theory differed from practice. The ESOP program did not stop new owners, especially international ones, from laying off large numbers of workers.

In theory, the laid-off workers would be taken care of by the Social Fund for Development (SFD), which the World Bank and the IMF stipulated should retrain workers and deploy them to other factories, as well as provide them with a social safety net and their families during their unemployment. Yet the SFD was not able to deal with the large number of workers. Ahmad Kamaly, Professor of Economics at AUC and previously an official in GAFI (General Authority for Investment and Free Zones), who was directly involved in the privatization program, explicitly criticized the SFD:

> If privatization was going to take place then unemployment was going to go up. SFD was supposed to find unconventional ways to absorb that surplus. They didn't do their job. I'd say the SFD is an example of doing nothing.... My objective as SFD from what I understand, I'd talk to the minister of public enterprise or investment to know the estimates of people who will be laid off and formulate a plan of action on how to re-skill and re-absorb them into the work force, especially knowing that privatizing has started to take place. If I don't do that, then I am not doing my job.[35]

Outcomes of ERSAP

From a macroeconomic standpoint, the World Bank and IMF-inspired liberalization program was arguably relatively successful. Egypt's economy, which had shrunk by 2 percent in 1990, was growing at a rate of 5 percent by 1996. Inflation, having reached 20 percent during the late 1980s, leveled at 7 percent.[36] Egypt was proclaimed the economic "Tiger of the Nile" and named by the IMF as a top economic performer. However, the disparity in wealth continued to increase. Even though the Mubarak regime attempted to reform the economy, it was at the expense of the lowest echelons of society. The arrival of neoliberalism in full force was symptomatic of a wider phenomenon across the region. Dodge writes that in the countries of the 2011 Arab uprisings:

> Neoliberal reforms produced a politically connected but small *nouveau riche*, with the majority of the population excluded and increasingly resentful. The transitional governments need to reformulate economic policies in a way that delivers meaningful growth to this previously alienated majority.[37]

This state of affairs was quite evident in Egypt, where the much-touted GDP growth rates had not trickled down to average Egyptians.[38] Similar to the Sadat era, major economic decisions were made to further integrate the Egyptian economy to the global one, with dire consequences for certain segments of the population. In 1995, Egypt joined the World Trade Organization (WTO), but this only made things worse for many Egyptian laborers, as reduced tariff and non-tariff barriers impeded the state's ability to protect certain labor-intensive sectors.

A 1997 report by ECES attempted to assess the impact of ERSAP on employment. It had found that even though the program may have had an overall positive impact on macroeconomic stability, nonetheless it had adverse effects on employment, specifically through the privatization program, where the new owners of state industries did lay off workers. The report concluded, rather optimistically, that "changes in the labor law are expected to address this issue" and that

> the IMF and the World Bank are quite aware of the problem, and some funds have been allocated through SAL and the Social Fund for training programs to enhance worker mobility. Also, unemployment insurance is recommended by ERSAP to minimize this effect of privatization … finance should be available for the retraining and creating jobs for laid-off workers.[39]

Despite such lofty ambitions and recommendations, none of the programs (e.g., SFD) designed to minimize adverse impacts had any substantive effect, as hundreds of thousands of workers became unemployed during the 1990s. Nonetheless, the IMF praised Egypt:

> By the standards of recent experience with economic stabilization, Egypt in the 1990s is a remarkable success story. Determined macroeconomic policy, together with some favorable external developments, has brought much reduced inflation, led to improved public finances, a stable currency, and a strengthened banking system, together with a sound balance of payments position.[40]

The IMF economist Arvind Subramaian wrote: "Egypt's economy has come a long way since the 1980s. Growth is recovering and confidence is rising. Tough macroeconomic policies and deep structural reforms are doing the trick."[41] Despite these stated macroeconomic successes, the poorest segments of society (especially public sector workers) were adversely impacted. The textile sector, long revered by Egyptians as a bastion of Egyptian industry, began to crumble as foreign producers took advantage of reduced tariffs to increase their market share. A report commissioned by USAID in 2004 forecasted that the textile industry would lose 22,185 jobs and approximately US$203.9 million in shipments, a figure that represented approximately 4 percent of the country's non-oil sector exports.[42]

In sum, it is not the role of the chapter to argue against economic reform during the early Mubarak era, for this was obviously needed considering the state of the economy, as well as the exploding population and rising unemployment. The argument rather is that the reforms were not effective long term and, coupled with corruption, would lead to the further disillusionment of the population over the years and contribute to the 2011 uprising.

Patronage and clientelism

Upon assuming power, Mubarak had tried to distance himself from some of the excesses and the corruption of the 'fat cats' of *infitāḥ* and the circle around Sadat. In a 1981 interview for *Al-Mosawar* magazine, Mubarak stated:

> My personal financial ambitions are humble and limited. I am not one of those who seek prosperity and even before I entered public life I never hated as much as those who steal from public funds ... what does it mean if I have a million pounds or more and in the same time have a loss of conscious with God and Country?... I will not wear except what I am wearing today[43] and I will not consume except what I consume today. I will not have anything except my family home, my sons and my personal life.[44]

Despite these grand ambitions, corruption during the Mubarak era would rise to new heights. Another by-product of the neoliberal program was the rise of a new class of businessmen and oligarchs with connections to the regime, who were able to reap the benefits of this economic liberalization. As Timothy Mitchell argued:

> The neoliberal program has not removed the state from the market or eliminated "profligate" public subsidies. These achievements belong to the imagination. Its major impact has been to concentrate public funds into different, but fewer hands. The state has turned resources away from agriculture, industry and the underlying problems of training and employment. It now subsidizes financiers instead of factories, speculators instead of schools.[45]

This manifestation of cronyism carried on from the Sadat era and became much stronger in the Mubarak era, as businessmen moved from influencing policy from afar to effectively legislating for themselves as the case of Ahmad Ezz would show. The parliamentary elections of 1984, 1987 and 1990 were the earliest manifestation of this phenomenon. The NDP, the Wafd and other political parties pushed businessmen onto their electoral lists, and many were successful in becoming members of parliament. Being selected for the electoral lists of the NDP was a highly prized objective. Businessmen seeking patronage from the regime donated large sums of money to the NDP to fund their expensive campaigns. Many with dubious backgrounds were successful in getting into parliament on the NDP list. The party itself, in collaboration with state security, coordinated ballot rigging, whether by bribery, intimidation or pure electoral fraud (including counting deceased persons' votes and ballot stuffing).

As economic conditions worsened, Cairo's elites chose to move out of the increasingly derelict and dysfunctional capital. New compounds with huge malls and plush golf courses were built on the outskirts of Cairo, selling mainly to the rich and aspirational upper middle classes.[46] These artificial compounds were christened with names like Dreamland and Beverly Hills, and came to personify the growing inequality between rich and poor. In a 2007 interview with the *Financial Times*, Nader Fergany, lead author of the Arab Human Development Reports from 2002 to 2005, stated:

> There's a vicious circle of the small clique getting filthy rich and the rest getting impoverished, we have returned this country to what it used to be called before the 1952 revolution: the one per cent society. One per cent controls almost all the wealth of the country.[47]

Many businessmen with close links to the regime were able to take advantage of the privatization program, similar to what happened in Russia during the dying hours of the USSR. The textbook example of crony capitalism in the privatization program is the case of Ahmad Ezz. He was able to take early advantage of the privatization program with the acquisition of a state factory, Alexandria Iron and Steel Company in Dekhila (AISCD), previously owned by state-affiliated petroleum companies and banks. After purchasing a stake, he was able to gradually consolidate his ownership of AISCD, eventually renaming it Ezz Steel.[48] Using cheap state credit, he acquired and increased his steel manufacturing capacity, ultimately controlling two-thirds of Egypt's steel industry. According to Ali Helmy, former chairman of the National Iron and Steel Company:

> The National Bank of Egypt and Bank of Cairo (Egypt's largest public banks) favored Ezz because of his relationship with Gamal Mubarak and helped him get the loans, while denying credit to viable businesspeople who lacked the right political pedigree; they had for instance refused to issue loans for the same company bought by Ezz (Alexandria National Iron and Steel Company) a few months earlier to help it get out of its devastating financial crisis.[49]

Ezz was to become a close associate and friend of Gamal Mubarak, and would enter politics, becoming a leading figure in the ruling NDP. This conflict of interest reached massive proportions as he entered parliament, becoming head of the industrial committee and thereby effectively legislating for himself as a steel manufacturer. Such corruption also extended to Mubarak's sons.[50] Initial investigations into the business dealings of Gamal Mubarak found that before he joined the NDP, he had created a company in Cyprus with a murky ownership structure named Bullion, which was an umbrella company that invested in several private funds in Egypt. These funds in turn reaped a windfall of profits as they invested in the various privatizations that started occurring in the 1990s.[51]

Corruption within the inner circle of Mubarak

Early in the 1990s, Gamal Mubarak was an investment banker involved in a deal that carried with it a huge conflict of interest. Through his connections, he was able to purchase a tranche of Egypt's international debt and sell it back to the Egyptian government at a reduced price, pocketing a handsome commission for himself and the bank. Mubarak himself confirmed this and denied that there is anything wrong with it:

> This is not a rumor. Gamal as part of the team at the Bank he worked for did indeed negotiate with China to buy an old Egyptian debt worth US$180 million at a discounted price. The Bank had already contacts with the Chinese government and when my son asked me if he can join the team that will negotiate the deal, *not as the president's son but as a member of the bank's investment committee*, I answered why not? You would be doing Egypt a patriotic service.[52]

Instances like these would only increase in the 1990s, and the stench of corruption around the Mubarak family grew as time passed. In 1991, Alaa Mubarak married the daughter of then relatively unknown businessman Magdi Rasekh, who would grow to become one of the richest men in the Middle East. By 2010, Magdi Rasekh became the head of the National Company for Gas (providing natural gas to Egyptian homes across Egypt), the CEO of SODIC (one of the largest real estate companies in Egypt, which acquired land at cheap prices), and the head of RINGO phone company (a phone booth company operating across Egypt), among other ventures.[53] This corruption would continue to grow and is elaborated on in the next chapter.

The labor movement

The rising power of the Islamist movement

While a full analysis of the Islamists in Egypt is beyond the scope of this book, it is clear that, led by the Muslim Brotherhood, they were the largest social movement able to benefit from the early and partial opening of the political system. Building on their successes on university campuses in the 1970s and emboldened by their success in the syndicates, the Muslim Brotherhood moved to contest parliamentary elections and made their initial debut in the 1984 elections in a coalition with the Wafd Party. Eight Muslim Brotherhood members won these elections and participated in the 1984 session of parliament. However, the 1984 parliament was dissolved in 1987, having been deemed 'unconstitutional' by the government.

Using a social movement theory approach, Wickham highlights some of the reasons why the Islamists were successful on campuses, syndicates and ultimately in parliament:

> Graduates became Islamists not because of the intrinsic appeal of the *daw'a* but because the networks of its transmission were deeply embedded in urban, lower middle-class communities; its social carriers were familiar and respected; and its content resonated with the life experience and belief system of potential recruits.[54]

As previously argued, in the absence of organizational structures, social movements find it increasingly difficult to sustain their collective action.[55] This had meant that the co-optation of both the student and the worker organizations did tend to negatively impact their ability to mobilize. However, in the case of the Islamist students, they had the opportunity to join the Muslim Brotherhood upon graduation (if they were not members already), and continue with their activism. This is because the Brotherhood was a viable organization, with members, a hierarchy, funds and a capacity to organize and mobilize not just for protest, but also to pursue democratic avenues when available to them. Arguably, the Brotherhood was the most successful organization that was able to harness the student movement in the long term.

In addition, the socio-economic dimension of the spread of Islamism also cannot be ignored. The structural adjustment and stabilization program had also meant cuts in social spending and welfare. State spending on welfare, education, health and other social services had also become more focused on urban areas.

This had allowed the Islamist current to build support in rural and more socio-economically disadvantaged areas of Egypt, through providing some of these services themselves. The speedy response of the Muslim Brotherhood to the 1992 earthquake, compared to the government's sluggish response, is a clear example of the retreat of the state and the rising (especially rural) influence of the Islamist movement. Wickham writes that the Brotherhood's doctors and engineers "were the first on the scene providing tents, blankets, food, and clothes to the victims, which they dispensed from first aid clinics and emergency shelters plastered with banners and posters declaring 'Islam is the Solution'."[56] The Muslim Brotherhood was able to leverage the support gleaned from such services in the elections it stood for during the Mubarak era and thereafter.

Labor activism during the first two decades of the Mubarak era

Early in Mubarak's era, the labor movement continued to be strangled by the official union structure, a legacy of the Nasser era. The GFETU continued to exercise leadership as the officially sanctioned union, ostensibly to mediate between the workers and management. The reality was much different. Shafer argues:

> Egyptian trade unions act as agents of the state inside the workers movement.... Even the lowest level of the trade union bureaucracy—the local union committees—is quite isolated from the workers struggles. Since members of these union committees are nearly powerless *vis-à-vis* high levels of the trade union structure, they tend to distance themselves from militant workers' actions in order to avoid punishment from their superiors.[57]

Nonetheless, workers were still a thorn in the side of the regime, even in its early days. Between 1984 and 1989 there was a number of strikes and collective actions taken by workers, with between 50 and 75 actions reported in the press.[58] This continued in 1989, with strikes in Mahallah that saw some of the most violent clashes between workers and the regime since the 1950s.[59] Benin writes:

> despite the insurgent character of some of the collective actions of 1984–9, most of them, as in the 1970s and early 1980s, were framed by a moral economy consciousness. They aimed primarily to restore the standard of living and working conditions that public sector industrial workers enjoyed in the Nasser era or to establish parity between private and public sector workers.[60]

Even though the Union leadership was co-opted and levels of activism fluctuated, nonetheless, Owen observes "In Egypt, as elsewhere, groups of workers were often able to obtain sufficient independence from official control to organize strikes and sit-ins or to develop a local leadership which was independent of the official union structure."[61] The phenomenon of independent unions would manifest itself strongly in the last decade of Mubarak's rule and will be elaborated on in the next chapter. With the privatization program implemented in the 1990s, industrial actions increased in ferocity, especially in Mahallah, the heartland of Egyptian textile manufacturing. Workers in Mahallah had been known for decades for their militancy and activism. They had been amongst the first workers to suffer from the economic policies of the Sadat and Mubarak eras; they would be at the forefront of opposition to the regime's economic policies in the 1990s, and to the regime as a whole in the last decade of Mubarak's rule. From 2004, the labor movement would lead the call for change and between 2004 and 2008, some of the largest strikes in Egyptian history took place in Mahallah.[62]

However, it would take some time for labor activism to gain proper momentum. The 1990s layoffs were absorbed in part into the informal economic sector, which partially explains the lack of a huge eruption of worker activism. Moreover, the 1990s had seen the rise of militant Islamism; the state's open combat with the Islamists yielded a general de-liberalization of the political environment. This allowed the government and the private sector to disingenuously unpick certain pre-existing labor protection laws. Rutherford describes how such laws in place since the Nasser era were routinely circumvented during the privatization process:

> It was common for firms on the verge of being sold to evade the ban on mass layoffs by undertaking a dramatic downsizing of staff immediately prior to the sale. They usually took the form of "early retirements" of thousands of workers. Under these plans, each worker received a lump-sum payment, combined with a monthly payment for life that was much lower than the pension he would have received had his factory remained state-owned. In other cases, pro-labor laws were simply ignored by the owners of the newly privatized firms. The regime was slow to prosecute these firms, and often allowed the transgression to pass without legal action.[63]

Continued corporatization of the union movement

Continuing the traditions of the Nasser and Sadat eras, the GFETU and its leaders continued to be closely allied with the regime. Its membership continued to increase across the national public sector. Amendments to the union laws in 1976 gave GFETU officials the right to invest union funds in several projects, creating countless opportunities for kickbacks and nepotism.[64] Effectively, the entire leadership of the GFETU was co-opted by the regime, and it was left to traditional leftist forces such as the Tagammu' Party to fight for union reform. Posusney writes:

> Most of the leftists were released from prison in Mubarak's first year and the Tagammu' began to publish al-Ahali again in the latter half of 1982. The

> left was in a much weaker position in the unions than it had enjoyed in 1976, but used its newfound freedoms to champion four causes: the curtailment of government interference in union elections, legalization of strikes, loosening the hierarchal control on the locals, and the end of the practice of *jam'*.[65]

The practice of *jam'* (combining) refers to the right simultaneously to hold a union position and a post at the ASU and later in the NDP. This dubious right, first legislated for under Nasser, had a direct impact on the co-optation and corruption of some leaders of the GFETU. For example, Saad Mohammed Ahmed, the leader of the GFETU, had also held the position of Minister of Labor, which was a glaring conflict of interest.[66] The left alleged that senior labor officials "had become part of a new elite class, since the *Infitah* gave them new ways to invest and spend the multiple salaries they earned by combining leadership positions, as well as numerous opportunities for illicit use of union funds."[67]

Protests would occur through the first two decades of the Mubarak era, usually in response to localized issues. The government sought to silence protest leaders through a variety of tactics, whether bribery, lay offs or relocation to factories in remote areas of Egypt. The experience of Hamdy Hussein, a veteran socialist labor activist from Mahallah, is a case in point. He recalls:

> In the late 1980s, Mubarak abolished the educational stipend, which was included in the September pay check of every year. It was given to the workers to help finance school requirements for their children (uniform, shoes, bags, notebooks and text books). We heard the news at about 1 p.m., we went out to spread the news and organically people came out. We spent the night at the factory to organize ourselves for the following day. On the second day we came out and for the first time called for the downfall of Mubarak and held a mock coffin for him. This was September 1988 and anti regime protests were not very frequent and the protest was a major event.
>
> I was arrested again and when I came back I was moved to Aswan. Others were moved to El Wady El Gedid, El Hamrawein (in the Red Sea Governorate) ... many of us were relocated. I filed cases to return back to Ghazl El Mahalla, and I won, but it was all on paper. From then on, I didn't return to Ghazl El Mahalla. They kept moving me between several factories in different governorates. The idea was to pull me away from the rest of the workers but also station me in a place where I will have a good income, as a way of shutting me up. They did not account for the awareness that has swept the working class, and the growing desire to better the livelihoods of workers.... In Aswan, I formed committees of workers and for it I was arrested again.[68]

Despite the regime's attempts to control the labor movement, starting from 2005 and 2006 the movement gained momentum unprecedented in its history, letting it present a direct challenge to the regime. This occurred in tandem with growing student and youth activism that crystalized in the 1990s, but would really gain momentum in the final decade of Mubarak's rule.

The student and youth movements

The numbers of university graduates across Egypt continued to grow exponentially. Sadat had opened several universities across Egypt, and several were located in rural areas and near agricultural zones, which further increased the number of enrolled students and university graduates. As noted earlier, although increasing numbers of university graduates is laudable in itself, there was an utter lack of any plan to absorb them into the workforce. Thus certain university graduates sought employment in sectors not related to their education, while others continued to wait for years for the promised government job, a legacy of the Nasser-era guarantee. The government was increasingly unable to absorb the new graduates into the public sector, so they "simply extended the waiting period between graduation and appointment ... from three years for the class of 1979 to nine to ten years for the class of 1985."[69] Table 5.1 illustrates the exponential student growth from the 1960s through the 1990s.

There were no substantial challenges by youth and student groups to the Mubarak regime in the 1980s and 1990s, only some sporadic anti-Israel and pro-Palestine demonstrations on university campuses which sometimes appended anti-regime slogans to their rhetoric. Student activism had seen a lull, especially after the 1977 uprising and the regime response. Sadat had warned:

> I am saying that strikes, sit-ins, disruption of studies, and gangster actions on campuses are forbidden. The incendiary kindling of youth must not be manipulated. It should not happen at the universities.... The mission of

Table 5.1 Change in university admissions, enrollments and graduates (1977/1978 to 1989/1990)

Year	*# of admissions*	*# of enrolled*	*# of graduates*
1977/1978	68,127	433,199	64,966
1978/1979	71,422	443,696	71,071
1979/1980	79,050	458,809	74,143
1980/1981	89,026	563,150	81,863
1981/1982	91,048	611,452	86,841
1982/1983	93,409	659,635	93,660
1983/1984	93,486	681,704	106,622
1984/1985	86,440	682,348	115,744
1985/1986	84,280	661,347	119,216
1986/1987	82,897	629,723	115,106
1987/1988	82,299	604,846	112,615
1988/1989	75,375	587,033	103,641
1989/1990	66,990	467,611	89,548
1990/1991	65,579	–	–

Source: Carrie Rosefsky Wickham, *Mobilizing Islam: Religion, Activism and Political Change in Egypt* (New York: Columbia University Press, 2002), 50.

> educational institutions is education. Political meetings should never be held at universities. Those who wish to engage in politics should find a political party outside.[70]

Late in the Sadat era and especially after 1977, the regime clamped down on student activism. The university guards and police were returned to campuses; wall magazines were banned. Many of the student clubs that discussed politics were also banned. All candidates who stood for any university union positions had to be first cleared by the security services to ensure they were pro-regime. Ironically, it was Sadat who had initially encouraged Islamist student activism. After his assassination, the security services clamped down on university campuses with a focus on eradicating Islamist activism.

Despite the clampdown, there was one final wave of student activism that coincided with the 1984 election and the slight opening of the political system initiated by Mubarak in the early part of his presidency. Protests erupted at the University of Mansoura after a university guard assaulted an engineering student in December 1983.[71] Over the next several months, students at universities in Cairo, Alexandria and Zagazig would join the protests and confront university authorities on issues that were not anti-regime, but concerned their rights on campus, including the presence of security on campus and free student elections. Abdalla writes that the government responded

> by agreeing to study proposals for a new constitution for the Student Union and for reform of the general student regulations. But it remained adamant about the University Guard, refusing to withdraw the force from university campuses, on the unconvincing pretext that the Guard's task was solely to protect university installations against theft and arson.[72]

Establishment of cross-ideological networks

Social movement theory literature points to the concept of informal networks as one of the key factors that form and sustain social movements. Della Porta and Diani argue that social movements are "informal networks, based on shared beliefs and solidarity, which mobilize about conflictual issues through the use of various forms of protests."[73] The process of network formation in the student movement can be clearly identified from the 1990s onwards, as students from across ideological divides came into contact on university campuses and worked together on certain campaigns. The relationships built in the 1990s and early 2000s would help form these networks of activism, which were important in the 2011 mobilization, as the Conclusion will highlight.

The regime continued to exert its control over campuses across Egypt. However, so did the legacy of Sadat's pro-Islamist policies. Islamist students were still the dominant force on campus. Mohammed el Qasas, a leading Muslim Brotherhood student activist who broke with the Muslim Brotherhood in 2011, described his experience:

> I joined Dar El Oloum of Cairo University in the 1990s. It was a very active university and the Islamists were dominating the scene, particularly the Muslim Brotherhood students. I was introduced to them from the start. They were first called "*Jama'a Islamiya*" then changed it to "Islamist Bloc." The titles changed but at the end the group represented the ideals of the Brotherhood. Their ideals were the closest to me at the time. In the 1990s, there was several other Islamic groups at the time, especially that Dar El Ouloum focused in Arabic and Islamic studies. There were *Jama'a Islamiya* and pro-militant groups and Salafis. To me the Brotherhood represented the moderate Islamic thought, so I joined their student union. I was in the athletic committee but also partook in all other activities that the union organized. That was my entry point during college years.[74]

Student activists would rally around causes involving the wider Muslim world. Qasas continued:

> We had a lot of resources at the time and restrictions were limited. Restrictions grew in 1995–1996 after many MB leaders were arrested and the government's stance towards Islamists started to shift. My political activism stemmed from my student activism. I was most involved in the Palestinian cause as well as causes that touched the Muslim world such as Kosovo and Bosnia/Herzegovina.[75]

The focus of activism was also on domestic issues pertaining to students such as student fees, free student elections and moving security off campus, as well as international issues. The first and second Palestinian Intifada was a cause that could rally both Islamist and leftist students, even though the former saw it within a religious and the latter within a nationalist prism. Although weakened during the Sadat era, the leftist current on university campuses was able to slowly reorganize and rebuild. The regime used the growing terror attacks and the rise of militant Islamism across the country as a pretext to fight the Islamists on campus. Islamist students reached across the ideological divide to find allies on campus, and the networks noted above began to emerge and consolidate. Qasas and many other Islamist students were arrested after protests in 1995. He argued:

> This was a turning point with respect to the government method of dealing with Islamists. At the time Mofid Shehab was appointed Dean and he paid close attention to the Islamists student movement, and at that point we realized that we couldn't mobilize on our own; we realized that we need another group of students to protest alongside against common issues, even if it was a much smaller group, and especially with regards to issues pertaining to student matters or the fight for freedoms and the current regime. This was the dramatic shift. The Islamist bloc knew it was the strongest student body, but upon being targeted realized it needs to ally with other groups. This

> ideological shift did not gather consensus from across the Brotherhood leadership. Conflict arose because both directions, the one taken by the Islamist movement and that of the student movement, were not always aligned.[76]

Qasas's point is apt, as it highlights the tension between the leaders of the Muslim Brotherhood and their university student members, showing that the students did not always follow the leadership and at times acted as part of a student movement. Such tension would boil to the surface in the early days of the 2011 uprising, causing a rupture between the Brotherhood's leadership and some of its university and youth cadres. Activism around the Palestinian issue in the 1990s allowed student activists from all ideological currents on campus to work together and build these informal networks, an experience that would later facilitate cooperation between activists from different currents. Qasas described this experience:

> The causes of the Muslim world were what consumed our time. We started to pay attention to local issues in 1995, when MB leaders were referred to military trials. In 1996–7 we started opening up to other movements. We started to get introduced to leftists, Nasserists and Wafidists within the university. I consider this a turning point because what we started at the time continued after we graduated and up until the revolution, which later led to the creation of the coalition. Many of the members of the coalition worked with us when we were in university. The coalition started with Khaled Abdel Hamid, who is a leftist, and myself. We were then joined by Islam Lotfy and Ziad El Eleimy. And then we started spreading it to Helwan University and we were joined by Khaled El Sayed and Mohammed Abbas.[77]

Islam Lotfy, Ziad El Eleimy, Khaled El Sayed and Mohammed Abbas would all be involved directly in the 2011 uprising as key participants, and their role will be discussed further in the next section. Osama Ahmad from the Faculty of Political Science at Cairo University and a socialist student leader and activist, also elaborated on this cooperation around the Palestinian cause:

> During the Palestinian uprising, students at Cairo University, and especially student from the leftist and Islamist blocs organized marches in solidarity. At that time I was still in school. My school was situated next to Cairo University. We organized marches and our goal was to reach the Israeli embassy. That was my first encounter with demonstrations. I remember very well the people I saw that day. Our protest was attacked. We were chased by the CSF (Central Security Forces). We were trapped in a small street the CSF running behind us. We eventually climbed a wall and ended up on campus and were trapped for the next 10 hours. I remember the huge numbers sitting in circles, as well as another less peaceful crowd torching KFC, precieved by some as a symbol of US economic power. There were other groups gathered, some singing, some reciting poetry, some painting.[78]

Another Muslim Brotherhood student leader, Amr Abdel Alim from the Law Faculty at Cairo University, also pointed to the cross-movement campus collaboration:

> There was a common platform in the Faculty of Law that brought us all student activists together. The causes that brought us together were the Palestinian issue and opposition to the State Security. When it came to specific political demands, we each had our own. But on one level we were all frowned upon by the authorities: the MB students, the Leftist students. The only group that was not frowned upon were the pro-government NDP students. This created a commonplace between us as well. The coordination differed from faculty to faculty. For example, Dar el Oloum and the faculty of Medicine barely included any Leftist students; they were more concentrated in the faculties of Commerce and Political Science.[79]

The relationship between the Islamist and the leftist student activists had previously been confrontational, largely as a legacy of the 1970s, when the Sadat regime had actively encouraged Islamist activism to confront the leftist students. What began to happen in the mid-1990s and early 2000s was that activists from both camps began to come together for common causes. First, students united in opposition to university officials over the issue of security officials on campus, as well as issues directly related to their studies, such as university fees, book costs and dormitory fees. Second, the students were united in many of their solidarity actions on Palestine, and later in their overwhelming opposition to the 2003 Iraq War. This collaboration between student activists would be the basis of many networks that came to have a strong impact on the 2011 uprising. After the Iraq War in 2003 and the protests that followed, a proliferation of anti-regime movements started taking root, both on university campuses and at an elite level. These started with the *Kefaya* movement, many of whose founders were themselves student activists in the 1970s. The period from 2001 and the *Kefaya* movement will be explored in the next chapter, for now the key point is to show the greater cohesion.

Opportunities and threats

This section focuses on threats faced by the labor and student movements, for arguably there were not many political process opportunities in the first two decades of the Mubarak era for the student and labor movements. As discussed previously, the other part of the political process model focuses on specific threats in a movement's environment that encourage the movement to respond. These may include state-attributed economic problems, erosion of rights and state repression.[80]

State-attributed economic problems: the perfect storm of population growth, urbanization, unemployment and poverty

Unknown to the government, several factors converging in the 1990s contributed to Mubarak's removal in 2011. First, population growth continued at unprecedented rates. The population of Egypt in 1985 was 50.3 million, by 1995 it grew to 61 million, and by 2005 to 71 million, meaning that the population increased by ten million people every decade.[81] If the current population growth rates continue as forecasted, by 2050 the population would become 121.7 million, effectively overtaking countries such as Russia and Japan.[82] Table 5.2 illustrates the population growth from 1990 to 2050. Second, urbanization continues to play a key role in regime instability. Even though the overall population distribution would stabilize at approximately at 43 percent in urban areas, the population growth in major urban centers like Cairo and Alexandria continued to increase.

The government attempted several policies to create a more balanced population allocation. Despite Mubarak's announcement of several mega-projects (such as Toshka) in the 1990s that were designed to shift population centers out of the capital cities and ease the rates of urban growth, this did not actually occur as they only attracted temporary workers as highlighted by Dennis.[83] This illustrates the seasonal nature of migratory patterns of workers who did indeed take up some work opportunities in the reclaimed land and mega-projects, but only temporarily—rather than move their families there, they then moved back to the Nile Delta and growing urban centers like Cairo and Alexandria.

The growth in urban centers also created a crisis of housing. Millions of Egyptians lived in informal housing slums (*'ashwa'iyyat*) that received minimal or no government facilities such as water, sewage, electricity, let alone schools or hospitals. Moreover, a majority of the housing developments were targeting mid- to high-level consumers, with a huge boom in the land developed for ultra-rich gated communities that included golf courses, malls and amusement parks. Mitchell writes, "structural adjustment was supposed to generate an export boom, not a building boom."[84]

Third, despite the liberalization of the economy, unemployment continued to increase, especially as thousands of workers were laid off as a result of the privatization program. Despite all stated macroeconomic successes, the poorest segments of society did not benefit from the liberalization program; in fact, they became worse off. According to the World Bank, the inequality gap continued to widen through the mid-1990s. In 1991, the poorest 10 percent of the population was responsible for 3.9 percent of the national income, while the richest 20 percent owned 26.7 percent. By 2001, the poorest had 3.7 percent of the income, and the richest received 29.5 percent.[85] Despite these alarming income disparity statistics, the IMF continued to consider the program a success. Nagarajan writes:

> The IMF itself had not considered the negative consequences of its SAP (Structural Adjustment Program). Only macroeconomic variables were targeted and based on progress achieved in those variables the program was

Table 5.2 Urban and rural population in Egypt (1980–2050)

Year	*Urban (000s)*	*Rural (000s)*	*Total (000s)*	*Percentage urban (%)*	*Percentage rural (%)*	*Year*	*Annual rate of change of percentage urban (%)*	*Annual rate of change of percentage rural (%)*
1980	19,715	25,237	44,952	43.9	56.1	1980–1985	0.04	–0.03
1985	22,259	28,401	50,660	43.9	56.1	1985–1990	–0.21	0.16
1990	24,714	32,129	56,843	43.5	56.5	1990–1995	–0.31	0.23
1995	26,572	35,492	62,064	42.8	57.2	1995–2000	–0.01	0.01
2000	28,951	38,697	67,648	42.8	57.2	2000–2005	0.11	–0.08
2005	31,927	42,276	74,203	43.0	57.0	2005–2010	0.16	–0.12
2010	35,186	45,935	81,121	43.4	56.6	2010–2015*	0.37	–0.2
2015*	38,969	49,210	88,179	44.2	55.8	2015–2020*	0.59	–0.48
2020*	43,145	51,665	94,810	45.5	54.5	2020–2025*	0.78	–0.68
2025*	47,751	53,158	100,909	47.3	52.7	2025–2030*	0.96	–0.90
2030*	52,864	53,630	106,498	49.6	50.4	2030–2035*	1.03	–1.07
2035*	58,328	53,294	111,622	52.3	47.7	2035–2040*	0.97	–1.12
2040*	63,764	52,468	116,232	54.9	45.1	2040–2045*	0.92	–1.18
2045*	69,044	51,164	120,208	57.4	42.6	2045–2050*	0.86	–1.23
2050*	74,040	49,412	123,452	60.0	40.0			

Source: United Nations Economic and Social Commission for Western Asia, "Egypt Demographic Profile 2012," www.escwa.un.org/popin/members/egypt.pdf (accessed October 1, 2014).

Note
* Projections.

> declared a resounding success. As Pfeifer notes, the IMF evaluation by Handy and the Staff Team (1998) rarely touched the subjects of employment, unemployment and human development. Even when these topics were mentioned, it was taken for granted that privatization and liberalization would lead to higher private investment which would take care of unemployment and poverty reduction.[86]

Later World Bank figures confirmed that both urban[87] and rural[88] poverty rates increased between 2000 and 2008, with the latter spiking at a staggering 30 percent (even given the Nazif government's reform attempts). Dunne and Revikin argued that "ordinary Egyptian citizens were facing high unemployment and rising prices on basic commodities, and were becoming increasingly aware of a painful disparity in the distribution of the material benefits of economic reform."[89] All these factors and more had begun to lead to worker mobilizations, coupled with a re-invigorated civil society and social movements in response to threats such as the erosion of rights and state repression.

Threat: erosion of rights and the neoliberalizing of labor laws

Within the context of economic reform, the regime sought to update labor laws to give investors and factory owners more flexibility with their workers, and to make Egypt a more attractive destination for FDI. Despite the weakness and co-optation of the union movement, it had earlier been able to fend off several attempts to sell public companies and adversely affect workers' employment, rights and entitlements. This would change in the 1990s, when Egypt's trade unions

> finally agreed to support the privatization legislation designed by the regime in 1991 (Law 203) to restructure the private sector, only with the proviso that all firms sold under the auspices of this law continue to abide by existing labor legislation, and that subsequent sales agreements contain clauses guaranteeing that work forces would not be reduced.[90]

While at face value the new laws seemed beneficial to workers, granting them (for example) the official right to strike after this had been banned for decades, it contained aspects that directly threatened workers' employment security. Posusney writes that "although all firms must still obtain government approval for mass layoffs, the new law makes such permission more likely, stating that employers have the right to adjust the workforce according to economic conditions."[91]

The new law, which applied to workers in both the public and private sectors, also allowed for casual labor to work in factories under temporary contracts. These could be renewed indefinitely but did not ensure the protections enjoyed by their permanent counterparts. This casualization of the workforce was designed to allow employers the flexibility to hire and fire. Until then, private sector employers had to bypass labor protection laws through various techniques, including firing workers on temporary contracts right before they were due to be renewed, forcing workers to sign blank contracts, and forcing workers to sign undated resignation letters upon hiring. The new law basically legalized such practices and was clearly designed to eliminate worker opposition to privatization.[92] It represented a legislated erosion of rights previously enjoyed by the workers, and as previously discussed such erosion does impact mobilization as it increases the economic grievances and provides impetus for activism.[93]

Threat: state repression

As previously highlighted, state repression can act as a powerful incentive for social movements to respond and challenge the regime. Regime challengers would wait for signs of weakness from the state to challenge its authority. While this did not occur at a massive scale in the first two decades of the Mubarak regime, the repressive measures of the 1990s would arguably have an impact on the mobilization in 2011. Desai *et al.* argue that "repression may solidify the regime's hold on power by neutralizing regime challengers, or it may make non-democratic regimes more vulnerable by decreasing the citizen's utility under the dictatorial *status quo*."[94]

Since the early 1990s, there had been a strong crackdown on any opposition to the regime as militant Islamists confronted the state in a mini-insurgency that caused severe loss of life for Egyptians as well as foreign tourists. Much of this insurgency was carried out in Upper Egypt, which was considered a hotbed of militant Islamists. These attacks against tourists and locals alike can be understood through the context of extreme poverty, rampant unemployment and shortage of state services in Upper Egypt, which allowed militant Islamists such as the *Jamāʿa Islāmiyya* to gain a foothold there. Fandy argues that

> the focus on poverty and injustice in the south seems to be the dominant theme in *Al Jemaa's* pronouncements. Unlike the Brotherhood, *Al Jemaa's* main writings do not dwell on larger Middle Eastern questions such as Pan-Arabism, the Palestinian question, or Israel and the West.[95]

The militant insurgency allowed the state to further justify its crackdown on opposition and the continued extension of the emergency laws. The combination of state-attributed economic problems, erosion of rights and increased state repression arguably furthered discontent with the regime. It would take international factors, such as the Palestinian Intifada of 2000 and the 2003 Iraq War, as well as advances in communication technologies to further bring these networks together in the years leading up to the 2011 uprising.

Notes

1 Interview with President Hosni Mubarak, *al-Mosawar Magazine*, October 30, 1981.
2 Dina Shehata, "The Fall of the Pharaoh," *Foreign Affairs*, May/June 2011, 26.

3 Ṣalāḥ Muntaṣir, *al-Su'ūd wal-suqūt: min al-manāsa ilā l-maḥkama* (The Climb and the Fall: From the Stand to the Court) (Cairo: The Egyptian Association for Printing, 2012), 78.
4 Hiekal, *Kharīf al-Ghadab*.
5 The Tunisians had already invested millions in building a new complex for the Arab League in Tunis and were initially furious with the decision, which represented a loss of status as well as a financial loss. See "Arab League Headquarters to Return to Cairo," *New York Times*, March 12, 1990, www.nytimes.com/1990/03/12/world/arab-league-headquarters-to-return-to-cairo.html (accessed October 1, 2014).
6 Alan Richards, "The Political Economy of Dilatory Reform: Egypt in the 1980s," *World Development* 19, no. 12 (1991): 1721.
7 Samer Soliman, *The Autumn of Dictatorship: Fiscal Crisis and Political Change in Egypt under Mubarak* (Stanford: Stanford University Press, 2011), 36.
8 Ibid.
9 Richards, "Political Economy of Dilatory Reform," 1722.
10 Bruce Rutherford, *Egypt After Mubarak: Liberalism, Islam and Democracy in the Arab World* (Princeton: Princeton University Press, 2008).
11 Francis Fukuyama, *The End of History and the Last Man* (New York: Free Press, 1992).
12 Emma C. Murphy, "The State and the Private Sector in North Africa: Seeking Specificity," *Mediterranean Politics* 6, no. 2 (2001): 2.
13 Milton Friedman had advised both Reagan and Thatcher. When he passed away in 2006, Thatcher eulogized him saying:

> Milton Friedman revived the economics of liberty when it had been all but forgotten. He was an intellectual freedom fighter. Never was there a less dismal practitioner of a dismal science. I shall greatly miss my old friend's lucid wisdom and mordant humour.
> (See Rupert Cornwell, "Milton Friedman, free-market economist who inspired Reagan and Thatcher, dies aged 94," *Independent*, November 17, 2006, www.independent.co.uk/news/world/americas/milton-friedman-freemarket-economist-who-inspired-reagan-and-thatcher-dies-aged-94-424665.html (accessed October 1, 2014))

14 See Lawrence H. Summers and Lant H. Pritchett. "The Structural-Adjustment Debate," *The American Economic Review* 83, no. 2 (May 1993): 383–389.
15 Dina Shehata, "The Fall of the Pharaoh," *Foreign Affairs*, May/June 2011.
16 Phillip Marfleet, "State and Society," in Rabab El-Mahdi and Philip Marfleet (eds.), *Egypt: The Moment of Change* (London: Zed Books, 2009), 21.
17 Raymond A. Hinnebusch, "Class, State and the Reversal of Egypt's Agrarian Reform," *MERIP*, September–October (1993): 21.
18 Ibid.
19 Ibid.
20 Aziza Sami, "Eid Abdel-Rahman," *Al-Ahram Weekly*, July 23–29, 1999.
21 Cited in Rabab El-Mahdy and Philip Marfleet (eds.), *Egypt: The Moment of Change* (London: Zed Books, 2009), 4.
22 The ECES was formed by a group of leading businessmen and government officials as a privately funded think tank to provide decision-makers with economic analysis. Its publications would play a policy role by advocating for more private sector growth and arguably promote the neoliberal economic agenda of its board. Rutherford highlights this agenda:

> In some respects, the reforms that the ECES advocates are classically liberal. It calls for a more efficient, accountable, and constrained state. It supports a strengthening of the rule of law, and it advocates an expansion of some rights (particularly property rights). Yet, it goes a step beyond this classical view by calling for a

> strong state that intervenes in the economy to achieve specific goals, such as subsidizing key economic activities and sectors, improving education, strengthening social services, and regulating the markets. This is a muscular liberalism that requires a powerful and invasive state. But, the invasiveness is targeted and constrained.
>
> (See Rutherford, *Egypt After Mubarak*, 217–218)

23 The Egyptian Centre for Economic Studies, "Egypt's Economic Reform and Structural Adjustment Program (ERSAP)," Working Paper 19 (October 1997), www.eces.org.eg/Uploaded_Files/%7BD83916F9–6CEF-4E7C-8F35–4A8CDC7AD78A%7D_ECESWP19e.pdf (accessed October 1, 2014).
24 Ibid.
25 Personal interview, Cairo, April 2, 2013.
26 Ibid.
27 Ayubi, *Overstating the Arab State*, 347.
28 Ibid.
29 See Bernard Black, Reinier Kraakman and Anna Tarassova, "Russian Privatization and Corporate Governance: What Went Wrong?" *Stanford Law Review* 52, no. 6 (July 2000): 1731–1808; for a less academically rigorous but more engaging account, see Naomi Klein, *The Shock Doctrine: The Rise of Disaster Capitalism* (London: Macmillan, 2007), 275–309.
30 According to the World Bank, public offerings are

> used for large, profitable, relatively well-known state enterprises. In addition to transferring ownership, share offers often raise additional capital for an enterprise through the issue of new shares. Share offers can also meet a government's objective of broadening share ownership by allocating a portion of shares to small investors. Shares can be offered on the domestic market as well as in international markets using American depository receipts (ADRs) or global depository receipts (GDRs).
>
> (Dick Welch and Olivier Frémond, "The Case-by-Case Approach to Privatization: Techniques and Examples," *The World Bank* (Washington, DC: The International Bank for Reconstruction and Development, 1998), http://elibrary.worldbank.org/doi/pdf/10.1596/0–8213–4196–0 (accessed October 1, 2014), 15)

31 According to the World Bank:

> Auctions are more common and more transparent than negotiated sales. First, the financial advisers or sales agents, working with state enterprise managers and government officials, prepare an information memorandum containing general information for potential investors. The memorandum is sent to potentially interested parties. In most cases the financial advisers or sales agents will have compiled a list of potential investors and will discuss it with the government prior to use. Then, nonbinding expressions of interest are received from interested buyers. Based on these expressions of interest and a review of the financial capacity of potential bidders, a short list of potential buyers is selected. These bidders then move to the second stage of the process. During the second stage the government signs confidentiality agreements with the short–listed bidders and gives them much more detailed, commercially confidential information on the state enterprise, access to management, and a draft sales agreement. Bidders that wish to proceed then submit a binding offer (bid) and a deposit. Finally, the government and its advisers choose the best offer, and the sale closes with payment for the shares (or in special cases, assets) of the state enterprise.
>
> (Ibid., 21)

32 Negotiated sales are

> a variant of the open bidding process. Once the government has chosen a buyer, it negotiates an agreement that is attractive to the buyer and protects the government's interests. Negotiated sales are used when there is only one bidder or a bidder has a marked advantage over other bidders in the government's eyes. It is difficult to get the highest price in such sales, however, and they are less transparent than open bidding.
>
> (Ibid., 23)

33 Karen Pfeifer, "Economic Reform and Privatization in Egypt," in Jeannie Sowers and Chris Toensing (eds.), *The Journey to Tahrir: Revolution, Protest, and Social Change in Egypt* (New York: Verso, 2012), 209.
34 Marsha Pripstein Posusney, "Egyptian Privatization: New Challenges for the Left," *Middle East Report* 210, Reform or Reaction? Dilemmas of Economic Development in the Middle East (Spring 1999): 39.
35 Personal interview, Cairo, February 26, 2013.
36 Arvind Subramanian, "Egypt: Poised for Sustained Growth?" *IMF Growth and Development* (December 1997).
37 Toby Dodge, "The Middle East After the Arab Spring," *London School of Economics (LSE) Ideas Report* (2012).
38 Dr. Heba Handoussa, World Bank Economist and lead author of the Egypt Human Development Report, personal interview, Cairo, April 1, 2013.
39 Karima Korayem, "Egypt's Economic Reform and Structural Adjustment (ERSAP)," Working Paper No. 19, *The Egyptian Center for Economic Studies (ECES)* (October 1997), 21–22.
40 Howard Handy, *Egypt: Beyond Stabilization, Toward a Dynamic Market Economy*, Occasional Paper No. 163 (Washington, DC: International Monetary Fund, 1998), 1.
41 Arvind Subramanian, "The Egyptian Stabilization Experience: An Analytical Retrospective," IMF Working Paper 97/105 (Washington, DC: International Monetary Fund, 1997), 44.
42 Nathan Associates, "Changing International Trade Rules for Textiles and Apparel," Report Submitted to Ministry of Foreign Trade, Egypt and USAID (January 2004).
43 Ironically, Mubarak, who had stated early in his rule that he would "wear nothing except what I am wearing today," toward the end of his rule would only wear bespoke British tailored suits, like one he wore in 2009 costing approximately 10,000 GBP and lined with his name microstitched as the suit stripes. See "Hosni Mubarak's Pinstripes Are Actually His Name Repeated Over And Over," *Business Insider*, March 4, 2011, www.businessinsider.com.au/hosni-mubarak-pinstripes-2011–3 (accessed October 1, 2014).
44 Interview with President Hosni Mubarak, *al-Mosawar Magazine*, October 30, 1981.
45 Timothy Mitchell, "Dreamland: The Neoliberalism of Your Desires," *MERIP* 210, Vol. 29 (Spring 1999), www.merip.org/mer/mer210/dreamland-neoliberalism-your-desires?ip_login_no_cache=90205cf5e7c2ad8f1dab4bddef9ab22a (accessed October 1, 2014).
46 Ibid.
47 Andrew England, "Wealth Disparities Cloud Progress," *Financial Times*, December 10, 2007.
48 Salma El-Wardani, "Money, Power and Law-Twisting: The Makings of the Real Ezz Empire," *Ahram Online*, May 7, 2011, http://english.ahram.org.eg/News/11480.aspx (accessed October 1, 2014).
49 Ibid.
50 After the 2011 uprising, Mubarak and his two sons Alaa and Gamal would stand trial for a variety of corruption charges. Due to the changing political environment post-2011, the trials to date have not convicted any of them of high-level corruption or for

the killing of protestors. The election of the Muslim Brotherhood presidential candidate Muhammad Morsi and his ouster by a popularly backed army coup in 2013 and the subsequent election of Abdel Fattah al-Sisi, naturally all impacted on the Mubarak trial. In a travesty of justice in Egypt, Ahmad Ezz was released on bail from jail in August 2014, and Gamal and Alaa Mubarak were released in January 2015. See "Mubarak-Era Egyptian Steel Tycoon Ahmed Ezz Released on Bail," *Al Ahram Online*, August 7, 2014, http://english.ahram.org.eg/NewsContent/3/12/107956/Business/Economy/Mubarakera-Egyptian-steel-tycoon-Ahmed-Ezz-release.aspx (accessed October 1, 2014) and David Kirkpatrick, "Mubarak Sons Released From Egyptian Jail," *New York Times*, January 26, 2015.

51 For further details, see Salma Hussein and Salma El Wardani, "All the King's Men: Who Runs Mubarak's Money?" *Ahram Online*, May 2011, http://english.ahram.org.eg/NewsContent/3/12/8793/Business/Economy/All-the-king%E2%80%99s-men-Who-runs-Mubaraks-money-.aspx (accessed October 1, 2014).

52 Muntaṣir, *al-Suʿūd wal-suqūt*, 151.

53 Ibid., 153–154.

54 Carrie Rosefsky Wickham, *Mobilizing Islam: Religion, Activism and Political Change in Egypt* (New York: Columbia University Press, 2002), 163.

55 For an elaboration on that argument, see Anthony Oberschall, *Social Conflict and Social Movements* (Englewood Cliffs: Prentice Hall, 1973).

56 Carrie Rosefsky Wickham, *The Muslim Brotherhood: Evolution of an Islamist Movement* (Princeton: Princeton University Press, 2013), 77.

57 Cited in El-Mahdi and Marfleet, *Egypt*, 29.

58 Joel Beinin, "Neo-Liberal Structural Adjustment, Political Demobilization and Neo-Authoritarianism in Egypt," in Laura Guazzone and Daniela Pioppi (eds.), *The Arab State and Neoliberal Globalisation: The Restructuring of State Power in the Middle East* (Reading: Ithaca Press, 2009), 23.

59 Omar el Shafie, "Workers, Trade Unions and the State in Egypt: 1984–1989," *Cairo Papers in Social Science* 18, no. 2 (Summer 1995): 1–43.

60 Beinin, "Neo-Liberal Structural Adjustment," 24.

61 Roger Owen, *State, Power and Politics in the Making of the Modern Middle East* (New York: Routledge, 2000), 39.

62 Joel Beinin, "The Militancy of Mahalla al Kubra," *MERIP*, September 27, www.merip.org/mero/mero092907?ip_login_no_cache=732608cc170a5ae9158e6ef3ee1df2e8 (accessed October 1, 2014).

63 Rutherford, *Egypt After Mubarak*, 226–227.

64 Marsha Pripstein Posunsney, *Labor and the State in Egypt* (New York: Columbia University Press, 1997), 114.

65 Ibid., 115.

66 Ibid., 89.

67 Ibid., 118.

68 Personal interview, Mahallah, March 30, 2013.

69 Wickham, *Mobilizing Islam*, 42.

70 Abdalla, *Student Movement and National Politics*, 228.

71 Ibid., 229–230.

72 Ibid., 231.

73 Donatella Della Porta and Mario Diani, *Social Movements: An Introduction*, (Oxford: Blackwell Publishing, 1999), 16.

74 Personal interview, Cairo, March 28, 2013.

75 Ibid.

76 Ibid.

77 Ibid.

78 Personal interview, Cairo, January 5, 2013.

79 Personal interview, Giza, April 18, 2013. At the time of the interview, Abdel Alim

was an administrator with the Muslim Brotherhood's Freedom and Justice Party. After the overthrow of Morsi, he was jailed and remains incarcerated at the time of writing (February 2015).

80 Paul Almeida, "Opportunity Organizations and Threat-Induced Contention: Protest Waves in Authoritarian Settings," *American Journal of Sociology* 109, no. 2 (September 2003): 345–400.

81 United Nations Economic and Social Commission for Western Asia, "Egypt Demographic Profile 2012," www.escwa.un.org/popin/members/egypt.pdf (accessed October 1, 2014).

82 Ibid.

83 Eric Denis, "Demographic Surprises Foreshadow Change in Neoliberal Egypt," *MERIP* 38 (Spring 2008), www.merip.org/mer/mer246/demographic-surprises-foreshadow-change-neoliberal-egypt (accessed October 1, 2014).

84 Mitchell, "Dreamland."

85 "Top Reformers in 2006/2007," Doing Business, *International Finance Corporation* (WB), www.doingbusiness.org/features/refomr2007.aspx.

86 K.V. Nagarajan, "Egypt's Political Economy and the Downfall of the Mubarak Regime," *International Journal of Humanities and Social Science* 3, no. 10 (Special Issue, May 2013): 31.

87 World Bank Data, "Egypt Poverty Headcount Ratio at Urban Poverty Line," http://data.worldbank.org/indicator/SI.POV.URHC/countries/EG?display=graph (accessed October 1, 2014).

88 Ibid.

89 Michele Dunne and Mara Revkin, "Egypt: How a Lack of Political Reform Undermined Economic Reform," Commentary, Carnegie Endowment for Peace, http://carnegieendowment.org/2011/02/23/egypt-how-lack-of-political-reform-undermined-economic-reform/crn (accessed October 1, 2014).

90 Mitchell, "Dreamland."

91 Marsha Pripstein Posusney, "Egypt's New Labor Law Removes Worker Provisions," *Middle East Report* 194/195, Odds Against Peace (May–August 1995), 63.

92 Ibid.

93 See Almeida, "Opportunity Organizations and Threat-Induced Contention," 353.

94 Raj Desai, Anders Olofsgard and Tarik Yousef, "The Logic of Authoritarian Bargains," *Economics and Politics* 21, no. 1 (2009): 116.

95 Mamoun Fandy, "Egypt's Islamic Group: Regional Revenge?" *Middle East Journal* 48, no. 4 (Autumn 1994): 610.

6 The Mubarak era (2001–2011)

> Egypt made significant progress in wide-ranging structural reforms that accelerated after 2004. This spurred rapid output growth—averaging 7 percent a year during FY2005/06 FY2007/08—underpinned by foreign investment-driven productivity gains and the favorable external environment. Reforms also reduced fiscal, monetary and external vulnerabilities, leaving some room to maneuver on macroeconomic policies in the event of negative shocks.
>
> IMF Executive Board Report on Egypt, April 2010[1]

> Those who continue to preach the trickle-down theory are likely to be the ones who do not really care whether anything trickles down at all.
>
> Egyptian economist Galal Amin[2]

> *al-Sha'b yurīd isqāt al-niẓām!* (The People Demand the Downfall of the Regime!)
>
> Protest chant during 2011 Egyptian uprising

Introduction

The last decade of Mubarak's rule was tumultuous, both domestically and internationally. Despite his advancing age, Mubarak was re-elected for the fourth time in a 1999 referendum and stood for elections for a record fifth time in 2005, even allowing for competition rather than the usual plebiscite. This decade would also see the political rise of Gamal Mubarak, the president's son, as well as a new cabinet led by Ahmad Nazif. While the government would achieve solid macroeconomic gains and be praised by the World Bank and the IMF, discontent would continue to simmer in those segments of society where the GDP growth was not improving people's livelihoods. Opposition to the regime would gain unprecedented momentum in the lead-up to the 2011 uprising. Internationally, the 9/11 attacks, the second Palestinian Intifada, and the 2003 Iraq War all had ramifications for domestic Egyptian politics. This chapter will explore the political economy of the last decade of the Mubarak regime and its impact on the labor and student movements, and how these movements responded in 2011.

The political economy of the late Mubarak era

The Ebied government at the turn of the new millennium

There was some optimism when Mubarak won his unprecedented fourth term in a referendum in September 1999, promising during the 'campaign' that the new millennium would bring untold prosperity and new riches to Egypt. However, pessimism soon returned, when Mubarak:

> named the ageing technocrat Atef Ebeid as the new prime minister and the cabinet reshuffle kept 19 of the old guard firmly entrenched, including all the main ministerial portfolios. The 13 new appointments have been met with considerable disappointment by commentators who have lamented another opportunity for meaningful reform. Ebied, like El-Ganzoury before him, is reported by the government press and some international agency commentators as the man to lead Egypt into the next millennium *because he is well known by the IMF*.... Ebied is confronted by economic reforms that have not delivered, even by their own measure, and created unprecedented levels of unemployment and poverty.[3]

The economic reforms initiated by the government during the 1990s were able to provide some macroeconomic stabilization, even though they had not translated strongly enough into improvements in the livelihoods of the poorer segments of the population. Under Ebied's leadership, Egypt would see increased levels of poverty. The year 2001–2002 was a particularly difficult year for the Egyptian economy, with lower revenues from oil and the Suez Canal, coupled with a decrease in tourism after the 9/11 attacks as well as increased regional instability with the renewed Palestinian Intifada that started in 2000. In 2001, the stock market crashed, with the value of trades falling sharply to 3 percent of GDP on average in 2001–2003, down from 10 percent in 1998–2000.[4] In 2001, the UNDP Human Development Index ranked Egypt 105 out of 162 countries, indicated illiteracy rates to be 45 percent, and estimated that 23 percent of the population lives below the national poverty line, with more than 12 percent of children under the age of five suffering from malnutrition.[5]

As Figure 6.1 shows, GDP growth slowed to 3.3 percent in 2000–2001, and then to 2.3 percent in 2001–2002, after reaching a high of 6 percent in the year 1998–1999.[6] By the end of the 1990s and also into the early 2000s, the economy stalled again, due to the factors previously stated. Another major factor was the pegging of the Egyptian pound to the dollar, which had made Egyptian exports less competitive in international markets. Moustafa writes:

> the government had maintained the peg in order to maximize hard currency revenues from tourism, despite its long-term negative effect on the country's growth potential. But the result was simply to delay the political turbulence that would follow the inevitable devaluation.[7]

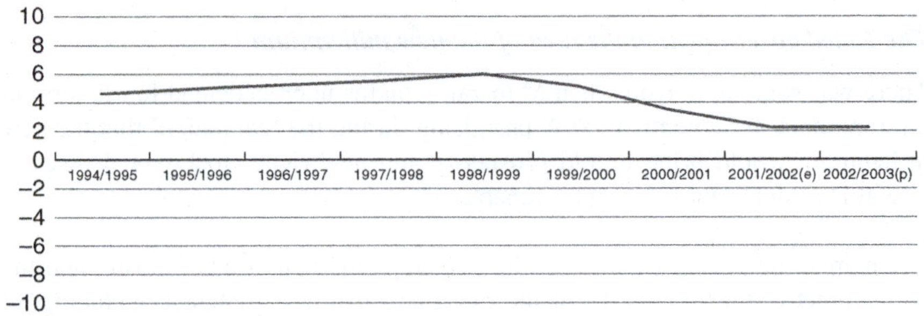

Figure 6.1 GDP growth rate (1994/1995 to 2002/2003).

The devaluation itself was always a goal of the government, and it was an economically sound one as the Egyptian pound was unnaturally overvalued and devaluation was necessary for long-term economic growth. However, the devaluation was done in a haphazard way in January 2003 with minimal societal consultation or parliamentary deliberation. The devaluation resulted in higher consumer prices, which affected the poorest segments of society negatively, and the government responded by announcing it would increase subsidies on basic food items as a stopgap measure to attempt to absorb the price increases. However, due to the haphazard devaluation, there was substantial short-term inflationary pressure. The 2003 UNDP Human Development Report on Egypt concluded:

> The inflationary episode of 2003–2004 in Egypt has disproportionately affected the poor. The significant increase in inflation that occurred in 2003–2004 followed a major devaluation of the pound that occurred in January 2003. Food prices tend to be more affected than other prices in exchange-rate induced price shocks and since food constitutes a larger share of the poor's budget, they tend to be disproportionately affected by such price shocks. Poor households are also less able to adapt to these price shocks than the non-poor because they tend to have lower labor force participation rates among adults and higher child dependency ratios.[8]

The 2008 report had shown that there was an improvement in several development indicators such as literacy and infant mortality rates, yet there was worsening sanitation, less access to fresh water, and higher poverty and unemployment rates. As shown in Table 6.1, in the worst-hit governorates in Upper Egypt such as Suhag, approximately 41 percent of the population was classified as 'poor,' and approximately 10 percent of the population classified as 'ultra poor.' In Assuit the indictors were even worse, with approximately 60 percent of the population classified as 'poor', and approximately 23 percent of the population as 'ultra poor.'[9] A Gini coefficient of 22.7 further underscores the inequality in Assuit.[10]

Table 6.1 Poverty levels in Egypt's poorest governorates (2008)

Governorate	*Poor persons (as a % of total population)*	*Ultra poor persons (as a % of total population)*	*Gini coefficient*	*Human Development Indicator (HDI)*
Fayoum	12.0	1.1	24.9	0.669
Menia	39.4	9.8	23.8	0.682
Assuit	60.6	22.7	24.8	0.681
Suhag	40.7	9.8	23.9	0.685
Beni Suef	45.4	11.8	25.7	0.697

Source: UNDP, *Egypt Human Development Report 2008* (UNDP, 2008), 37.

Nationally, the report also had some stark findings regarding the poorest segments of society. Even the poorest areas of Cairo had some alarming statistics in 2005–2006, though it fared better in some indicators. These statistics would come from the *ʿashwaʾiyyat*, whose conditions were comparable to Brazilian favelas or South African shantytowns. As the rich and well-off continued to move to gated communities at the outskirts of Cairo, conditions only worsened in these *ʿashwaʾiyyat.*

As per Table 6.2, in the years from 2004 to 2006, Cairo had approximately 16,000 people without access to piped water, 37,000 people without access to proper sanitation, 26,000 children dying before the age of five, 464,000 children not enrolled in basic or secondary schools, 59,000 malnourished children, 356,400 people classified as poor, and 41,000 people classified as 'ultra poor.'[11] The table also shows this pattern across the country. These statistics continued to worsen in the lead-up to 2011, and constituted a clear failure of state policy to address these socio-economic issues.

ERSAP 1991–2001: Keynes versus Friedman

Although by the turn of the millennium the regime had silenced much political dissent, the economic reforms continued to be debated in the public arena on the pages of *Al-Ahrām Al-Iqtiṣādī*. In December 2001, after approximately ten years of ERSAP, *Al-Ahrām Al-Iqtiṣādī* held and published a debate titled *al-iṣlāḥ al-iqtiṣādī: injizāʾāt haqīqiyya aw farīḍa ghaʾiba?* (The Economic Reform: Real Achievements or Absent Duty?).[12] It turned out to be more of a confrontation between Gouda Abdel Khaleq, the leftist economics professor and then deputy leader of the Tagammu' Party, and Mahmoud Mohiedin, economics professor and head of the economic subcommittee of the NDP's Policies Secretariat.

Abdel Khaleq vigorously attacked ERSAP and argued that the developmental model being followed in Egypt was only developmental in name. To him, true development involved economic growth that improved people's livelihoods, increased productivity, sharing the gains of development across broad segments of society, and improving Egypt's global competitive position. Moheidien

Table 6.2 Profile on human deprivation 2004/2006 (in 000s)

Area	*People without access to*		*Children dying before age 5*	*Children not in basic or secondary schools*	*Illiterates (15+)*	*Poor persons*		*Malnourished children below age 5*	*Unemployed persons*	
	Piped water	*Sanitation*				*Total*	*Ultra poor*		*Female*	*Total*
	2006	*2006*	*2005*	*2005/2006*	*2004/2005*	*2004/2005*	*2005*	*2006*	*2005*	*2006*
Cairo	16.2	37.2	26.2	464.23	1,243.8	356.4	41.2	59.0	284.5	120.8
Alexandria	4.3	246.5	9.7	163.27	692.9	306.8	44.3	24.0	130.8	47.6
Port Said	8.8	15.0	0.9	26.39	85.0	41.0	5.0	3.0	21.4	10.3
Suez	0.9	13.2	1.2	18.32	75.3	11.8	3.2	6.3	18.4	9.9
Urban	30.2	311.9	38.5	672.21	2,097.0	716.1	93.7	92.3	455.0	188.6
Governorates										
Damietta	3.8	94.6	1.6	54.58	210.0	28.2	2.6	2.5	27.0	30.7
Daqahlia	39.6	210.3	11.6	271.81	1,144.1	346.7	24.2	14.8	153.9	116.2
Sharqia	124.0	762.7	14.2	229.01	1,360.1	1,440.0	148.3	18.7	167.6	121.5
Qalyoubiya	25.4	495.9	8.5	257.55	931.0	435.6	38.8	22.9	115.3	74.8
Kafr el Sheik	19.2	326.3	4.4	143.05	738.8	341.8	22.5	24.5	54.8	54.1
Gharbia	19.6	644.9	7.7	260.37	862.0	238.9	31.4	11.4	132.6	89.4
Menoufia	38.4	508.1	6.9	227.38	731.6	564.4	13.9	22.8	75.7	39.9
Behera	99.3	754.6	8.6	306.85	1,418.7	960.7	130.5	16.8	134.8	102.2
Ismailia	10.7	94.8	2.0	38.60	180.4	55.2	4.1	2.5	22.8	35.2
Lower Egypt	380.0	3,892.3	65.4	1,789.20	7576.8	4,411.5	416.2	137.0	884.3	664.0
Urban	–	–	–	–	1,447.4	–	–	–	291.7	
Rural	–	–	–	–	6,129.4	–	–	–	592.7	
Giza	24.1	474.2	12.1	283.39	1,349.7	737.7	79.6	65.4	187.6	47.1
Beni Suef	56.4	420.1	11.2	124.55	731.5	1,024.5	265.7	26.3	27.8	21.4
Fayoum	16.0	363.8	9.2	156.29	816.6	290.7	26.6	32.0	25.4	25.2
Menia	94.2	798.4	19.4	185.56	1362.6	1,592.2	396.8	56.3	70.2	81.6

Assuit	29.4	659.5	23.0	198.06	1,032.4	2,072.5	776.9	80.0	85.1	63.6
Suhag	51.2	719.5	18.4	162.35	1,120.4	1,551.0	373.9	42.8	85.1	54.8
Qena	45.5	572.1	12.4	82.38	835.7	988.6	175.8	14.0	98.7	52.8
Luxor	1.4	52.9	1.6	7.41	106.3	25.5	7.0	0.9	24.5	10.3
Aswan	2.6	157.9	3.8	48.66	226.0	268.2	53.3	2.0	65.0	31.5
Upper Egypt	321.0	4,218.5	111.0	1,248.64	7,581.3	8,553.9	2,155.7	319.8	669.4	388.3
Urban	–	–	–	–	1,597.8	–	–	–	313.6	–
Rural	–	–	–	–	598.5	–	–	–	355.8	–
Red Sea	6.5	23.0	0.5	2.07	32.7	–	–	2.4	8.4	1.9
New Valley	0.4	20.5	0.3	5.59	30.6	–	–	0.7	6.4	1.5
Matrouh	15.8	44.6	0.8	7.02	90.8	–	–	0.9	5.5	5.5
North Sinai	14.2	36.9	1.2	11.38	66.1	–	–	1.4	6.3	3.9
South Sinai	3.5	6.0	0.2	0.94	18.8	–	–	0.1	4.7	1.9
Frontier Governorates	40.3	130.9	3.0	27.00	239.1	292.6	96.9	5.4	31.3	12.8
Urban	–	–	–	–	124.3	–	–	–	23.8	–
Rural	–	–	–	–	114.8	–	–	–	7.6	–
Total Egypt	771.6	8,553.6	217.9	3,737.05	17,494.1	13,974.1	2,762	554.5	2,040.1	1,253.7
Urban	–	–	–	–	5,266.5	–	–	–	1,048.1	–
Rural	–	–	–	–	12,227.7	–	–	–	956.0	–

Source: UNDP, *Egypt Human Development Report 2008* (Cairo: UNDP, 2008), 303.

responded that the economic reform undertaken could not be accurately assessed in such a short time span, and that GDP growth rates of up to 6 percent during the 1990s were a testament to the positive impact of the reform. He argued that more structural reform was needed so that the individual would able to feel the impact of development, and that the NDP's economic policies were reconfiguring the Egyptian economy to become fully market based over the next several years, and finally that ultimately this would improve popular livelihoods in the long run.[13]

The debate between these economists could be viewed within the intellectual debate between Keynesian and the neoliberal Chicago school views of economics as espoused by Milton Friedman. Keynesian and left-oriented economists in Egypt had viewed the liberalization experiment as a failure that actually worsened people's livelihoods. Its neoliberal proponents held that more reform was needed. While this debate raged on in the pages of *Al-Ahrām Al-Iqtiṣādī* and between elites, the actual economic direction of the country had already been set by the NDP and the incoming Nazif government.

Ironically, in the following decade, the careers of the two men would take them through different but intertwining paths that reflected their economic points of view, and Abdel Khaleq's point of view would arguably ultimately stand the test of time. Mohiedin would enjoy his moment in the sun as Minister of Investment in the Nazif government, overseeing the further structural reforms he had advocated. He would resign from the Ministry in 2010 to take up a position as Managing Director at the World Bank—lucky to avoid being charged and arrested with Nazif and most of his Cabinet in 2011—and remains at the World Bank at the time of writing (February 2016). Gouda Abdel Khaleq would spend the decade from 2001 to 2011 on the fringes of economic debates and political power, and after the 2011 uprising would be appointed to the first post-Mubarak Cabinet as Minister of Supply and Domestic Trade, appointed to tackle rising food prices.[14] When asked about his view on taking the GDP as a sole indicator of development, Abdel Khaleq replied:

> The GDP has some significance but it should not be overestimated. If you are concerned with poverty, then a higher growth rate means you are pushing everybody above a certain limit by raising the per capita income. Presuming that inequality does not increase, then that may reduce poverty. Particularly in the context of neo-liberal policies, inequality will rise so you may end up having faster growth rate and rising levels of poverty alongside, which is what happened in Egypt preceding 25 January 2011. The trouble with over emphasizing GDP growth is that for one thing it hinges on the so-called trickle down effect, which no evidence proves it takes place.
>
> People usually think of social justice as justice among-socio-economic groups, but one has to add to that the inter-generational justice, which takes on more importance in countries that rely on depletable resources when the current generation exhausts the resources leaving nothing for the next. The mention of social justice is inter-regional as well … 2/3 of Egypt's poor are

> in Upper Egypt. What happened during the 1991–2011 period was that GDP growth did provide some benefits to middle and higher strata of income urban based populations, however this means its significance in terms of social justice is very low as the most disadvantaged in society continue to suffer.... Furthermore, if you are dealing with a case of a repressive regime, national accounts are constructed so that government spending is part of national income. So if the government spends more on prisons and central police, it means people are getting more repressed, more unhappy and GDP is rising, which is an anomaly.[15]

Within the context of political economy, Abdel Khaleq raises some highly relevant points regarding the over-emphasis of GDP as an indicator of growth. While indeed the Nazif government achieved high GDP growth rates, yet as previously outlined many human development indicators actually worsened in the decade leading up to the 2011 uprising. This highlights the point that Richards and Waterbury make regarding the difference between "economic growth" (measured by the GDP) and "economic development" (measured by human development indicators).[16] The government's inability or reluctance to make such distinctions would ultimately prove detrimental to the regime's survival.

Gamal Mubarak and the Nazif government

Abdel Khaleq's views would remain on the fringe until 2011. In the meantime, after 2004, the Ebied government was showing it was increasingly inept in dealing with the challenges that the country was facing, especially the rising discontent and emerging political opposition after the 2003 Iraq War. Moreover, rumors had begun to swirl around Ebied himself, allegations that would be corroborated after 2011 when he was charged and convicted of corruption. He passed away in 2014, during the appeal process. One of the main charges he was facing was that he facilitated the illegal seizure of a natural reserve island in Luxor by fugitive business tycoon and long time Hosni Mubarak confidant Hussein Salem.[17]

Despite an increase in FDI in 2004, at closer inspection much of these investments are shown to have been acquisitions in the privatization program, which showed foreigners and well connected locals acquiring Egyptian state assets at very lucrative prices.[18] Again, this highlighted the debate between Keynes and Friedman. To neoliberals in the Egyptian government, rising FDI was a sign of success of the reform program. Leftist critics however argued that FDI was non-productive, as it was focused on acquisition and did not stimulate industrial and job growth at the levels expected.[19]

Through backroom machinations of the ruling NDP, the president's son had become involved in the party since 1999. Gamal Mubarak had returned to Egypt in the late 1990s after a few years working in London as an investment banker at Bank of America, where he was involved in some of the deals to acquire a portion of Egypt's external debt and re-sell them to the government at a discounted price.

Mubarak Sr. had appointed his son to the NDP General Secretariat in February 2000. The NDP had performed poorly in the parliamentary elections of 2000, and this had allowed Gamal the opportunity he was waiting for to enter the fray.[20]

In 2004 Atef Ebied was dismissed, and a new Cabinet led by Ahmad Nazif was sworn in. The NDP 'old guard' was represented by Kamal el Shazly, Youssef Waly, Safwat el Sherif, Zakariyah Azmi, and others who had been stalwarts of the Mubarak regime since its inception, and who saw little value in reform or change. The 'new guard' was led by Gamal and a group of technocrats and businessmen, who believed that the system could be improved politically, economically and socially from within.[21] The vehicle for Gamal and his group would be the NDP's Policies Secretariat, which quickly became the most powerful of all the NDP's secretariats and its leaders began to establish their own networks of patronage and would directly influence the formation of the new Cabinet.[22] The new Cabinet included members of the Policies Secertariat such as Mahmoud Mohiedin, as well as businessmen who had direct commercial interests in the portfolios they were leading, which went beyond the realm of conflict of interest into outright corruption in some cases.[23]

In addition to the Cabinet changes, there was a slight electoral opening in the political system. For the first time, Mubarak would run for president in a ballot that was not a plebiscite but an election proper, against two opponents: Nuʿmān Gomʿa of the Wafd Party and the independent Ayman Nour. The 2005 parliamentary elections, while not entirely transparent and democratic, were nonetheless more competitive than before, leading the Muslim Brotherhood to win 88 seats.[24]

Despite these seemingly liberalizing efforts, the regime remained authoritarian in nature and people suspected that these moves were designed to orchestrate the ultimate ascendance of Gamal Mubarak as the ruling party's candidate for the presidency. Cook argues that although multi-party parliamentary and presidential elections were indeed noteworthy developments nonetheless "there is a tendency among analysts to see genuine democratization in what are essentially tactical liberalizations and modifications of authoritarian political order."[25] Extending this line of analysis, such liberalizing efforts could be construed as an attempt by the ruling elite to coat Gamal's dynastic rise with a liberal veneer. The limitations of this veneer were clearly exhibited in the 2010 parliamentary elections where the results were pre-engineered and falsified by the NDP.[26] Amr El Shobaky, a senior researcher at Al-Ahram Center and ex-member of parliament (2012) argues that the falsification of the 2010 elections contributed to an unprecedented loss of legitimacy of the Mubarak regime that further encouraged previously unpoliticized everyday people to protest in the 2011 uprising.[27]

GDP growth rate versus sustainable development

The focus of the Nazif government on GDP growth by any means had allowed businessmen and foreign investors to make higher returns, under the belief that growth will eventually trickle down. Dr. Hala el Said, Dean of the Faculty of

Economics and Politics at Cairo University and member of the governing board of the Egyptian Central Bank, says that while the government was focused on GDP growth and well-needed structural transformation, there was minimal focus on social justice and preventing the exploitation of the poor. She concludes that the lack of attention paid to social justice during the Nazif government was one of the main reasons for the January 25 uprising.[28] Egyptian World Bank economist Heba Handoussa, the lead author of the Egypt Human Development Report, concurs and argues:

> Welfare is much more indicative than GDP, because you have to take into account how this growth is shared. The theory of Nazif's cabinet was that there would be a good trickle down effect and people should not worry about equality and equity as long as there is growth. His theory was that we should worry about distribution once we have a sustainable growth rate that is high enough to create jobs, as job creation is a very good way to create equity. The problem was that there weren't enough jobs created. Many of the jobs that were created were in the informal sector where there is little social security and social protection, and they are not very stable or "decent" jobs. That was the part of the problem. On the equity front, the minimum wages were ridiculously low, creating a lot of exploitation of workers.
>
> I know among businessmen, especially the textile and garment industry, were willing to admit that there was exploitation. And of course you see it in terms of how much of a margin or profit is made by a particular sector because wages are kept so low. When you talk of garments, you know they are getting export subsidies, and they were paying wages way below the 700EGP. They were making huge profits. There is evidence that exploitation existed in a political economy context. It was fair enough that one of the three main slogans of the revolution was social justice.[29]

Within the political economy framework and specifically the impact of state policy on economy growth and social actors, Handoussa's remarks are apt. Much of the GDP and FDI growth came from sectors that did not stimulate job creation, like mobile phones, luxury imports and real estate development. Unemployment continued to rise to unprecedented levels. A perfect storm of growing unemployment, population growth, urbanization and the 'youth bulge' was combining and presented an eminent danger to the regime's stability. The perception of regime corruption and cronyism further alienated the people from the Mubarak family and the Nazif government.

Zawāj al-sulṭa bil-māl

The last years of Mubarak's rule would see actual marriages that would signify the ultimate culmination of the alliance between power and business, which became known as *zawāj al-sulṭa bil-māl* (the marriage of authority to money). According to Soliman, the liberalizing efforts during the Mubarak era were underlined by "political marriage between the state bureaucracy and capitalism under the umbrella of the regime and the NDP."[30] At the apex of this alliance, lay the president's sons themselves. Alaa Mubarak was married to the daughter of Magdi Rasekh, as discussed in the previous chapter, and cementing the alliance was Gamal Mubarak's marriage to the daughter of Mahmoud el Gammal, a wealthy businessman and developer. Magdi Rasekh, whose wealth had exploded exponentially after the marriage of his daughter to Alaa, would be convicted of several counts of corruption after the 2011 uprising, and at the time of writing remains an escaped convict. Mahmoud el Gammal, who was already a wealthy businessman before the marriage of his daughter to Gamal, was charged but the evidence against him was found lacking and he was not convicted. Despite his family association with the Mubarak family, el Gammal was careful not to be perceived as too politically close to the ruling NDP.[31] Through their real estate development companies, both Rasekh and el Gammal were able to acquire highly lucrative land plots on the outskirts of Cairo as well as on the north coast, which they developed and were able to gain handsomely from.

Businessmen and bureaucrats in the state took their cue from this apex, and many were involved in corruption themselves. Mohammed Soliman, Minister of Housing, is one glaring example of this. Soliman was "charged with violating laws regulating tenders and auctions including profiteering, illegal seizure of state land and squandering public funds. During his term from 1993 to 2005, Soliman was involved in corrupt land deals with various private entities."[32] One of these private entities was SODIC, a company led by Magdi Rasekh himself, which, through Soliman, was able to acquire an extensive land bank which was developed as gated communities on the outskirts of Cairo and sold to Egypt's ultra-wealthy. After 2011, several of the ministers in Nazif's Cabinet, as well as Nazif himself, were guilty of corruption and received varying jail sentences. The continued corruption and cronyism, coupled with the negative impact of the neoliberal policies on the welfare state and the rise in poverty levels, would eventually erode the support base of the regime itself.

International economic context

Objectively analyzing the economic performance of the Nazif government, there were two interrelated international factors that were out of the government's control that would have negative domestic economic consequences. The first factor was rising global food prices. In a research paper published months after the uprising, Lagi *et al.* have linked rising global food prices directly to the uprisings in the Middle East and instability elsewhere. By conducting a study that combines data from the United Nations Food and Agricultural Organization (FAO) and incidents of social unrest in a large number of developing countries, they have been able to show some correlation between food prices and political instability.[33] While their paper at times overreaches and oversimplifies, especially when local dynamics and drivers of instability are not fully taken into consideration, the work does make some valid points within the Egyptian context.

As the global price of cereals rose, Egyptian food prices rose 37 percent from 2008 to 2010.[34] The ramifications of such price hikes cannot be underestimated.

The second international factor was the Global Financial Crisis (GFC). Despite the rising GDP, increased macroeconomic stability and increased flows of FDI, the GFC would hit Egypt hard. The first sector that was impacted was tourism, where statistics indicate that overall tourist arrivals declined by 12 percent from 2008 to 2009.[35] As a result of a decline in world trade after the GFC, there was a corresponding decline in ships passing through the Suez Canal, which showed a decrease of 19.6 percent from 2008 to 2009, after post-GFC global stabilization measures were taken.[36] In addition, the stock market declined by 56 percent by the end of 2008, making the Egyptian stock exchange one of the worst hit in the world.[37] These two international economic factors were beyond the control of the Nazif government, but did have a negative domestic impact, further heightening popular economic grievances against the regime.

The military: ruling but not governing

While it is beyond the scope of this book to conduct a full analysis of civilian–military relations in Egypt, it is apt to critically discuss them within the context of a political opportunity that would inadvertently aid the mobilization of 2011: elite divisions. Aside from the NDP's 'old guard' and 'new guard,' there was another cleavage at an elite level. All Egyptian presidents since 1952 had been from the military, and this to a certain extent had meant the military would side with the presidency (should the need arise). Naturally, the relationship would not be as seamless.

In his influential book on civil–military relations, Huntington argues that military institutions are shaped by two forces:

1 a functional imperative stemming from threats to society's security; and
2 a societal imperative arising from "social forces, ideologies, and institutions dominant within society."[38]

At the core of civil–military relations is the relationship between the officer corps and the state.[39] From the eighteenth century onwards, states have aimed to professionalize their armies, bringing them under the control of a civilian authority.

Following from that, for Feaver the central issue in military–civil relations is the attempt to "reconcile a military strong enough to do anything the civilians ask them to with a military subordinate enough to do only what civilians authorize them to do."[40] Huntington describes two forms of civilian control of the military:

1 subjective civilian control, which denies the military an independent sphere of power to operate in and which maximizes the power of civilian groups over the military;[41] and

2 objective civilian control, which is built on the professionalism of the officer corps and which rests predominantly on efforts to professionalize the military.

Huntington postulates that a "highly professional officer corps stands ready to carry out the wishes of any civilian group which secures legitimate authority within the state."[42] While Huntington's approach is not without its critics,[43] his points on civilian control of the military are pertinent, as is his argument that objective control works best to ensure that the military obeys the elected civilian leadership.

Egypt's army had been undergoing a process of professionalization that started in the Muhammad Ali era and continued into the twentieth century.[44] While civil–military relations in Egypt had not corresponded directly to Huntington's analysis as all of Egypt's presidents (until 2013) had come from the military and not through elections, this analysis became more pertinent during the Mubarak era. Mubarak would spend three decades as an ostensibly civilian president, but he would maintain the privileges of the military in an unspoken social contract. Such an arrangement uses a combination of Huntington's approaches to keep the army from interfering directly in political affairs. Nordinger postulates that "The great majority of coups are partly, primarily, or entirely motivated by the defense or enactment of the military's corporate interests."[45] In the same vein, Needler argues that the

> military typically intervenes in politics from a combination of motives in which defense of the institutional interests of the military itself predominates, although those interests are frequently construed so as to be complementary to the economic interests of the economic elite.[46]

Bearing out Needler's hypothesis, Waterbury argues that after the 1967 defeat, army officers lost some of their legitimacy to continue as an effective political power at the time.[47] During the Sadat era, the military's role in defense matters and its role in policy-making, even in defense matters, decreased.[48] Sadat's symbolic victory in the October War strengthened his position with the military, as well as with the general population. However, after the Camp David Accords, the restrictions enforced on the Egyptian army (particularly in the Sinai Peninsula) caused some resentment in the ranks. Fearing the military, Sadat began to attempt to curb its influence, making several changes in the command chain and decreasing the number of state posts offered to ex-military personnel. Upon assuming power, Mubarak knew that the military would be a potential threat to his rule, so he used a gentler approach. He assured the high command that there would be no more cutbacks, brought new weapons from the United States to replace Soviet equipment, and drastically increased the privileges enjoyed by the officer corps.[49]

The political economy of the Egyptian military

Mubarak gave the military a green light to become involved in the economy. The military began to increase its role in civilian industries as well as in arms manufacturing. Ayubi writes:

> The "economic wing" of the Egyptian army grew significantly throughout the 1980s. In 1978 a National Service Projects Organization (NSPO) was created and in 1981 a Military Organization for Civil Projects was established, engaging itself in a variety of public works such as the construction of roads and bridges, telecommunications networks, and other engineering projects. The army is now involved in all kinds of civilian activities that include the building of railways, flyovers, irrigation canals and water pipelines, transport and communications networks, and a wide range of factories, laboratories, clinics and training centers. Other activities include the running of poultry batteries and a large set up of bakeries and other projects for "food security" and at one point even extended to the rather un-military task of organizing an opera performance.[50]

The military's economic interests continued to grow during the Mubarak era. While the interests of the Mubarak regime and the military had mostly aligned, Mubarak did remove the widely popular Abu Ghazalah from office, perceiving him as a threat, and selecting the supposedly blindly loyal Tantawi to replace him. Arguably, the interests of the military and the 'new guard' began to diverge especially after the appointment of the technocrats and the businessmen of the Nazif government. Businessmen were on the ascendancy, and were now operating in areas that had been previously been the sole purview of the military. The military's involvement in the economy had always been a closely guarded secret; for instance, the army's budget, revenue and expenses were often a vague single line in Egypt's annual budget. The official explanation is that the army's budget is a matter of national security. Abul Maged disagrees and argues that the budget is kept secret so that the army avoids civilian oversight and does not have to declare the huge profits it accrues from the production of non-military goods and services.[51]

The issue of civilian oversight over the military's economic affairs is part of the overall question of the role of the army in civilian affairs. Nordinger identifies three general models of military intervention in civilian affairs:

1. as moderators, the military does not control the government directly, but exercises veto powers on a range of issues;
2. as guardians, the military maintains stability, but has no qualms against direct intervention through a coup should the status quo be threatened—as in the case of Turkey; and
3. as rulers, where the military rules directly.[52]

The case could be argued then that the Egyptian military was initially (post-1967) a moderator; in response to threats to their interests, as well as demands from society, they became outright guardians; finally, they stepped in directly in 2011. Abul Magd argues:

> Generally speaking, the Egyptian military establishment does not believe in US-style neoliberalism or free market policies, particularly those that would result in the army's loss of its valued companies and assets. Such feared measures include limiting the state's economic role, privatization, and promoting the role of private capital. For instance, in a 2008 Wikileaks cable, a former US ambassador to Egypt indicated that Field Marshal Tantawi was critical of economic liberalization on the ground that it undermined the state's control over the economy. Tantawi's skepticism of neoliberal economics has little to do with his loyalty to the socialist model of the Soviet Union, where he received his training as a young officer. Rather, it is privatization's potential encroachments against the vast economic empire owned by the military that Tantawi fears the most.[53]

A less cynical view, and not necessarily wholly contradictory, is that the army (and in particular some mid-level officers of the corps) had empathized with the January 2011 uprising, and that the high command had further impetus to withdraw its support from Mubarak. The case of the 8th of April Officers supports this argument. The officers, who took to Tahrir Square on April 8, 2011 to support the uprising, were all arrested for military insubordination.[54] While this does not necessarily mean that their sentiments were widespread in the officer corps, it illustrates that there were elements of the officer corps who did indeed support the uprising. These elite schisms between Mubarak and the army will be built upon later in the opportunity and threat section.

The student and youth movements

Political context and regional dynamics

In the last few years of the 1990s, there was a decrease in protests across Egypt, as the state was engaged in a confrontation with militant Islamists, which had raised the levels of repression to unprecedented levels. Several attacks on tourists, locals and the authorities convinced many Egyptians that it was better to fall in line as the state fought the militant Islamists. By 1999–2000, the state had been successful in fighting off many of the militants, with some killed and many thousands jailed. For now, the militant insurgency was defeated; it would not return until 2012, and even then not where it was based (in Upper Egypt) but in the Sinai Peninsula, particularly after the ouster of President Morsi.

At the turn of the millennium, after the defeat of the militant insurgency, there was relative calm, which was soon shattered by events outside Egypt's border. After the Middle East summit at Camp David that was mediated by US President Bill Clinton, the Palestinians and Israelis blamed each other for the failure of the talks. The failed talks had been led by Israeli Labor Party Prime Minister Ehud

Barak. The opposition leader, Ariel Sharon, made a very public visit to Al-Aqsa Mosque, which arguably contributed to the outbreak of the Second or Al-Aqsa Intifada. Sharon himself was elected in 2001 and in the following years there would be an unprecedented escalation of violence between Palestinians and Israelis that would have domestic consequences in Egypt.

Re-invigorating the student movement part one: the Al-Aqsa Intifada

As previously highlighted, the social movement literature has investigated the impact of changes in the international system on social movements.[55] These processes could be observed in Egypt, where massive protests would occur in support of the Palestinians. Much of these protests occurred on university campuses. The Intifada had galvanized and re-invigorated the student movement, as well as mobilizing solidarity activists at large. As outlined in the previous chapter, the Intifada caused the ideological divide between leftist and Islamist students to weaken as they both worked together across university campuses not only to protest, but also to set up committees to gather medicine to send to the Occupied Territories. Ahmad Ezzat, a human rights lawyer who was one of the youth leaders during the 2011 uprising, was himself a student leader of the Revolutionary Socialists group in Cairo University at the time of the Al-Aqsa Intifada. He recalled:

> In 2000–2001 there was general anger on the street, even amongst those who are not politically engaged. Average Egyptians watching the news on TV sympathized with the Palestinians in their plight against the Zionist enemy. They were enraged by the ineffectiveness of Arab countries. This lead to a series of protests and caravans in support of Palestinians, which gave birth to the Popular Committee in Solidarity with Palestine which was largely manned by students from different currents. The Caravan collected food and medical supplies and organize convoys to deliver them to Palestine.[56]

The Popular Committee in Solidarity with Palestine would provide an incubator for activists from different ideological backgrounds to work together. The committee would also give the current generation of students its first experience of protest in Tahrir Square. In September 2001, the committee called for a demonstration in solidarity with Palestine, and approximately 1,000 people gathered in Tahrir Square. The group comprised of leftist and Islamist students, as well as veteran activists from older generations.[57] While thousands of policemen prevented the protest from marching on the US embassy, the 2001 protest would be the first major protest in Tahrir Square since the 1977 Bread Intifada. It would not be the last. The student presence in the protest signifies and underlines the historic resonance of Palestine as a cause across university campuses in Egypt. On the campus of Cairo University, Ezzat recalled how the Al-Aqsa Intifada had a direct impact on the student movement:

> During the Palestinian intifada there was a chance to re-create the student movement. This resonated on campus; students started to organize haphazard protests against the massacres that were perpetrated by the Zionists. Then, political forces started to join efforts, including leftist movements, Nasserists and the MB. Supporting the Palestinian intifada was uncontested among the different political forces. It also represented the university's thirst for political activism. For years since 1981, most student activities were limited to social work spearheaded by the Islamist bloc, none of which touched upon issues that are of interest to the public or that cater to a public cause, be it political, economic or social. Hence, the intifada created a chance for students to pour out their energy and readiness for organized movements.[58]

There were further protests in 2002 when the Israelis attacked the Jenin refugee camp, leading university campuses across Egypt to erupt in protest. Al Ahram Online reported that thousands of students took part; even the more affluent and historically less politicized AUC students took part and blocked Qasr el Aini street.[59] The ongoing Palestinian–Israeli conflict was an opportunity for the overall student movement to mobilize, and more specifically a chance for the leftist students to make a comeback on campus, after years of repression and disorganization. Ezzat recalled:

> At that time, the socialist student blocs seized the chance to really solidify themselves as an entity. If we put aside what occurred during the 25th of January revolution, this was the peak of the socialist movement inside Cairo University, as well in other major universities. Prior to that, there were only about a handful of members of the socialist student movement; the ones you could rely on and consider leaders were only a few. During the intifada, this number rose up exponentially. They referred to themselves as socialists, joined protests whilst carrying the socialist flag, introduced themselves to the public as socialists, gave out leaflets at protests, and so on. This was novel. It hadn't happened since the 1960s and 1970s and it would only happened again during the 25th of January revolution.[60]

The framing of the protests: 'liberating Jerusalem starts by liberating Cairo'

As previously outlined, framing refers to the process of interpreting issues within a specific context that is able to resonate with the wider group and induce them to mobilize. Within the context of social movement theory, a frame denotes "an interpretive schemata that simplifies and condenses the 'world out there' by selectively punctuating and encoding objects, situations, events, experiences, and sequences of action within one's past or present environment."[61] The use of the word 'framing' denotes:

> An active, processual phenomenon that implies agency and contention at the level of reality construction. It is active in the sense that something is being done, and processual in the sense of a dynamic, evolving process. It entails agency in the sense that what is evolving is the work of social movement organizations or movement activists. And it is contentious in the sense that it involves the generation on interpretive frames that not only differ from existing ones, but that may also challenge them.[62]

In the Egyptian context, even though the protests were directed against Israel and in support of the Palestinian cause, slowly but surely people began to make a connection with domestic politics and the seemingly toothless response from the Egyptian regime. The Palestinian issue provided an opportunity for anti-regime activism without directly challenging the regime.[63] Activists themselves began a process of framing the Palestine issue not solely as a regional concern but as an issue that is related directly to the Mubarak regime. This was the first of three main framing processes that can be construed occurring between 2000 and 2011. The first was the framing of the Palestinian Intifada as a domestic issue. Examples of this can be seen in the chants during the protests. Ezzat recalled:

> The intifada created some sort of internal turmoil; people started to look within and realize Egypt's problems, and that Egypt was in fact partaking, in one way or the other, in the occupation. But we had to ask, why is Egypt a stakeholder in this? There was a crucial question to answer: how does the intifada relate to Egypt's internal affairs? No one wanted to solely speak of internal affairs without looking out for the plight of Palestinians, adhering to a strictly nationalistic rhetoric. Likewise, people did not want to only act in support of Palestine and Arab nationalism and fail to include the average man on the street. From here on, ways to tie both realities together came about. For example, it was then that the slogan "Liberating Al Quds (Jerusalem) starts by Liberating Cairo" was widely iterated within the university.[64]

The second would be the framing of the *Kefaya* protests as relating to people's everyday lives. Gunning and Baron argue that, "Following a process known in social movement theory as 'frame bridging', Youth for Change activists recognized that the masses would not be mobilized unless they saw the linkage between their daily concerns and the toppling of Mubarak."[65] Therefore, the *Kefaya* activists made a concerted effort to connect their campaign to economic concerns, as well as concerns about *mashrūʿ al-tawrīth* (the hereditary project). The third process of framing would be the workers' movement, who moved from framing their activism from exclusive economic grievances to broader political opposition to Mubarak, which will be discussed later in this chapter.

Re-invigorating the student movement part two: the 2003 Iraq War

The 2003 Iraq War was another external event that helped galvanize protests, initially against the United States but ultimately against the Egyptian regime. The regime itself had inadvertently helped mobilize people, when it initially encouraged protests against the United States—even organizing a state-sanctioned demonstration 'carnival' at Cairo stadium, complete with popular singers and food stalls, which was aired live on Egyptian state TV.[66]

Several unofficial protests were also organized, and university campuses erupted again, further further bringing down the ideological divides between leftists and Islamist students. Arm Abdel Hakim, the Muslim Brotherhood student leader, recalls that during the Iraq War:

> The Iraq war united Cairo University. In March 2003, after the invasion, we organized a huge demonstration that brought almost all activists together. Several protests continued in the following days and we worked closely with all the students from various political currents.[67]

Even though the regime responded with violent repression and arrests, the Iraq War protests would provide the second opportunity for activists from different political currents to work together.

The rise (and fall) of Kefaya

Kefaya was formed in 2004, building on the various mobilizations against the Iraq war. Meaning 'enough' in Arabic, *Kefaya* was directed at Mubarak, specifically his 2005 campaign for ostensible 'reelection,' and at Gamal Mubarak, his heir apparent. The secret of the movement's success was its simplicity, spreading the simple message that enough was enough. Its catchy slogan, *lā lil-tamdīd, lā lil-tawrīth* (no to extension, no to inheritance) was effective in channeling the public's anger at the regime. Although over the following years the *Kefaya* movement would lose steam, it paved the way for other movements that challenged the status quo. In the years leading up to 2011, there were many other manifestations of activism in Egyptian civil society. Protest groups would mobilize and challenge the authority of the regime in a variety of ways, including groups like Students for Change, University Professors for Change, Artists for Change, and the People's Campaign For Change.[68] Indeed, the Arabic word for change, *al-taghyīr*, was part of many slogans and campaigns used by activists. El-Mahdy and Marfleet argue:

> For the first time in decades those in power have been confronted by diverse forms of action: protests about water and bread; village mobilizations against de-sequestration; street demonstrations for democracy; solidarity marches and convoys for Palestine; campus protests over war and repression; sit ins by state employees; strikes in industry; and a host of actions by

judges, teachers, university professors, physicians and pharmacists. Millions of Egyptians have participated.[69]

The *Kefaya* protests would also find traction on university campuses. Mohammad al Qasas, the ex-Muslim Brotherhood student leader, recalls:

> Kefaya put a call out and the students responded, and we were supportive of Kefaya during 2004 and 2005. In 2005 there was a huge movement bringing together all university students to call for freedoms on campus and in wider society. Also in 2005 a group called *Jāmiʿatunā* (Our University) was created, bringing students from different political backgrounds to protest issues related to the university campus and dorms. The movement also partook in several conferences; certain *herak* (movement) was taking place among the Leftist students; MB students and students from the labor party and then joined by Kefaya. 2004 witnessed the revival of the student movement. Kefaya's members were from across generations from the student movement.[70]

As Qasas elaborates, while *Kefaya* itself was not a student movement, many of its founding were student activists themselves during the 1960s and 1970s, despite being on opposing ideological sides. Ahmad Bahā el Dīn Shaʿbān, the veteran leftist leader, was a socialist student activist in the 1970s. Another *Kefaya* founder, Abu el Ela Madi, was a veteran Muslim Brotherhood activist in the 1970s who left the organization in the 1990s to create the Wasat Party. Gunning and Baron argue that

> the protests served to reconnect long term activists who had become politicized in the student and workers protests of the 1970s, but who had become fragmented and had gone their separate ways in the intervening decades, following different ideological trends.[71]

In clear processes of diffusion and spillover, the Aqsa Intifada and the 2003 Iraq War had brought people together in unprecedented fashion. As previously discussed, the absence of organizational structures negatively affects social movements. While *Kefaya* was not an organization per se, nonetheless it provided a vehicle for activists to network and coordinate anti-regime protests.[72] Gunning and Baron argue:

> The protests provided a unifying focal point for ideologically and socially divided activists. Through the 1980s and 1990s but especially during the 1990s, the schism between secularists and Islamists had widened, as key secular ideologues had been hounded out of Egypt, or, in some cases, assassinated. Opinions were deeply divided on how to oppose the Mubarak regime, and what alternative system would be put in place. The Al-Aqsa Intifada provided a rallying call behind which all sides could unite. The Popular Committee for the Support of the Palestinian uprising, for instance,

> and later the Popular Committee Opposing US aggression Against Iraq, brought together Arab nationalists, Marxists, Islamists, civil society and professional organizations, intellectuals, public figures and artists.[73]

Even though the *Kefaya* movement would ultimately lose momentum, it paved the way for a variety of other interconnected groups to actively oppose the regime. These included the 20th March Movement for Change, the March 9th Movement for the Independence of Universities, the Judges Clubs, and the National Coalition for Democratic Change. In clear processes of spillover, activists in one group would be also part of another group, as well as supporting a third—like the support that the Judges received in 2005, when the Judges Club confronted the executive by denouncing the fraudulent results of the constitutional referendum, as well as 2005 presidential and legislative elections.[74]

The labor movement

The previous section has highlighted how university and elite-centric activism was re-invigorated in the 2000–2005 period. While *Kefaya* did lose steam, student and professional organizations would continue to protest, with varying degrees of success. However, starting from 2005–2006, another segment of society would carry the mantle of activism in the face of the regime. The labor movement was becoming increasingly militant in response to the continued structural adjustment. Table 6.3 shows the rise in worker activism. Beinin argues that

> the largest and most politically significant industrial strike since a dispute in the same workplace in 1947 took place in December 2006 at the Misr Spinning and Weaving Company in Mahalla al-Kubra, where nearly a quarter of all public sector textile and clothing workers are employed.[75]

Worker protests were not only localized in the public sector. They had also begun to include workers in the private sector, as well as public servants. Abdel Rahman observes:

> A particularly interesting feature of labor protests during the 2000s was the widening of the base of protestors. Traditional factory-based industrial workers were joined by vast numbers of public civil servants who were adversely affected by privatization policies which targeted them in the same way as industrial workers. Civil servants, traditionally reliant on the state for their livelihoods, had enjoyed a relative degree of security under the populist regimes of Nasser and to lesser extent under Sadat and the early years of Mubarak. However, in the second half of the 1990s the government began to implement aggressive neoliberal policies under the dictates of multilateral and bilateral donors, downsizing its own bureaucracy and chipping away at many of the privileges civil servants had enjoyed for decades.[76]

Table 6.3 Collective action and number of workers involved (1998–2010)

Year	*Strikes*	*# of workers involved*
1998	114	
1999	164	
2000	135	
2001	115	
2002	96	
2003	86	
2004	266	386,346
2005	202	141,175
2006	222	198,088
2007	614	474,838
2008	609	541,423
2009	432	
2010	371	
Total	3,426	

Source: Joel Beinin, "Workers and the Egyptian January 25th Revolution," *International Labor and Working-Class History* 80, no. 1 (September 2011): 191.

Indeed, the widening base of worker protests to include civil servants would be another crack in the regime's control of workers. More specifically, the strike of the real estate tax collectors would resonate widely and lead to the formation of an independent union that would inspire other workers to follow suit. The formation of independent unions was clearly an attempt to address the consistent weakness in labor mobilizations that dated back to the pre-1952 era, where workers were only allowed to organize through co-opted union structures, or not allowed to organize independently at all. Hisham Fouad, a veteran leftist journalist and member of the Revolutionary Socialists group, recalls:

> In 2009–10 the independent union/syndicate of real estate taxes was formed. This was an important turning point; by then the struggle had reached civil servants, which mean that the problem was getting bigger. These workers decided to better their lives without turning to corruption. They were also able to organize themselves and challenge the existing workers' laws and form independent unions. This would have a mobilizing effect for the whole workers movement across Egypt.[77]

As discussed earlier in this chapter, there were clear framing processes unfolding and used by the activists, first during the protests supporting the Palestinian cause, second during the *Kefaya* wave of activism, and third with the labor protests. What had begun as a struggle for economic rights began to transform into a political struggle against the regime. Beinin postulates that after 2007:

> Important elements among the Mahalla strikers are now framing their struggle as a profoundly political fight with national implications. They are

> directly challenging the economic policies and political legitimacy of the regime of President Husni Mubarak. In this challenge, they have received the support of not only the bulk of the population of Mahalla, but also workers from the textile mills of Kafr al-Dawwar and Shibin al-Kom, railway workers and urban intellectuals.[78]

Kamal al Fayoumy, the veteran activist and labor leader in the Mahallah textile factory, stated that the protests in Mahallah had begun with the simple issue of receiving a promised two-month incentive pay.[79] His testimony illustrates the growing dissent in the ranks of workers that contributed to the 2011 uprising:

> Because of worsening economic conditions, workers started to realize the need to dissent through strike action. This coincided with Nazif's decision that workers have the right for a 2 months bonus. Local union lections for the factories in Mahallah were underway under heavy security involvement and presence. The factory and security approved candidates had announced that they would also adhered to the same promise. After they were elected and in coordination with management, they went back on their word. As a result the workers decided they would not cash any of their upcoming salaries. They thought that if they can get what they are entitled to (2 months' pay), they did not want anything.
>
> We started a campaign for the workers not to receive their pay at all, if they would not have the two months included. When it was payday, the cashiers thought that once the pay cheques are issued, workers would automatically cash them; they were stunned when after issuing the cheques the workers refused them.... On 6 December, 2006 we announced a strike until two months of pay were released. This was the first major strike of the decade known as *idrab al-shahrayn* (the Two-Month Strike, referring to the two-months' pay). We issued several statements before the strike outlining the following demands: the 2 months of pay promised, higher allowances for lunch, higher wages connected to inflation, and better incentives. We wanted to lift our standards; textile workers are the least paid in Egypt. Around 27,000 workers protested at the time. From a small number of protestors through out the decade for Palestine and *Kefaya,* and in direct opposition to the brutality of the Mubarak regime, having a protest with 27,000 workers was a great achievement in itself, and it showed to all urban based democracy and student activists that the workers were now mobilizing in numbers never seen in Egypt for decades. The spark of the 2011 Egyptian revolution started here in Mahallah in 2006.[80]

The strike was successful; management was forced to pay out the two months' incentive bonuses. This highlighted to workers across the country that carefully organized strikes could yield positive outcomes. It also highlighted to all anti-regime activists that cracks were beginning to appear in the authoritarian façade. In 2007 there were further demands by the workers for increased benefits to help alleviate the nationwide increase in prices. The management and the authorities fought back on these demands, paving the way for the April 6, 2008 strike.

The labor movement and the birth of the 6th of April Movement

A large strike was planned in Mahallah for April 6, 2008. Activists in Cairo responded and magnified the call for strike, arguing that April 6 should be a general strike across Egypt. Even though the strike was unsuccessful, the 6th of April Youth Movement was born. Using grassroots mobilization techniques and social media, the movement was able to reach various sectors of society over the following years. Although the starting point of the movement was a cry for workers' rights, it had transformed into a movement calling for political reform.[81] Again, the establishment of the 6th of April Movement was an attempt to bypass the continued weakness of oppositional groups in Egypt manifest in their inability to build sustainable organizations. The organization was built after the events that unfolded on April 6, 2008. Kamal el Fayoumy, who was present at the time, describes how the events unfolded:

> On 6 April, there were large numbers of CSF trucks surrounding the factory. There were more than 3000 civil dressed officers within the workers. Cars were hired to lift workers home upon stepping outside the factory. It didn't look too good. They managed to create a wide split among the workers group.... At 2:30 p.m. I was arrested by state security.... We learnt later that the people of Mahalla rose against the high levels of unemployment and rising prices.... Arrests were made and people were tortured.... We were blindfolded and questioned then we were later transferred to Tanta and then to Borg El Arab, Karim El Beheiry, a worker, myself and Tarek Belal ... El Badeel and Al Dostour papers were covering our arrest closely. Due to the support we received from fellow workers and from the press, we were released 2 months after adamant to keep up the fight for workers rights.... A remarkable sit-in at the time was that of Tanta Lenin factory which kept their sit-in for 180 days. They received a lot of support from other workers who joined their sit-in in solidarity.[82]

Clear processes of diffusion and spillover could be viewed through the April 6 strike and the formation of the 6th of April Movement, as this represented another connection between the labor movement and the youth and democratization movement. Even though many of the workers had initially framed their protests within a moral economy view, seeking to maximize their economic gains and recover some of their rights, after 2008 the workers' protests would take increasingly political shape. According to el Fayoumy, "after 2007–2008 it became evident that textile workers shifted from calling for economic demands to calling for political demands and calling directly for the fall of the regime."[83] Mohammed Abdel Hamid, a worker in Mahallah, stated:

> I took part in all the sit-ins inside the company starting 2006.... The video of Shoman Square with Mubarak's picture falling was the first sign of a revolution trigger in Mahalla. It positioned Mahalla as a city with a strong workers front. Mahalla is the center of industries, even more so than Tanta. The workers here started to become fed up with the high cost of living. My base salary is EGP500 per months. My expenses are EGP1,500 per month. Where do I get the difference? You borrow from here and there. You end up pressuring yourself to make ends meet.
>
> After 2006, the demands shifted from being economic to be political. The succession plan was the turning point.... We were living in a bottleneck for 30 years, when would we have gotten out of it? Workers were performing well and producing a lot. If wealth distribution were fair, they would have lived better than doctors. Even if the worker only retained part of the profit of what he produced daily, he would live better than a doctor, a teacher, an engineer.[84]

However, it is impossible to say that all the workers made this shift from economic to political demands. Some of the workers I met in Cairo, Mahallah and Alexandria were less politicized and more focused on bread and butter issues. This inconsistency can be attributed to their varying degrees of politicization as well as their political inclinations. Veteran activists like el Fayoumy and Hussein are both considered leftist activists, and tend to politicize their activism and combine economics and politics. There are other currents within the labor movement who are more focused on strictly economic issues. Kamal Abbas, a leader in the independent union movement, illustrates this discrepancy:

> With all due to respect to the workers, the most important thing about strikes is their effect on the economic future and wellbeing of the individual workers. For example when the metro workers announced their intent to go on strike next week (March 2013), this generated an immediate response [from authorities] to address their grievances. I think this is what matters. You should note that many of the strikes from 2006 to 2011 were for economic reasons, and continue to be so. They didn't always call for the downfall of Mubarak. The demands usually revolved around higher pay and better working conditions. This is because for the longest time the workers fight in Egypt had been an economic fight.
>
> What happened between 2006 and 2011 was the most active time for workers strikes, and all of them were calling for economic demands, but some workers *are more politicized* than others. However in the final years of the Mubarak regime, workers across the country saw the horrific corruption and unequal opportunities. This worsened the perception of the regime across society, and including the workers. People's livelihoods were getting worse, and in the same time people saw the grooming of Gamal Mubarak and the benefits gained by the regime's business cronies. To the workers, this hit close to home.[85]

Hamdy Hussein, a veteran labor activist and worker in Mahallah, concedes that not all workers had made the connection between the economic and the political demands:

> The predominant awareness among the workers is of an economic nature. The more educated among the workers are generally the ones with an increased awareness in politics; there is a group of such workers that can tie both economic and political demands together, and explain them to the rest of the workers. This is done by tying maximum and minimum wage to the need for better pay (a worker's demand), and linking both to similar models in foreign countries. Nonetheless, this process is not straightforward or easy as many workers would want to focus solely on the economic to be able to feed their families in harsh economic times.[86]

These contrasting views on the politicization of the labor movement illustrate how fragmented the movement is. Yet it is arguably clear that the workers' strikes from 2006 to 2011 were driven by economic demands; the dislike of the regime then affected the politicization of the demands of certain workers, predominantly those based in Mahallah, who have a long history of activism. This discrepancy will be further illustrated in the next section by showcasing how workers were involved in the 2011 uprising: some were involved in their professional capacity as workers while others were involved as private citizens.

The 2011 uprising

This section will focus on the events that unfolded in the lead up and during the 18 days of the uprising in 2011. Rather than provide a day-by-day anthology of the events, it will seek to showcase selected processes that unfolded within the context of social movement theory, and the interplay between elites, students, youth and workers.

Opportunity: Tunisian uprising

As previously outlined, the social movement literature has highlighted the impact of international and regional changes on social movements.[87] The Tunisian Revolution,[88] which started on December 18, 2010 and ended with the ouster and eventual flight of Tunisian President Zine El Abidine Ben Ali on January 14, 2011, arguably had a galvanizing effect on the Egyptian uprising. The local official papers intentionally kept their coverage of the events in Tunisia vague so as not to show that a neighboring authoritarian regime was being challenged to its core. Nonetheless, the advent of satellite television and ICT (Information and Communication Technology) platforms ultimately ended the state's ability to control information, and Egyptians were very closely watching on satellite television and on the Internet the events unfold in Tunisia.

This is corroborated by my own experience in the weeks before January 25, 2011, as seen in my own networks of family, friends, contacts, as well as online. Tunisia was being watched very closely by Egyptians, and in a way it showed that the people could challenge and indeed oust an authoritarian ruler in the Middle East. While this did not necessarily mean that those about to protest on January 25 expected their rallies in Tahrir and elsewhere would lead to the ouster of Mubarak, it did demonstrate that political and economic concessions might be gained from the regime through protests of a certain scale. The overthrow of Ben Ali could be construed as a regional political opportunity, which, according to Tarrow, provides "incentives for collective action by affecting people's expectations for success or failure."[89]

ICT was used to connect Tunisia and Egypt. After the ouster of Ben Ali and seeing the impartiality of the Tunisian army, the 'We Are All Khaled Said' Facebook page began to direct some of its posts to the Egyptian army and relate it to the events in Tunisia. The page made this post on January 15, one day after the ouster of Ben Ali and ten days before the planned protests in Egypt:

> All respect to the Tunisian army chief Rasheeh Ammar who absolutely refused to shoot the protestors and asked the army to defend the people. Egypt has tens and hundreds of Rasheeds, those who were willing to sacrifice themselves in the 1973 war to liberate the country. Believe me, our army is a patriotic army and most of the members of the army are with us in our cause. We need to move to make them stand by us as it happened in Tunisia.[90]

After the unprecedented turnout and events that unfolded on January 25, 2011, the Facebook page followed up with a post directed at army personnel:

> To all members of the Egyptian army on Facebook: I know that there are at least a thousand members of the army following this page. We are your brothers, we are fighting injustice and corruption. You have to go into the streets. Please be with us and say no to the injustice and corruption. Do not shoot your bullets against your brothers. The bullets should be used against an enemy, not against your brother. To all members of the Egyptian army, we are all citizens of this nation.[91]

While the impact of the Tunisian Revolution on the Egyptian uprising cannot be easily quantified, arguably it had further emboldened people in Egypt to take to the streets in January 2011. This was also reflected in the chants used. From January 25 onwards, pro-Tunisia chants would be heard in Tahrir and across Egypt: *thawra thawra hatta an-nasr; thawra fi Tunis; thawra fi Masr!* (Revolution until victory, revolution in Tunisia, revolution in Egypt!).[92] In clear processes of diffusion between Tunisian and Egyptian protestors, some of the chants that were used in Tunisia would be directly appropriated by the Egyptian protestors[93] such as *al-sha'b yurīd isqāt al-niẓām!* (The people want the fall of the regime!). That specific chant would go on to be chanted in Libya, Syria, Bahrain and Yemen.[94]

Opportunity: elite conflict

While it is unlikely that the 'We Are All Khaled Said' Facebook page had a direct impact on the army, the posts on the page highlight how the activists knew that the role of the army would be critical to the success or failure of the protests. O'Donnell and Schmitter postulate that "there is no transition whose beginning is not the consequence—direct or indirect—of important divisions within the authoritarian regime itself."[95] Such a split could be seen during the uprising, especially between the president and his inner core on one hand, and the military high command on the other. In O'Donnell and Schmitter's view, generally the military is unlikely to support the removal of authoritarian leader from power if they took part in repression.[96] This was not the case in 2011. After the police withdrew after clashes on January 28, the army was called in. The army went to considerable lengths to present itself as siding with the people, differentiating itself from the hated Ministry of the Interior, which was involved in battles with the protesters from January 25–28 and incriminated in various cases of abuse and torture in the decade before the uprising. Some army tanks and armored personnel carriers (APCs) were draped in Egyptian flags, some even allowed protestors to sit on their tanks, paint nationalist and anti-Mubarak graffiti on them, and army officers posed for photos with the protestors.[97] This was also reflected in the chants of the protestors: *el-gaysh wal-sha'b ayd waḥda!* (the army and the people are one hand!).[98] This illustrates how the protestors, at least during those 18 days, viewed the army. It became obvious that the military high command would not follow Mubarak blindly and would refuse orders to fire on protestors.

In the years before 2011, there were reports that the military high command viewed the rise of Gamal Mubarak with suspicion. US Embassy cables from Cairo published by Wikileaks confirm this view. After a secret meeting between Anwar Sadat's nephew, the parliamentarian Esmat el Sadat, and the embassy's political officer (POLOF), the US Embassy cabled the following to Washington in April 2007:

> Sadat noted to POLOF his assessment that the recently approved constitutional amendments package is largely aimed at ensuring Gamal Mubarak's succession of his father, and "a more controllable, stable political scene when he does take the reins." Opining that "Gamal and his clique" are becoming more confident in the inevitability of Gamal's succession, and are now angling to remove potential "stumbling blocks," Sadat said that speculation among Cairo's elite is that there could be a cabinet reshuffle as soon as May or June, in which Minister of Defense Tantawi and/or EGIS head Omar Suleiman would be replaced. "Those two are increasingly viewed as a threat by Gamal and those around him," and thus Gamal is reportedly pushing Mubarak to get them out of the way, so they "could not pose any

> problems" in the event of a succession. Sadat speculated that "hitches" to a Gamal succession could occur if Mubarak died before installing his son: "Gamal knows this, and so wants to stack the deck in his favor as much as possible now, while Mubarak is firmly in control, just in case his father drops dead sooner rather than later." Sadat said Tantawi had commented to him in a recent private meeting that, "he has had it 'up to here' with Gamal and his cronies, and the tremendous corruption they are facilitating."[99]

Other sources close to the military also corroborated the view that the high command was against the succession of Gamal Mubarak.[100] During the uprising, the army had begun to distance itself from the presidency. The Minister of Defense himself, Field Marshall Tantawi, went to Tahrir Square on January 30.[101] Egyptian fighter jets flew over Tahrir, prompting chants of support from the protestors. Mubarak had met SCAF (Supreme Council of the Armed Forces) that same day. The photos of that meeting were on the cover of *Al-Ahram* on February 1, 2011, and were arguably designed to show Mubarak in control of the military and sitting among its offers, but this was not really the case. Arguably, the protests in Tahrir Square and major urban centers, as well as the strikes that were beginning to occur across Egypt, pushed the military to finally support the ouster of Mubarak.

Mostafa Bakry, a journalist and parliamentarian with close contacts with the military, published a book titled *al-Gaysh wal-thawra: qiṣṣat al-ayyām al-akhīra* (The Army and the Revolution: The Story of the Last Days). While it is impossible to corroborate all the facts in the book, his assertions can be taken seriously due to his personal connections with Tantawi and Enan. Bakry reports that the decision to support the protetors, not Mubarak, was made in a secret meeting between Tantawi and members of SCAF on January 31. In that meeting, SCAF members drafted a communiqué to the public and made sure that it was broadcast live on television without the prior approval of Mubarak's Minister of Information, who was the eyes and ears of the presidency in the Maspero TV building.[102] The communiqué stated that "freedom of expression in peaceful manner is a right for everyone" and crucially that "the Armed Forces is *aware* of the people's legitimate demands." It concluded by saying that the army would never use force against the people. That communiqué could be construed as the first public expression of the elite schism. The key sentence here is "*aware* of the people's demands": the military's communiqué on February 10 showed a clear break with the presidency, using instead the phrase "*support* the people's legitimate demands." This change of terminology from 'aware' to 'support' denotes a conscious decision made within SCAF as it responded to events unfolding on the ground. The communiqué read by General Ismail Osman stated:

> Emanating from the responsibility of the Armed Forces and its responsibility to protect the people and care for his interests and security, and watching over the safety of the nation and the people, and the gains of the great

> Egyptian people and their property, and in confirmation and support of the people's legitimate demands, on Thursday 10th of February 2011, SCAF has convened to follow the developments. The council decided to be in continues meeting to see what can procedures and plans can be done to keep the nation safe and preserve the gains and the ambitions of the great Egyptian people.[103]

Finer argues that "the military's consciousness of themselves as a profession may lead them to see themselves as servants of the state [or nation] rather than of the government in power."[104] This could partially help explain why the military had abandoned Mubarak, first to preserve its privileges and second to preserve the existing social order. After the announcement by General Ismail Osman on television, SCAF continued to send unofficial messages to the protestors. SCAF general Hassan el Rowiny was seen walking freely amongst the people in Tahrir and was videotaped on February 5 saying cryptically, "don't worry, all your demands will be met."[105]

The elite schism between the presidency and the military would be a crucial factor in the ouster of Mubarak, which arguably would not have happened had the military not abandoned him. However, to give the military all the credit for the ouster of Mubarak is to deny the agency of the millions of protestors. Arguably, the protestors had shown the military that if it would stand by Mubarak, there would be a risk of bloodshed on an unimaginable scale.

Threat: regime repression

As previously argued, state repression can either suppress protest, or act as a powerful incentive to inflame protests. A variety of empirical studies have focused on the mobilizing impact of state repressive measures in semi- and non-democratic settings.[106] Almeida argues:

> Activists can use state repressive acts as empirical verifications of the unworthiness of state managers to rule as well as for motivational appeals within organizations and interorganizational units to participate in future protest actions. These organizational settings provide solidarity incentives, normative pressures, and shared activist identities to engage in high risk protest.... In addition, repressive acts grant occasions for emotionally charged focal events, such as funeral processions and homage ceremonies for fallen victims of state violence, to rally challengers.[107]

In the Egyptian context, this is relevant on two different levels. First, in the lead up to the uprising, various videos and photos of police brutality were disseminated on the Internet. This helped fuel the anger of everyday people and aided the grievance construction process used by the activists, who showed the brutality of the regime up close and personal. The case of Khaled Said in particular is pertinent. The photos of the light-skinned middle-class Khaled while alive, and the image of his body after the autopsy were particularly powerful. It sent the message that state repression was no longer predominantly directed at the subaltern classes, but that now repressive measures targeted even the more privileged middle-class youth.

At a second level, during the uprising itself police repression would help in mobilizing people. The first deaths at the hands of the police in Suez on January 25–26, 2011, mobilized the population of Suez to rise up against the police, attacking and torching several police stations. When the news reached Cairo, this helped further mobilized people on the 'Friday of Anger.' As highlighted by my personal experience in the Preface, many people were no longer afraid of the regime. State repression had the exact opposite effect of what it intended to do: it helped mobilize people in larger numbers.

Resource mobilization: use of technology and social media

The role of social media in the Arab uprisings, particularly Egypt, continues to generate considerable debate and scholarly interest. Much of the initial conceptualizations of the uprisings in the Western world were arguably simplistic, with descriptions such as the 'Facebook' and 'Twitter revolutions.' This made the uprisings more palatable in the Western world, showing a sanitized version of people's struggles, where the focus is mostly on middle-class urban youth on smartphones using social media to challenge the authority of the state.[108]

That noted, it is undeniable that the Internet played a role in mobilizing people during the January 25 uprising. In the decade before the uprising, Internet use was becoming more and more widespread, especially in urban areas. As previously discussed, the Palestinian Intifada, the Iraq War and the *Kefaya* movement had created political awareness and facilitated mobilizations unseen for decades. This was also occurring online; from 2005 onward, there was an explosion of blogs from leftist, Muslim Brotherhood and independent activists directly criticizing the regime. Crucially, blogs such as *al-Waʿi al-Miṣrī* (The Egyptian Conscience), run by journalist and activist Wael Abbas, began to show widely circulated leaked videos of police brutality. The effects of this online activism cannot be understated, as it gave people examples of police brutality in the working class (e.g., the torture of the driver Emad el Gelda) and the middle class (the case of Khaled Said). Similarly, social media was instrumental in magnifying the effects of the Tunisian revolution. El-Tantawy and Wiest argue:

> As Egyptians were carefully watching events unfold in Tunisia while also planning their own movement, activists from both countries were exchanging information, ideas, and words of encouragement online. During the Tunisian revolution, Egyptian bloggers were on Twitter, Facebook, and personal blogs posting updates and uploading images and videos of the Tunisian protests. On January 17, 2011, Egyptian female activist and blogger Nawara Negm posted a video message from an Egyptian actress with words of encouragement for Tunisians. Negm also posted information and cell

> phone numbers, urging Egyptians to send text messages to encourage Tunisians during the protests.[109]

El-Tantawy and Wiest's article at times overreaches to credit the uprising almost solely to the Internet, which is not the view of this book. However, the main gain from such technology was that it ultimately ended the state's ability to control information. Egyptians had grown up accustomed to tight control of the media, both on television and in print. Since the early 1990s, satellite television and the so-called 'Aljazeera' effect had begun challenging the authoritarian regime's ability to craft and control the messages to the population.[110] The Internet came and further disrupted (indeed outright destroyed) the regime's ability to act as information gatekeeper. Garrett identified three key mechanisms that highlight ICT's influence on social movements. ICTs

1 potentially link technology and participation;
2 reduce participation costs; and
3 promote a collective identity and the creation of community.[111]

All three mechanisms can be seen in the Egyptian context in the years leading up to 2011. The third mechanism is particularly pertinent. Egypt had a long history of labor and student activism, as discussed throughout the book; however, the ability of movements to connect with each other, as well as promote a sense of community, was severely restricted to its inability to communicate and publish. ICTs effectively changed this paradigm forever, as they facilitated the organization of networks.

In addition to helping form networks, ICTs had also impacted the mobilization for the uprising. The Facebook event of the Khaled Said Facebook page did indeed help mobilize people and direct them to Tahrir Square and other places of mobilization across Egypt. Similarly, the April 6 Facebook page, as well as the emotional YouTube video of activist Asmaa Mahfouz calling people to join the protests on January 25, did have a mobilizing impact. Wael Ghonim and other activists created an open Google Document titled "All You Need to Know about the Protests of the 25th of January." In the well-laid out documents, there were eight clear sections:

1 Who we are
2 Why are we protesting
3 What are our demands
4 Places and times of the protests
5 Guide how to protest
6 Important numbers in case of emergency
7 Important links
8 Who will be participating.[112]

The document was used and viewed hundreds of thousands of times. Interestingly, the people behind the organization of the protests were not expecting or demanding a revolution or the ouster of Mubarak. The 'demands' section called only for more jobs, cancelling the emergency laws, changing the Minister of Interior Habib el Adli, and limits on presidential terms.[113] There was no mention of the ouster of Mubarak. As the protests unfolded over the 18 days, protestors were emboldened by their success and only then upped their demands to *al-sha'b yurīd isqāt al-niẓām!* (The people demand the ouster of the regime).

The size of the protests came as a shock to the government. After the success of the initial mobilization on January 25, the regime ordered the shutdown of the Internet and cellular phone networks on January 28. The shutdown of the Internet, instead of de-mobilizing people, helped further mobilize them.[114] The debate on exactly how much social media has contributed to the uprisings in the Arab world is likely to continue. This book acknowledges the role it played, but postulates that reducing causality in the Egyptian uprising to social media is reductionist, to say the least. As Gunning and Zvi Baron conclude:

> The Uprising was clearly not a "Facebook" Revolution in that hundreds of thousands were mobilised offline and those who were online needed additional triggers to translate their online support into offline participation in street protests. Nevertheless, social media played a significant role in creating online protest communities, facilitating informational cascades about regime failure and protest frames, communicating the protests and providing (at least the perception of) a level of protection through broadcasting police abuses.[115]

The Revolutionary Youth Coalition (RYC)

The formation of the RYC was another example of the cross-ideological networking in the student movement that had been occurring between students in the decade and a half before. Many Muslim Brotherhood activists, such as Mohammed el Qasas, Islam Lotfy and Mohammed Abbas, had known secular and leftist activists like Ziad el Elimy and Ahmad Ezzat from their student activism days. During the 18 days of the uprising, a coalition was formed to bring together activists from the Muslim Brotherhood, Nasserites, 6th of April, the Revolutionary Socialists, El Baradei supporters and the activists behind the 'We Are All Khaled Said' page together to form a cohesive block.[116] Mohammad Qasas describes some of the networking that was occurring on the ground in Tahrir:

> The relationship between us and the other student activists from other currents goes a long way back. I am of the older generation. Islam Lotfy and Mohammed Abbas are a bit younger. So you have more than one generation within the University from different political bloc, so it was easy to link up and work together on the coalition. After pitched battles with the police on the January 28th, we successfully reached Tahrir Square, we [Khaled, Ziad,

> Islam Lotfy] started organizing ourselves and working with the 6th of April group.
>
> Before 25 January 2011, we held preparatory meetings were we discussed our plans and started recruiting people we know from among the MB youth. But on 25 January we started to adopt a more detailed structure to the group in preparation for the protests on 28 January. We also planned marches/protests for 26 January in case the square was cleared out by the end of 25 January. We joined the huge protests on 28 January and we were amongst the first group of activists to think of holding the first million man march on Tuesday 1 February. Each political bloc had one or two representatives. We drafted a list of thirteen members in addition to three independent members. That was the shape the coalition was emerging as, and we announced to the public on 5 February from within the Square.[117]

This coalition would grow to prominence during the uprising, and in the period immediately following it, when it met with SCAF members to outline the demands of the youth. Some of its members, like Ziad el Eliemy, would enter into parliament in 2012. The collaboration between youth activists from different ideological backgrounds is a trend not only in Egypt, but also regionally. Murphy argues that Arab youth activists across the region "continue to reject the impermeable ideological boundaries of the previous generations. They have forged rainbow coalitions and lobby groups, which draw in activists from diverse political parties."[118]

However, highlighting the limitations of such cross-ideological cooperation after the ouster of Mubarak, the RYC would disband and activists would go back to supporting their mother organizations, as well as form new parties for those who broke with their organizations during the uprising. Abdelrahman concludes that despite some networking activities during the uprising and the period right after,

> neither the RYC nor any other coalitions managed to create abroad-based alliance or to give rise to any other form of organization which could claim a meaningful degree of representation … One major problem facing these coalitions is that they were formed along binary secular/Islamist lines as a focal point of unity among disparate groups.[119]

Despite efforts to blur these sharp lines, they would continue and would prove disastrous to Egypt's transition to democracy in 2013 with the ouster of Mohamed Morsi.

Spillover and diffusion between workers and students

In the decade leading up to 2011, there was contact between the students and the workers, but it had happened in a haphazard way, and only became more organized after April 6, 2008. Ahmad Ezzat, the student leader from the Revolutionary Socialists, argued:

> The relationship between the workers' movement and the student movement was different from that of the 1970s, where student were seen leading marches from inside the factories. The relationship in 2000s was complementary in that students would raise awareness about the workers plight outside of the sit-in, through writing articles in the socialist paper, for example. They would also show their solidarity by joining the sit-ins and bringing blankets…
>
> The student movements have always showed their solidarity with workers' movements by visiting them at their sit-ins and joining their protests. But both movements have not fully integrated up to this day. For several reasons, there did not exist real cooperation. The absence of true organization for the workers' movement in Egypt has resulted in the fact that economic demands were never tied to political demands. As a result, politicians hijacked the workers' call for a strike in Mahalla in 2008, and turned it into a general strike.[120]

On the workers' side, many viewed the students and the youth as engaged in futile protest against the regime. Abdel Hamid, the worker from Mahallah, described how the workers viewed the youth groups:

> At first the workers used to mock the student and youth groups, wonder what they have to offer. They didn't realize that young people are initiators of change. That's because some workers view their sons and daughters as a bunch of kids, not adults.… When workers see that political forces are protesting against the entire country/regime, not against a specific leadership, they refuse to join force. For example, we joined forces when people were calling for minimum wage, although the law would harm us, because we have already surpassed it. But it stood because it is a general demand that will benefit the next generation.[121]

The activists behind the 'We Are All Khaled Said' Facebook page, having seen the success of the mobilization in urban areas, began to call directly for the participation of the workers, as well as the students. On February 7, 2011, the page posted:

> The revolution is not demonstrations and protests only. The revolution is legitimate and it is imposed by the people. And this long confrontation with the regime is in our favor because the system's defenses are collapsing. So why don't the labor unions and student unions start to choose their own representatives rather than the current fake representatives?[122]

The call was an attempt by the activists to rally the workers, some of whom had gone on strike, while others combined work with protesting. When asked what his crew did throughout the 2011 uprising, Abdel Hamid answered:

> I went to work everyday and the factory was running. We were following the news, but we were adamant on continuing our work because that was our role. We supported the sit-in but that did not mean we had to ruin our work. Some must work while others protest. Workers would join the protests after their shift ended.[123]

Abdel Hamid's testimony suggests that he was part of the group of workers that viewed their activism within a moral economy prism; that is, that their struggle contained and focused on gaining and protecting their economic rights. In all the worker interviews conducted, a majority supported that view, while more politicized workers viewed themselves as part of the larger opposition movement against Mubarak. This points to a main difference between the worker and the youth movements in 2011. Workers tend to come from disadvantaged socio-economic backgrounds and thus are primarily concerned with bread and butter issues. Middle-class urban-based activists tend to be better off than the workers, and therefore have the luxury to be able to protest. Also, university students, by virtue of the time they have during their studies and their exposure on campus to different ideas, are arguably more open to becoming more politically active. In Mahallah, many of the workers interviewed took pride in the fact that their machines never stopped and they continued producing, but joined the protests in their individual capacity after their shift ended. Kamal Abbas and other union leaders used the uprising to form an independent union and called for the disbanding of the GFETU and forming the Egyptian Federation of Independent Trade Unions (EFITU). He recalled:

> Having seen the uprising unfold around me in Tahrir Square, I called for the meeting on January 30, 2011. The idea initially was not to create a union. After 25 and 28 January, I wanted the workers to join the protests not as individuals but as a movement. Also at the time the government-backed union was releasing statements in support of the regime. The idea behind this meeting was to create an authority whose task is to collectively mobilize workers nationwide to join the revolution.
>
> When we sat down there were representatives from the Health Technology Syndicate (where the meeting was held), the Real Estate Tax and Pensions Syndicate. These were the only independent syndicates under Mubarak. In addition to that some labor leaders from Helwan, Mahalla and Sadat City joined. After the discussion, some of the participants proposed announcing the formation of an independant union, the Egyptian Federation of Independent Trade Unions [EFITU].
>
> We organized a committee to prepare for the formation of the union, and subsequent statements came out representing/signed by the new entity. Our mission was to distribute the statements in a number of factories with the goal to bring workers into the revolution and encourage them to strike. This worked as you started to see strikes in Mahalla and within the steel factories, for example. There was discussion around some companies affiliate with the Suez Canal Authority joining as well.[124]

Starting from February 6–7, 2011, strikes began occurring in several factories across Egypt. Beinin writes:

> Facilitated by the government's closure of all workplaces in early February, many workers participated in the popular uprising as individuals. On February 6 they returned to their jobs; just two days later, EFITU called for a general strike demanding that Hosni Mubarak relinquish power. Tens of thousands of workers—including those employed at large and strategic workplaces like the Cairo Public Transport Authority, Egyptian State Railways, the subsidiary companies of the Suez Canal Authority, the state electrical company, and Ghazl al-Mahalla—answered the call, engaging in some 60 strikes and protests in the final days before Mubarak's fall on February 11.[125]

It is impossible to prove the motivations of each individual worker, especially whether the strikes were economically or politically motivated. But it could be argued that as a whole, having seen the events of Tahrir Square unfold in the early days of the uprisings, some workers who went on strike at factories moved as a 'movement' as Kamal Abbas claimed, while others joined in their individual capacity. When asked about the involvement of Mahallah workers on January 25 in Shoun Square (the Tahrir of Mahallah), Hamdy Hussein said, "As for the workers, some of them had come out in an organized fashion, while others joined the protests as individuals."[126] Asked about what he did during January 25 and afterwards, Sayyed Abū el Suʿūd, a union leader in Alexandria, said:

> On 25 January in the morning I was at work, and at night I was at home with my family. We knew what was happening in Cairo, we had heard. I spent 25–27 January at work as I could not leave, but on 28 January there was no escape. I skipped work for 11 days from then on.... In Alexandria, we did not join the marches as workers, or any political group. We all joined as Egyptians. The company did not close; it worked on 15 to 20 percent capacity. Some workers stayed at home while others were in the squares.[127]

Regardless of why they joined, they would have a decisive impact: the military and civilian elites in Cairo now saw that the uprising was not only urban and middle class based, but was now spreading to rural and working-class areas and factories. Bienin argues that

> on February 9, Kamal ʿAbbas, abandoning the "bread and butter" approach he insisted on during the previous decade, called on workers to strike in support of the demand to oust Mubarak. According to the Sons of the Land Centre for Human rights the worker strikes which occurred in the last days of the uprising was detrimental in the decision of the Military to finally abandon Mubarak.[128]

To reiterate, the haphazard networking between the movements illuminates a point within the context of social movement theory, specifically framing and the process of grievance construction. It is clear that the urban-based student and youth activists engaged in anti-regime protests in the decade before 2011 had framed their grievances within the context of a pro-democracy, anti-authoritarian and anti-torture context. The workers had framed their grievances within a socio-economic context. In the final years of the Mubarak regime, they developed what Snow and Benford term a "master-frame,"[129] which denotes an overarching frame that can be used by several movements. The master-frame became the opposition to the Mubarak regime, and it encompassed political, social and economic elements. The conversion of demands could be seen in one of the main chants raised during the uprising: *'aysh! ḥurriya! 'adāla ijtimā'iyya!* (bread, freedom, social justice!), which ingeniously combines the economic (bread) with the political (freedom) with the socio-economic (social justice). The disunity that has unfolded between all the movements that participated in the 2011 uprising points to a lack of master-frame post-Mubarak. The success of any future Egyptian mobilization will partially depend on the construction of a new master-frame to facilitate any future democratic transformation in Egypt.

Notes

1 "IMF Executive Board Concludes 2010 Article IV Consultation with the Arab Republic of Egypt" (Washington: IMF, April 2010), www.imf.org/external/np/sec/pn/2010/pn1049.htm (accessed October 1, 2014).
2 Galal Amin, "Nothing Trickles Down," *Daily Star Egypt*, November 15, 2007.
3 Ray Bush and David Seddon, "Editorial: North Africa in Africa," *Review of African Political Economy* 26, no. 82 (December 1999): 435–439.
4 Anton Dobronogov and Farrukh lqbal, *Economic Growth in Egypt: Constraints and Determinants*, World Bank Working Paper Series No. 42, October (Washington, DC: World Bank, 2005), http://siteresources.worldbank.org/INTMENA/Resources/WP42SEPTEMBER2006.pdf (accessed October 1, 2014).
5 UNDP, *Egypt Human Development Report 2003*, The United Nations Development Program in Cairo and the Institute of National Planning (Cairo: UNDP, 2003), 16.
6 OECD, *African Economic Outlook: Egypt*, 2003, 123, www.oecd.org/countries/egypt/2498037.pdf (accessed October 1, 2014).
7 Tamer Mostafa, "Protests Hint at New Chapter in Egyptian Politics," *MERIP*, April 9, 2004, www.merip.org/mero/mero040904?ip_login_no_cache=f78b5695fa9cbcb6e47487aa2a7f37b6 (accessed October 1, 2014).
8 UNDP, *Egypt Human Development Report 2008* (Cairo: UNDP, 2008), 32.
9 Ibid.
10 Ibid. There are a variety of ways to show inequality levels and varying standards of living. The Gini index popularized by Dalton (1920) is the most extensively used measure of welfare distribution. See Sami Bibi and Mustapha Nabili, *Equity and Inequality in the Arab World*, Economic Research Forum PRR No. 33, February (Cairo: ERF, 2010), www.erf.org.eg/CMS/uploads/pdf/PRR33.pdf (accessed October 1, 2014).
11 UNDP, *Egypt Human Development Report 2008* (Cairo: UNDP, 2008), 303.
12 Hassan Qamhawy, *al-iṣlāḥ al-iqtiṣādī: ingazaa't haqiqiya aw farīda gha' iba?* (The Economic Reform: Real Achievements or Absent Duty?), *Al-Ahrām Al-Iqtiṣādī*, December 31, 2001, http://economic.ahram.org.eg/Ahram/2001/12/31/INVE1.HTM (accessed October 1, 2014).

13 Ibid.

14 "Egyptian Minister of Solidarity Abdel Khaleq Will Also Take on Food Prices in Latest Reshuffling," *Al Ahram Online*, December 3, 2011, http://english.ahram.org.eg/NewsContent/3/12/28359/Business/Economy/Egyptian-Minister-of-Solidarity-Abdel-Khaleq-will-.aspx (acessed October 1, 2014).

15 Personal interview, Cairo, August 5, 2013. Anecdotally, the electricity cut when I was in the elevator heading up to meet Dr. Abdel Khaleq, and I was stuck there for hours until I was freed. Dr. Abdel Khaleq was very sympathetic to my plight and was very hospitable (perhaps a reflection on his own views on social justice), granting me a lot more time than was originally allocated for the meeting, as well as food and copious amounts of tea.

16 Ibid., 12.

17 "Mubarak-Era Prime Minister Atef Ebeid Dead at 82," *The Cairo Post*, September 2014, http://thecairopost.com/news/124779/news/mubarak-era-prime-minister-atef-ebeid-dead-at-82 (accessed October 1, 2014).

18 Ahmad al-Said al-Naggar, *Kashf hisāb Atef Ebied* (Balance Sheet for Atef Ebied) (Cairo: Al Ahram, 2004), 7.

19 Ibid., 7–9.

20 A.M. Lesch, "Egypt's Spring: Causes of the Revolution," *Middle East Policy* 18, no. 3 (2011): 35.

21 See Safinaz El Tarouty, "Reinventing the Party: Reform and Internal Dynamics of Egypt's National Democratic Party," *PSI Papers in Culture, Ideas and Policy*, University of East Anglia Working Paper 2 (2008), www.uea.ac.uk/polopoly_fs/1.103897!s%20el-tarouty%20final%20dec%202.pdf (accessed October 1, 2014).

22 Joshua Stacher, *Adaptable Autocrats: Regime Power in Egypt and Syria* (Stanford: Stanford University Press, 2012), 103–106.

23 The new cabinet represented the 'all-star' team of neoliberal economic thought and practice in Egypt. Mahmoud Mohiedin became Minister of Investment. Youssef Boutros Ghali, who had started his career as an economist at the IMF, became Minister of Finance. Rashid Mohammed Rashid, an ultra-wealthy Egyptian entrepreneur and head of Unilever in the MENA region and also member of the Policies Secertariat, became Minister of Industry and International Trade. Amin Abaza, another ultra-wealthy Egyptian agriculture entrepreneur, became Minister of Agriculture. Mohammad Mansour, the Egyptian tycoon who owned represented and manufactured on behalf of multinationals such as Caterpillar and Chevrolet, became Minister of Transportation. Ahmad el Maghraby, Mansour's cousin, and a business tycoon in his own right in real estate, became Minister of Housing. Zuhier Garanah, owner of one of Egypt's largest travel companies and hotel chains, became Minister of Tourism. Dr. Hatem el Gabaly, owner of Egypt's largest and most exclusive private hospital, became Minster of Health. In addition to Mahmoud Mohiedien, Dr. El Gabaly would be among the few in the Cabinet who was not arrested and charged with corruption after 2011. See Lesch, "Egypt's Spring."

24 For a full analysis of the 2005 presidential and parliamentary elections, see Yoram Meital, "The Struggle over Political Order in Egypt: The 2005 Elections," *The Middle East Journal* (2006): 257–279.

25 Steven Cook, *Ruling but Not Governing: The Military and Political Development in Egypt, Algeria and Turkey* (New York: Johns Hopkins University Press, 2007), 148.

26 See Tarek Masoud, "The Road to (and from) Liberation Square," *Journal of Democracy* 22, no. 3 (2011): 20–34.

27 Personal interview, Cairo, February 7, 2013.

28 Personal interview, Cairo, February 1, 2013.

29 Personal interview, Cairo, February 8, 2013.

30 Soliman, *The Autumn of Dictatorship*, 154.

31 Muḥammad Shabāb, *Maḥmoud el Gammal: Nahb al-arḍī fī himāyat al-niẓām*

(Mahmoud el Gammal: The Robbery of Land with the Protection of the Regime), *al Wafd*, February 17, 2011.

32 Sung Un Kim, "Egypt Court Sentences Former Housing Minister for Corruption," *Jurist*, March 30, 2012, http://jurist.org/paperchase/2012/03/egypt-court-sentences-former-housing-minister-for-corruption.php (accessed October 1, 2014).

33 M. Lagi, K.Z. Bertrand, and Y. Bar-Yam, "The Food Crises and Political Instability in North Africa and the Middle East," *New England Complex Systems Institute* (August 10, 2011).

34 "Let Them Eat Baklava: Today's Policies are Recipes for Instability in the Middle East," *The Economist*, March 17, 2012.

35 Ahmad Badr, Enas Zakarareya and Mohamed Saleh, "Impact of Global Economic Crisis on Tourism Sector in Egypt: A System Dynamics Approach," *Information and Decision Support Center (IDSC)*, Economic Issues Program (EIP), Egyptian Cabinet (2009).

36 Tamer Mansour, "Egypt and the Financial Crisis," *Faculty of Economics and Political Science Paper*, Cairo University (December 2011), 7, http://mpra.ub.uni-muenchen.de/37370/2/MPRA_paper_37370.pdf (accessed October 1, 2014).

37 Ibid., 17.

38 Samuel Huntington, *The Solider and the State: The Theory and Politics of Civil-Military Relations* (Cambridge, MA: Harvard University Press, 1985 edn), 2.

39 Ibid., 3.

40 Peter Feaver, *Armed Servants: Agency, Oversight, and Civil-Military Relations* (Cambridge, MA: Harvard University Press, 2005), 149.

41 Huntington, *Soldier and the State*, 80–83.

42 Ibid., 70.

43 For an alternative view, see Samuel E. Finer, *The Man on Horseback: The Role of the Military in Politics* (New York: Praeger, 1962) and Morris Janowitz, *The Military in the Political Development of New Nations* (Chicago: University of Chicago Press, 1964).

44 See Khaled Fahmy, *All the Pasha's Men: Mehmed Ali, His Army and the Making of Modern Egypt* (Cairo: American University in Cairo Press, 2002).

45 Eric Nordlinger, *Soldiers in Politics: Military Coups and Governments* (Englewood Cliffs: Prentice Hall, 1977), 78.

46 Martin Needler, *The Problem of Democracy in Latin America* (Lexington: Lexington Books, 1987), 59.

47 John Waterbury, *Egypt: Burdens of the Past, Options for the Future*, (Bloomington: Indiana University Press, 1978), 267.

48 Hinnebusch, *Egyptian Politics Under Sadat*, 125.

49 Roger Owen, *State, Power and Politics in the Making of the Modern Middle East* (London: Routledge, 2000), 203.

50 Ayubi, *Overstating the State*, 275.

51 Zeinab Abul Magd, "The Army and the Economy in Egypt," *Jadaliyya*, December 23, 2011, www.jadaliyya.com/pages/index/3732/the-army-and-the-economy-in-egypt (accessed October 1, 2014).

52 Nordlinger, *Soldiers in Politics*, 22.

53 Abul Magd, "Army and Economy in Egypt."

54 Ivan Watson and Mohamed Fadel Fahmy, "Army Officers Join Cairo Protest," *CNN*, April 9, 2011, http://edition.cnn.com/2011/WORLD/meast/04/08/egypt.protests (accessed October 1, 2014).

55 See David S. Meyer, Nancy Whittier and Belinda Robnett (eds.), *Social Movements: Identity, Culture and the State* (Oxford: Oxford University Press, 2002).

56 Personal interview, February 25, 2013.

57 Khaled Dawoud, "Message to the 'Castle'," *Al Ahram Online*, September 13–19, 2001, http://weekly.ahram.org.eg/2001/551/eg4.htm (accessed October 1, 2014).

58 Ibid.
59 Amira Howeidy, "Solidarity," *Al Ahram Online*, April 4–10, 2002, http://weekly.ahram.org.eg/2002/580/eg4.htm (accessed October 1, 2014).
60 Personal interview, February 25, 2013.
61 David Snow and Robert Benford, "Master Frames and Cycles of Protest," in A.D. Morris and C.M. Mueller (eds.), *Frontiers in Social Movement Theory* (New Haven: Yale University Press, 1992), 137.
62 Robert Benford and David Snow, "Framing Processes and Social Movements: An Overview and Assessment," *Annual Review of Sociology* 26 (2000): 612.
63 Robert Bowker, *Egypt and the Politics of Change in the Arab Middle East* (London: Edward Elgar, 2010), 170–171.
64 Personal interview, February 25, 2013.
65 Jeroen Gunning and Illan Zvi Baron, *Why Occupy a Square: People, Protests and Movements in the Egyptian Revolution* (London: Hurst and Co, 2013), 56.
66 Steven Lee Myers, "Egypt Sanctions Massive Demonstration Against Iraq War," *New York Times*, February 28, 2003.
67 Personal interview, April 18, 2013.
68 Angela Joya, "The Egyptian Revolution: Crisis of Neoliberalism and the Potential for Democratic Politics," *Review of African Political Economy* 38, no. 129 (September 2011): 369.
69 El-Mahdy and Marfleet, "Introduction," 11.
70 Personal interview, Cairo, March 28, 2013.
71 Gunning and Baron, *Why Occupy a Square*, 41.
72 For an elaboration on that argument, see Anthony Oberschall, *Social Conflict and Social Movements* (Englewood Cliffs: Prentice Hall, 1973).
73 Gunning and Baron, *Why Occupy a Square*, 41.
74 Sarah Wolff, "Constraints on the Promotion of the Rule of Law in Egypt: Insights from the 2005 Judges' Revolt," *Democratization* 16, no. 1 (2009): 100–118.
75 Joel Beinin, "Workers' Struggles under 'Socialism' and Neoliberalism," in Rabab El-Mahdi and Philip Marfleet (eds.), *Egypt: The Moment of Change* (London: Zed Press, 2009), 79.
76 Maha Abdelrahman, "In Praise of Organization: Egypt between Activism and Revolution," *Development and Change* 44 (2013): 577.
77 Hisham Fouad, personal interview, Cairo, March 20, 2013.
78 Joel Beinin, "The Militancy of Mahalla al Kubra," *MERIP*, September 27, 2007, www.merip.org/mero/mero092907 (accessed October 1, 2014).
79 Osman El Sharnoubi, "Revolutionary History Relived: The Mahalla Strike of 6 April 2008," *Al Ahram Online*, April 6, 2013, http://english.ahram.org.eg/NewsContent/1/64/68543/Egypt/Politics-/Revolutionary-history-relived-The-Mahalla-strike-o.aspx (accessed October 1, 2014).
80 Personal interview, Mahallah, March 30, 2013.
81 Robert Dreyfuss, "Who's Behind Egypt's Revolt?" *The Nation*, www.thenation.com/blog/158159/whos-behind-egypts-revolt (accessed October 1, 2014).
82 Personal interview, Mahallah, March 30, 2013.
83 Ibid.
84 Personal interview, Mahallah, March 31, 2013.
85 Personal interview, Cairo, March 24, 2013.
86 Personal interview, Mahallah, March 30, 2013.
87 See Anthony Oberschall, "Oppurtunities and Framing in the Eastern European Revolts of 1989," in Doug McAdam, John D. McCarthy and Mayer N. Zald (eds), *Comparative Prespectives on Social Movements* (Cambridge: Cambridge University Press, 1996), 93–121.
88 The term 'Revolution' is used here rather than uprising, as arguably in the Tunisian case there was a transformational change of the political system after 2011, unlike Egypt.

89 Tarrow, *Power in Movement*, 85.
90 Translated in Hani Shehada, "Social Movement 2.0: An Analysis of Mobilization Through Facebook in the 2011 Egyptian Revolution" (M.A. thesis, International Institute of Social Studies, Netherlands, 2012), 31.
91 Ibid., 31–32.
92 My personal observations in Tahrir Square and other protest locations, Cairo, January 25–February 11, 2011.
93 Rashid Khalidi, "Reflections on the Revolutions in Tunisia and Egypt," *Foreign Policy*, February 25, 2011.
94 See Gilbert Achcar, *The People Want: A Radical Exploration of the Arab Uprising* (London: Saqi Books, 2013).
95 Guillermo O'Donnell and Philippe C. Schmitter, *Transitions from Authoritarian Rule* (Baltimore: Johns Hopkins University Press, 1986), 19.
96 Ibid., 35.
97 My personal observations of the protests, Tahrir Square, Cairo, January 30, 2011.
98 Ibid.
99 US Embassy Cairo, Cable 07CAIRO974, *Prominent Independent MP on Presidential Succession*, April 4, 2007, https://wikileaks.org/cable/2007/04/07CAIRO974.html (accessed October 1, 2014).
100 See Abdel Latif al-Manawy, *al-Ayyām al-akhīra al-niẓām Mubarak: 18 Yawm* (The Final Days of the Mubarak Regime: 18 Days) (Cairo: al-Dār al-Maṣriyya al-Libnāniyya, 2012).
101 Egypt Independent Staff, "Egypt's Minister of Defense Joins Protesters in Tahrir Square," *Egypt Independent*, January 30, 2011, www.egyptindependent.com/news/egypts-minister-defense-joins-protesters-tahrir-square (accessed October 1, 2014).
102 Mostafa Bakry, *al-Jaysh wal-thawra: qiṣṣat al-ayyām al-akhīra* (The Army and the Revolution: The Story of the Last Days) (Cairo: Akhbar Al Youm, 2011), 204.
103 Egypt State Information Service, 1st Announcement by SCAF, www.sis.gov.eg/Ar/Templates/Articles/tmpArticles.aspx?ArtID=44081 (accessed October 1, 2014).
104 Finer, *The Man on Horseback*, 25.
105 "General Hassan al Roiny speaking to the Protestors in Tahrir Square," *Al Ahram Gate Online*, February 6, 2011.
106 See Marwan Khawaja, "Repression and Popular Collective Action: Evidence from the West Bank," *Sociological Forum* 8, no. 1 (1993): 47–71; Ronald Francisco, "The Relationship between Coercion and Protest: An Empirical Evaluation in Three Coercive States," *Journal of Conflict Resolution* 39, no. 2 (1995): 263–281; Mara Loveman, "High-Risk Collective Action: Defending Human Rights in Chile, Uruguay, and Argentina," *American Journal of Sociology* 104, no. 2 (1998): 477–525; and Mark Beissinger, *Nationalist Mobilization and the Collapse of the Soviet State: A Tidal Approach to the Study of Nationalism* (Cambridge: Cambridge University Press, 2001).
107 Paul Almeida, "Opportunity Organizations and Threat-Induced Contention: Protest Waves in Authoritarian Settings," *American Journal of Sociology* 109, no. 2 (September 2003): 353–354.
108 See Rabab el Mahdy, "Orientalising the Egyptian Uprising," *Jadaliyya*, April 11, 2011, www.jadaliyya.com/pages/index/1214/orientalising-the-egyptian-uprising (accessed October 1, 2014).
109 Nahed El Tantawy and Julie Wiest, "Social Media in the Egyptian Revolution: Reconsidering Resource Mobilization Theory," *International Journal of Communication* 5 (2011): 1214.
110 See Mohammed El-Nawawy and Adel Iskander, *Al-Jazeera: The Story of the Network That is Rattling Governments and Redefining Modern Journalism* (Boulder: Westview, 2003), Hugh Miles, *Al-Jazeera: The Inside Story of the Arab News Channel that is Challenging the West* (New York: Grove Press, 2005), Abdallah

Schleifer, "The Impact of Arab Satellite Television on Prospects for Democracy in the Arab World," *Transnational Broadcasting Studies* 15 (2006) and Mohamed Zayani (ed.), *The Al Jazeera phenomenon: Critical Perspectives on New Arab Media* (Boulder: Paradigm Publishers, 2005). For examples of how Arab states like Egypt, Jordan and the UAE are attempting regain control of the media space see Emma C. Murphy, "The Arab State and (Absent) Civility in New Communicative Spaces," *Third World Quarterly* 32, no. 5 (2011): 959–980.

111 Kelly Garret, "Protest in an Information Society: A Review of Literature on Social Movements and New ICTs," *Information, Communication and Society* 9, no. 2 (2006): 204.

112 Anonymous, *Kul ma turīd an taʿrifah ʿan thawrat 25 yanayer* (All You Need to Know About the 25th of January Revolution), Cairo, January 2011, https://docs.google.com/document/d/1qU3TnumUD5ZzZN9CEBbDRIzNvcjbOtJX5CkcBcC9OjI/preview?sle=true (accessed October 1, 2014).

113 Ibid.

114 See Tim Eaton, "Internet Activism and the Egyptian Uprisings: Transforming Online Dissent into the Offline World," *Westminster Papers in Communication and Culture* 9, no. 2 (April 2013): 3–23.

115 Gunning and Baron, *Why Occupy a Square*, 302.

116 Salmah Shukrallah, "Egypt Revolution Youth Form National Coalition," *Al Ahram Online*, February 9, 2011, http://english.ahram.org.eg/t/NewsContent/1/64/5257/Egypt/Politics-/Coalition-of-The-Revolutions-Youth-assembled.aspx (accessed October 1, 2014).

117 Personal interview, Cairo, January 20, 2013.

118 Emma C. Murphy, "Problematizing Arab Youth: Generational Narratives of Systemic Failure," *Mediterranean Politics* 17, no. 1 (2012): 18.

119 Abdelrahman, "In Praise of Organization," 581.

120 Personal interview, Cairo, February 25, 2013.

121 Personal interview, Cairo, March 31, 2013.

122 Translated in Shehada, "Social Movement 2.0," 33.

123 Personal interview, Cairo, March 31, 2013.

124 Personal interview, Cairo, March 24, 2013.

125 Joel Beinin, "The Rise of Egypt's Workers," *Carnegie Papers* (June 2012), 7.

126 Personal interview, Cairo, March 30, 2013.

127 Personal interview, Alexandria, April 6, 2013.

128 Beinin, "Rise of Egypt's Workers," 7–8.

129 David Snow and Robert Benford, "Master Frames and Cycles of Protest," in A.D. Morris and C.M. Mueller (eds.), *Frontiers in Social Movement Theory* (New Haven: Yale University Press, 1992), 133–155.

Conclusion

> One thing that the IMF has learned as a result of the Arab transition is that numbers do not tell the whole story and we have to really examine precisely what is behind the numbers. Who benefits from growth? Who benefits from subsidies? How are the fruits of growth allocated in a particular country?
>
> Christine Lagarde, Head of the IMF, 2012[1]

Contemporary Egyptian history has shown that successful mobilizations occur when social movements come together to challenge the state. While the concept of success or failure is subjective, in this case when social movements achieve their demands, even in part, it is considered a success. From 1919 to 2011, this book has shown that indeed both the labor and student movements were able to get some of their grievances partially addressed. My ambition was not to show a continuous and simplistic line of historical mobilization over nine decades, but rather to understand Egyptian mobilizations and the dynamics between the labor and student movements within the context of the socio-economic and political conditions of the respective eras investigated.

The political economy context of mobilizations

Social movements do not operate in vacuums, but rather act and react to the political economy dynamics surrounding them. In the pre-1952 era, economic conditions were part of the motivation for mobilizations, but the main driver of protests at the time was the anti-colonial struggle. Having said that, the struggle for economic self-determination cannot be ignored. Within the broader nationalist movement, Egyptian workers had mobilized and protested to demand better wages and improved working conditions. The dominant role of foreigners in the Egyptian economy was arguably one of the key rallying calls for the anti-colonial struggle.[2]

The 1979 'Bread Intifada' was a direct reaction to the economic austerity measures undertaken by the Sadat regime under the auspices of the World Bank. Similarly, during the Mubarak era, economic factors created the conditions for Egypt's most successful mobilization to date. Structural adjustment policies and the focus on GDP growth at the expense of human development directly contributed to the downfall of Mubarak. As noted by IMF head Christine Lagarde, growth figures do not tell the whole story. The debate between a pure focus on GDP growth versus a focus on human development needs to be further engaged with in Egypt if some of the root causes of the 2011 uprising are to be addressed.

Opportunities and threats for the Egyptian labor and student movements

When political opportunities opened up, both the labor and student movements were able to take advantage of them. Domestic political opportunities—such as institutional access—have been an important and formative break for movements, providing avenues for growth and organization, however limited. During the Sadat era, the regime's willingness to provide increased access to Islamist students at the expense of leftist students was an opportunity for the Islamist groups to broaden their support base on campus, and across Egypt in general.

Regime weakness is another political opportunity that provides social movements with a chance to mobilize. The Egyptian defeat in the 1967 War revealed a fundamental weakness of the Nasser regime and the gap between its militant rhetoric and actual performance in military engagement against Israel. When the regime used senior air force generals as scapegoats for the Egyptian defeat, worker and student protests erupted against the Nasser regime, highlighting that following the 1967 defeat, the aura of invincibility and infallibility of the regime had been greatly diminished.

Further, elite conflict presents an opportunity for regime challengers to pursue their demands. The discord between Mubarak and the army during the 2011 uprising provided impetus for mobilizations not only for the labor and student movements, but also for all the individuals and groups that participated in the 2011 uprising. As the protests spread across the country, the Egyptian army began distancing itself more and more from the presidency. Arguably, increased protests and the threat of nationwide strikes had pushed the army high command to end its support of Mubarak.

Changes in the international environment also create opportunities for mobilization of wide segments of Egyptian society, including the labor and student movements. The lead-up to World War II, and the weakening of British colonial power, created the conditions for the anti-colonial movement to advance their demands. Approximately seven decades later, the Tunisian uprising and the early successes of the Tunisian people against Ben Ali helped inspire a similar mobilization of the Egyptian people against the Mubarak regime. In this regard, ICTs have played an increasingly important role not only in the dissemination of dissent between Tunisia and Egypt, but in Egypt itself during the 18 days of the uprising.

In terms of threats, state-attributed economic problems played a fundamental role in almost all Egyptian mobilizations, highlighting the strong impact of economic conditions on protests. In addition, factors such as population growth, urbanization and declining human development indicators that further exacerbated state-attributed economic problems, are crucial for understanding the mobilizations investigated in this book. This was seen in all the eras investigated, and was most apparent in the conditions that led to the downfall of Hosni Mubarak. In addition to state-attributed economic problems, threats such as regime repression and erosion of rights also helped galvanize labor and student mobilizations against successive regimes in Egypt.

Cooperation between movements

In authoritarian environments, cross-movement cooperation bolsters social movement activism. The 1946 mobilization in particular showed how two different movements—one anchored in the working class and another in the middle class—transcended economic and urban socio-economic divides to challenge the authorities. *al-Lajna al-Ṭullābiyya wa al-ʿUmmāliyya* (The Committee for Students and Workers) arguably set the precedent for the student–labor cooperation that did occur throughout the century.

While in certain instances, there was consciously planned cooperation between movements, at other instances the cooperation between them was disorganized and haphazard, such as during the mobilizations of 1968 and 1977. While some limited networking occurred between movements before and during these mobilizations, ultimately they were spontaneous uprisings in response to specific situations. Although both did effect some change and forced the state to respond to some of the demands of the protestors, the outcome was limited and the state was swiftly able to quell the protests. This was seen through Nasser's March 30th Program issued after the 1968 mobilization, and the retreat by the Sadat regime in implementing proposed austerity measures after the 1977 mobilization.

Barriers to mobilization

One of the main limitations affecting coordination between movements, as well as their activism in general, is the co-optation of these movements by regimes and established political forces. The mobilizations of 1935, 1936 and especially 1946 showed how the student and labor movements were an integral part of the nationalist struggle, but at times nationalist politicians attempted to co-opt the movements to further their own goals. The attempts to co-opt both movements by the authorities would manifest themselves regularly over the following decades. The regime of Gamal Abdel Nasser from its earliest days attempted to co-opt both movements through a process of corporatization, and it did so initially with a high degree of success. Sadat attempted to maintain the corporatization of both movements.

In addition to co-optation, the lack of organizational structures independent of the government had consistently undermined the ability of both movements to mobilize and advance their objectives. To attempt to overcome this weakness, workers built independent unions in the late Mubarak era. The ability to maintain these independent unions in the post-Mubarak era will be a key factor in determining the ability of the labor movement to successfully pursue its goals.

While students enjoyed some limited success in mobilizing around issues pertaining to their studies and their immediate surroundings, they were not entirely successful in building lasting organizational structures, in large part due to the transient nature of their time as students. However, student activists would go on to join political organizations, illustrating how university activism has acted as an incubator for successive generations of activists, politicians and intellectuals.

Future avenues for research

While this study aimed to be as comprehensive as possible, there are several facets of mobilization in Egypt that were outside its scope, the most significant being the role of the Islamist movement at the various historical junctures. This investigation warrants its own research project. In addition, the coverage of the book intentionally ends at 2011, and does not include the 2013 mobilizations against ex-President Mohamed Morsi, despite my presence in Cairo at the time while conducting research.

While it was tempting to have included a chapter on the Morsi era, there was not enough information to investigate the year critically and I did not want to depart from the realm of academia to journalism by providing a running commentary on events currently unfolding in Egypt. However, the year of Morsi rule and the worker/student mobilizations during his era, as well as the role of the army and the deep state within it, is another potential research project. There is also a need for further investigations to understand the unprecedented wave of mobilizations organized by Islamist student groups in campuses across Egypt since the election of Abdel Fattah el-Sisi.

Breaking the barrier of fear

As I highlighted in the Preface, the book was inspired by my own participation in the January 25 uprising, where I personally witnessed the barrier of fear breaking down around me. The year 2011 was one of optimism not just for me, but also for my generation and the country at large. Unfortunately, as I write this conclusion in early 2016 I am disheartened by developments in Egypt as a resurgent authoritarianism attempts to make a comeback. However, I am comforted when I view the events of January 25 in broad historical terms, in which the 2011 uprising is simply another milestone in the Egyptian people's march toward freedom.

To help contextualize such history, in this book I sought to investigate labor and student mobilizations in Egypt since the early twentieth century. The key difference between the first three mobilizations and the final mobilization needs to be stated clearly: unlike earlier mobilizations, the 2011 uprising helped produce a politically empowered generation of workers and students able to challenge and threaten a regime. This is the main gain of the 2011 uprising: the political empowerment of not only the workers and students, but society at large. The impact of such political empowerment is likely to manifest itself in the coming decades in Egypt.

Notes

1 Avi Asher-Shapiro, IMF Amnesia in Egypt, *Muftah*, September 7, 2012, http://muftah.org/imf-amnesia-in-egypt/ (accessed October 1, 2014).
2 Robert Mabro, *The Egyptian Economy, 1952–72* (Oxford: Oxford University Press, 1974), 18–24.

Bibliography

Fieldwork interviews

Abbas, Kamal. Independent trade union leader. Cairo. March, 2013.

Abdel Khaleq, Gouda. Economist and ex-Minister of Supply and Domestic Trade. Cairo. August, 2013.

Ahmad, Osama. Student leader from Revolutionary Socialists group. Cairo. February, 2013.

El Fayoumy, Kamal. Labor leader. Mahallah. March, 2013.

El Said, Hala. Dean of Faculty of Economics and Politics, Cairo University. Cairo. January, 2013.

El Shobaky, Amr. Senior researcher, Al-Ahram Center and ex-member of parliament. February, 2013.

Ezzat, Ahmad. 1990s–2000s student activist and Revolutionary Socialist. Cairo. February, 2013.

Fouad, Hisham. Revolutionary Socialist activist and journalist. Cairo. March, 2013.

Galal, Ahmad. Previous director of ECES and Minister of Finance. Cairo. April, 2013.

Ghany, Nabil. 1960s student activist and current independent union official. Cairo. March, 2013.

Handoussa, Heba. World Bank economist and lead author of UNDP Egypt Human Development Reports. Cairo. August, 2013.

Hussein, Hamdy. Veteran labor activist. Mahallah. March, 2013.

Kamaly, Ahmad. Professor at the American University in Cairo and ex-government official. Cairo. February, 2013.

Name Withheld. Government official. Cairo. March, 2013.

Name Withheld. Ex-government official. Cairo. March, 2013.

Name Withheld. Worker. Mahallah. March, 2013.

Name Withheld. Worker. Mahallah. March, 2013.

Qasas, Mohammad. 1990s student leader, ex-Muslim Brotherhood member and leader of al-Tayyar al-Misri Party (merged with Strong Egypt Party). Cairo. January, 2013.

Shabaan, Ahmad Bahaa el Din. 1970s leader, *Kefaya* founding member and head of the Egyptian Communist Party. Cairo. March, 2013.

Shukrallah, Hani. 1970s student leader and intellectual. Cairo. March, 2013.

Su'ūd, Sayyed Abū el. Independent labor activist. Alexandria. April, 2013.

Books

Abdel Alim, Taha. 1987. *Bināyat al-tabaqa al-'amila al-sina'iya al-misriyya* (The Composition of the Egyptian Industrial Working Class). Cairo: NP.

Abdel-Fadil, Mahmoud. 1975. *Development, Income Distribution and Social Change in Rural Egypt*. London: Cambridge University Press.

Abdel Fatah, Nahed. 2006. *al-'Ummāl wa rijāl al-a'māl: taḥawulāt al-furas al-siyāsiyya fi maṣr* (Workers and Businessmen: The Changes in Political Opportunities in Egypt). Cairo: Al Ahram Center for Political and Strategic Studies.

Abdel Khaleq, Gouda, ed. 1982. *al-Infitāḥ: al-juzur wal-hassad wal-mustaqbal* (*Infitāḥ*: Roots, Outcomes, and the Future). Cairo: RAPAC.

Abdel Khaleq, Gouda. 1986. *al-Iqtiṣād al-dawlī min al-maza'iyya al-nisbiyya ilā al-tabādul al-lā-mutakāfi'ī* (The International Economy, from Relative Privileges to Asymmetrical Exchanges). Cairo: Dār al-Nahda al-'Arabiyya.

Abdel Malik, Anwar. 1967. *Dirāsat fī-l-thaqāfa al-waṭaniya* (Studies in the National Culture). Beirut: Dār al-Taliya.

Abdel Moteleb, Assem. 2007. *al-Talabah wal-harakat al-waṭaniya fī masr 1922–1952* (The Students and the Nationalist Movement in Egypt 1922–1952). Cairo: Dār al-Kutub wal-Wathā'iq al-Qawmiya.

Abdel Nasser, Gamal. 1996. *Falsafat al-thawra* (The Philosophy of the Revolution). Cairo: Bayt al-'Arab.

Abdel Rāziq, Ḥusayn. 1979. *Miṣr fī-l-thāmin 'ashr wal-tāsi' 'ashr min yanayer: Dirāsa siyāsiyya watha'iqiyya* (Egypt on 18 and 19 January: A Documentary Political Study). Beirut: Dār al-Kalima.

Achchar, Gilbert. 2013. *The People Want: A Radical Exploration of the Arab Uprising*. London: Saqi Books.

Ahmed, Jamal Mohammed. 1960. *Intellectual Origins of Egyptian Nationalism*. London: Oxford University Press.

Amer, Abdel Salam Abdel Halim. 1987. *Thawrat ulio wal-tabaqa al-'āmila* (The July Revolution and the Working Class). Cairo: al-Hay'a al-'Āmma lil-Kitāb.

Amer, Ibrahim. 1956. *Thawrat maṣr al-qawmiya* (Egypt's National Revolution). Cairo: NP.

Amin, Galal. 1995. *Egypt's Economic Predicament: A Study in the Interaction of External Pressure, Political Folly and Social Tension in Egypt, 1960–1990*. Leiden: E.J. Brill.

Amin, Galal. 2011. *Egypt in the Era of Hosni Mubarak, 1981–2011*. Cairo: American University of Cairo Press.

Amin, Galal. 2012. *Qiṣṣat al-iqtiṣād al-maṣri: min 'ahd Muhammad Ali ilā 'ahd Mubārak* (The Story of the Egyptian Economy: From The Era of Muhammad Ali to The Era of Mubarak). Cairo: Dār al-Shurūq.

Anderson, Benedict. 1983. *Imagined Communities: Reflections on the Origin and Spread of Nationalism*. London: Verso.

Ansari, Hamied. 1986. *Egypt: The Stalled Society*. New York: SUNY Press.

Attia, Shohdi. 1957. *Taṭāwur al-ḥaraka al-waṭaniya al-miṣriya 1882–1956* (The Development of the Egyptian Nationalist Movement 1882–1956). Cairo: al-Dār al-Maṣriya lil-Kutub.

Attia, Shohdi. 1980. *Bureaucracy and Politics in Contemporary Egypt*. London: Ithaca Press.

Ayubi, Nazih. 1995. *Overstating the Arab State: Politics and Society in the Middle East*. London: I.B. Tauris.

Baer, G. 1969. *Studies in the Social History of Modern Egypt*. Chicago: University of Chicago Press.

Baker, Raymond William. 1978. *Egypt's Uncertain Revolution under Nasser and Sadat*. Cambridge: Harvard University Press.

Baker, Raymond William. 1990. *Sadat and After: Struggles for Egypt's Political Soul*. Cambridge: Harvard University Press.

Bakry, Mostafa. 2011. *al-Jaysh wal-thawra: qiṣṣat al-ayyām al-akhīra* (The Army and the Revolution: The Story of the Last Days). Cairo: Akhbar al-Youm.

Beattie, Kirk. 2000. *Egypt During the Sadat Years*. New York: Palgrave.

Beblawi, Hazem and Giacomo Luciani, eds. 1987. *Nation, State and Integration in the Arab World*. London: Croom Helm.

Beinin, Joel and Zachary Lockman. 1987. *Workers on the Nile: Nationalism, Communism, Islam and the Egyptian Working Class, 1882–1954*. Princeton: Princeton University Press.

Beinin, Joel and Fredric Vairel, eds. 2011. *Social Movements, Mobilization and Contestation in the Middle East and North Africa*. Stanford: Stanford University Press.

Beissinger, Mark. 2001. *Nationalist Mobilization and the Collapse of the Soviet State: A Tidal Approach to the Study of Nationalism*. Cambridge: Cambridge University Press.

Berk, Richard. 1974. *Collective Behavior*. Dubuque: WC Brown.

Bianchi, Robert. 1989. *Unruly Corporatism: Associational Life in Twentieth Century Egypt*. Oxford: Oxford University Press.

Blumer, Herbert. 1986. *Symbolic Interactionism: Perspective and Method*. Berkeley: University of California Press.

Botman, Selma. 1988. *The Rise of Egyptian Communism, 1939–1970*. Syracuse: Syracuse University Press.

Botman, Selma. 1991. *From Independence to Revolution: Egypt, 1922–1952*. New York: Syracuse University Press.

Bowker, Robert. 2010. *Egypt and the Politics of Change in the Arab Middle East*. London: Edward Elgar.

Bush, Ray. 1999. *Economic Crisis and Political Reform in Egypt*. Boulder: Westview Press.

Calhoun, Craig J. 1997. *Neither Gods Nor Emperors: Students and the Struggle for Democracy in China*. Berkeley: University of California Press.

Cohen, Robin, Peter Gutkind and Phyllis Brazier, eds. 1979. *Peasants and Proletarians: The Struggle of Third World Workers*. London: Hutchinson and Co.

Cole, Juan Ricardo. 1999. *Colonialism and Revolution in the Middle East: Social and Cultural Origins of Egypt's Urabi Movement*. Cairo: American University in Cairo Press.

Coleman, J.S., E. Katz and H. Menzel. 1966. *Medical Innovation*. New York: Bobbs-Merril.

Cook, Steven. 2007. *Ruling But Not Governing: The Military and Political Development in Egypt, Algeria and Turkey*. New York: Johns Hopkins University Press.

Cooper, Mark. 1982. *The Transformation of Egypt*. Baltimore: Johns Hopkins University Press.

Crouchley, Arthur Edwin. 1938. *The Economic Development of Modern Egypt*. London: Longmans and Green.

Daigle, Craig. 2012. *The Limits of Detente: The United States, the Soviet Union, and the Arab-Israeli Conflict, 1969–1973*. New Haven: Yale University Press.

Deeb, Marius. 1979. *Party Politics in Egypt: the Wafd and its Rivals, 1919–1939*. London: Ithaca Press for the Middle East Centre, St Antony's College, Oxford.

Dekmejian, Hrair. 1971. *Egypt Under Nasser: A Study in Political Dynamics*. Albany: SUNY Press.

Della Porta, Donatella and Mario Diani. 1999. *Social Movements: An Introduction*. Oxford: Blackwell Publishing.

DeNardo, James. 1985. *Power in Numbers: The Political Strategy of Protest and Rebellion*. Princeton: Princeton University Press.

Dodwell, Henry. 1931. *The Founder of Modern Egypt: A Study of Muhammad Ali*. Cambridge: Cambridge University Press.

Dubois, Ellen. 1978. *Feminism and Suffrage*. Ithaca: Cornell University Press.

Dunne, J. 1938. *An Introduction to the History of Education in Egypt*. London: Luzac and Co.

El-Banna, Gamal. 1962. *Nash' at al-ḥarakat al-niqābiyya wa taṭāwurihā* (The Birth of the Union Movement and its Development). Cairo: al-Mu'assasat al-Thaqāfiya al-'Umaliya.

El-Mahdy, Rabab and Phillip Marfleet, eds. 2009. *Egypt: The Moment of Change*. London: Zed Books.

El-Massry, Ahmad. 1979. *48 Sa'āt ḥazzat Miṣr: Ri'yat shāhid a'yān* (48 Hours that Shook Egypt: An Eyewitness Account). Cairo: Maṭbu'āt al-Tadāmun.

El-Nawawy, Mohammed and Adel Iskander. 2003. *Al-Jazeera: The Story of the Network That is Rattling Governments and Redefining Modern Journalism*. Boulder: Westview.

Erlich, Haggai. 1989. *Students and University in 20th Century Egyptian Politics*. London: Frank Cass.

Esposito, John. 1984. *Islam and Politics*. New York: Syracuse University Press.

Esposito, John and John Voll. 1996. *Islam and Democracy*. New York: Oxford University Press.

Evans, Sarah. 1980. *Personal Politics: The Roots of the Women's Liberation Movement in the Civil Rights Movements and the New Left*. New York: Knopf.

Ezz el-Din, Amin. 1967. *Tārīkh al-tabaqat al 'amilah al-miṣriyya mundh nash'atihā ḥatta thawrat 1919* (The History of the Egyptian Working Class since its Beginnings Until the 1919 Revolution). Cairo: Dar al-Kitāb al-'Arabi.

Fahmy, Khaled. 1997. *All the Pasha's Men: Mehmed Ali, His Army and the Making of Modern Egypt*. Cambridge: Cambridge University Press.

Faksh, Mahmud. 1983. *Egypt Under Mubarak: The Uncertain Path*. Toronto: Canadian Institute for International Affairs.

Feaver, Peter. 2005. *Armed Servants: Agency, Oversight, and Civil-Military Relations*. Cambridge: Harvard University Press.

Finer, Samuel E. 1962. *The Man on Horseback: The Role of the Military in Politics*. New York: Praeger.

Fukuyama, Francis. 1992. *The End of History and the Last Man*. New York: Free Press.

Gamson, William A. 1990. *The Strategy of Social Protest*. Homewood: Dorsey.

Gamson, William A., B. Fireman and S. Rytina. 1982. *Encounters with Unjust Authority*. Homewood: Dorsey Press.

Gershoni, Israel and James P. Jankowski. 1986. *Egypt, Islam, and the Arabs: The Search for Egyptian Nationhood, 1900–1930*. New York: Oxford University Press.

Gervasio, Gennaro. 2010. *al-Ḥaraka al-markisiyya fi Maṣr 1967–1981* (The Marxist Movement in Egypt, 1967–1981). Cairo: al-Markaz al-Qawmi lil-Tarjama.

al-Ghazali, Abdel Monem. 1958. *21 Febrayer: Yawm al-nidal ḍidd al-isti'mar* (21 February: The Day of Resistance against Colonialism). Cairo: NP.

Ghonim, Wael. 2012. *Revolution 2.0: The Power of the People is Greater than the People in Power: A Memoir*. New York: Houghton Mifflin Harcourt.

Gillespie, Kate. 1984. *The Tripatriate Relationship: Government, Foreign Investors and Local Investors During Egypt's Economic Opening*. New York: Praeger.

Gitlin, Todd. 1987. *The Sixties*. New York: Bantam.

Goffman, Erving. 1974. *Frame Analysis: An Essay on the Organization of Experience*. Boston: Northeastern University Press.

Goldberg, Ellis. 1987. *Tinker, Tailor and Textile Worker: Class and Politics in Egypt 1930–1954*. Berkeley: University of California Press.

Gorman, Anthony. 2003. *Historians, State, and Politics in Twentieth Century Egypt: Contesting the Nation*. London: Routledge.

Gunning, Jeroen and Illan Zvi Baron. 2013. *Why Occupy a Square: People, Protests and Movements in the Egyptian Revolution*. London: Hurst and Co.

Hagerstrand, T. 1967. *Innovation Diffusion as a Spatial Process*. Chicago: University of Illinois Press.

Hall, Stuart and Paul Du Gay. 1996. *Questions of Cultural Identity*. London: Sage.

Hansen, Ben and Samir Radwan. 1982. *Employment Opportunities and Equity in a Changing Economy: Egypt in the 1980s*. Geneva: International Labour Office Publications.

Harik, Illiya. 1974. *The Political Mobilization of Peasants: A Study of An Egyptian Community*. Bloomington: Indiana University Press.

Harik, Illiya. 1997. *Economic Policy Reform in Egypt*. Gainesville: University Press of Florida.

Hassanin, Gamal Magdi. 1971. *al-Mumizāt al-ʿama lil-tarkīb al-tabāq fī maṣr ʿāshiya thawra 23 Yunio* (The General Indicators of Class Structure Before the Revolution of the 23rd of June). Cairo: NP.

Heikal, Muhammad Hassanin. 1978. *Sphinx and Commissar: The Rise and Fall of Soviet Influence in the Arab World*. New York: Collins.

Heikal, Muhammad Hassanin. 1988. *Kharīf al-ghaḍab* (The Autumn of Fury). Cairo: Al-Ahram.

Hierich, Max. 1971. *The Spiral of Conflict: Berkeley 1964*. New York: Columbia University Press, 1971.

Hinnebusch, Raymond A. 1988. *Egyptian Politics Under Sadat: The Post-Populist Development of an Authoritarian–Modernizing State*. Cambridge: Cambridge University Press.

Hirst, David and Irene Beeson. 1981. *Sadat*. London: Faber & Faber.

Hishām, Aḥmad, ed. 2012. *Min tārīkh al-ḥarakah al-ṭullābiya al-maṣriyah, kulliyat al-handasah Jāmiʿat al-Qāhira, October 1961–October 1972* (Of the History of the Egyptian Student Movement, Faculty of Engineering, Cairo University, October 1961–October 1972). Cairo: Eeon Publishing.

Huntington, Samuel. 1985. *The Solider and the State: The Theory and Politics of Civil-Military Relations*. Cambridge, MA: Harvard University Press.

Hussein, Adel. 1982. *al-Iqtisad al-Misri Min al-Istiqlal Ila al-Tabaʾiyah* (The Egyptian Economy from Independence to Dependency). Cairo: Dar al-Mustaqbal.

Hussein, Mahmoud. 1973. *Class Conflict in Egypt, 1945–1970*. New York: Monthly Review Press.

Ikram, Khaled. 1980. *Egypt: Economic Management in a Period of Transition*. Baltimore: Johns Hopkins University Press for the World Bank.

Ikram, Khaled. 2006. *The Egyptian Economy, 1952–2000: Performance, Policies, Issues*. London: Routledge.

Ismael, Tareq Y. and Rifʿat el-Saʿīd. 1990. *The Communist Movement in Egypt, 1920–1988*. Syracuse: Syracuse University Press.

Issawi, Charles. 1954. *Egypt at Mid-Century: An Economic Survey*. London: Oxford University Press.

Issawi, Charles. 1963. *Egypt in Revolution*. London: Oxford University Press.

Issawi, Charles. 1984. *The Economic History of the Middle East and North Africa*. New York: Columbia University Press.

Janowitz, Morris. 1964. *The Military in the Political Development of New Nations*. Chicago: University of Chicago Press.

Kassem, Maye. 2004. *Egyptian Politics: The Dynamics of Authoritarian Rule*. Boulder: Lynne Rienner.

Kassow, Samuel D. 1989. *Students, Professors, and the State in Tsarist Russia*. Berkeley: University of California Press.

Keohane, Robert. 1984. *After Hegemony: Cooperation and Discord in the World Political Economy*. Princeton: Princeton University Press.

Kepel, Gilles. 1985. *The Prophet and the Pharaoh: Muslim Extremism in Egypt*. London: Saqi Books.

Kepel, Gilles. 2002. *Jihad: The Trail of Political Islam*. Cambridge, MA: Harvard University Press.

Khalid, Muhammad. 1975. *al-Ḥaraka al-niqābiya bayn al-māḍī wal-ḥāḍir* (The Union Movement Between the Past and the Present). Cairo: Dār al-Taʿāwun.

Khalil, Azza, ed. 2006. *al-Ḥarakāt al-ijtimāʿiyya fī-l-ʿālam al-ʿarabī* (Social Movements in the Arab World). Cairo: Matbouly.

Klein, Naomi. 2007. *The Shock Doctrine: The Rise of Disaster Capitalism*. London: Macmillan.

Kornhauser, William. 1959. *The Politics of Mass Society*. Glencoe: The Free Press.

Lamborn, Alan. 1991. *The Price of Power: Risk and Foreign Policy in Britain, France and Germany*. Boston: Unwin Hyman.

Landes, David. 1981. *Bankers and Pashas: International Finance and Economic Imperialism in Egypt*. Cambridge, MA: Harvard University Press.

Laroui, Abdallah. 1976. *The Crisis of the Arab Intellectual: Traditionalism or Historicism?* Berkeley: University of California Press.

Le Bon, Gustave. 1896. *The Crowd: A Study of the Popular Mind*. New York: Macmillan.

Mabro, Robert. 1974. *The Egyptian Economy, 1952–72*. Oxford: Oxford University Press.

McAdam, Doug. 1982. *Political Process and the Development of the Black Insurgency, 1930–1970*. Chicago: Chicago University Press.

McAdam, Doug. 1988. *Freedom Summer*. New York: Oxford University Press.

McAdam, Douglas, Sidney Tarrow and Charles Tilly. 2004. *Dynamics of Contention*. Cambridge: Cambridge University Press.

Mahmud, Zayid. 1965. *Egypt's Struggle for Independence*. Beirut: NP.

al-Manawy, Abdel Latif. 2012. *al-Ayyām al-akhīra al-niẓām Mubarak: 18 Yawm* (The Final Days of the Mubarak Regime: 18 Days). Cairo: al-Dār al-Maṣriyya al-Libnāniyya.

Marlowe, John. 1965. *A History of Modern Egypt and Anglo-Egyptian Relations, 1800–1953*. 2nd edn. Hamden: Archon Books.

Marlowe, John. 1974. *Spoiling the Egyptians*. London: Andre Deutsch.

Mead, Donald. 1967. *Growth and Structural Change in the Egyptian Economy*. Homewood: R.D. Erwin.

Meyer, David S., Nancy Whittier and Belinda Robnett, eds. 2002. *Social Movements: Identity, Culture and the State*. Oxford: Oxford University Press.

Migdal, Joel S. 1988. *Strong Societies and Weak States: State-Society Relations and State Capabilities in the Third World*. Princeton: Princeton University Press.
Miles, Hugh. 2005. *Al-Jazeera: The Inside Story of the Arab News Channel that is Challenging the West*. New York: Grove Press.
Miller, James. 1987. *Democracy in the Street*. New York: Simon & Schuster.
Mitchell, Richard. 1969. *The Society of the Muslim Brothers*. Oxford: Oxford University Press.
Mitwallī, Maḥmūd. 1973. *al-Uṣūl al-tārīkhiyya lil-rasmaliya al-miṣriyya wa-tata'wurihā* (The Historical Roots of Egyptian Capitalism and Its Development). Cairo: GEBO.
Morris, Aldon. 1984. *The Origins of the Civil Rights Movement*. New York: Free Press.
Mosco, Vincent. 2009. *The Political Economy of Communication: Rethinking and Renewal*. London: Sage Publications.
Muntaṣir, Ṣalāḥ. 2012. *al-Su'ūd wal-suqūt: min al-manāsa ilā l-maḥkama* (The Climb and the Fall: From the Stand to the Court). Cairo: The Egyptian Association for Printing.
al-Naggar, Ahmad al-Said. 2004. *Kashf ḥisāb Atef Ebied* (Balance Sheet for Atef Ebied). Cairo: Al Ahram.
Needler, Martin. 1987. *The Problem of Democracy in Latin America*. Lexington: Lexington Books.
Nordlinger, Eric. 1977. *Soldiers in Politics: Military Coups and Governments*. Englewood Cliffs: Prentice-Hall.
Oberschall, Anthony. 1973. *Social Conflict and Social Movements*. Englewood Cliffs: Prentice Hall.
O'Brien, Patrick. 1966. *The Revolution in Egypt's Economic System, From Private Enterprise to Socialism, 1952–1965*. London: Oxford University Press.
O'Donnell, Guillermo. 1988. *Bureaucratic Authoritarianism: Argentina 1966–1973 in Comparative Perspective*. Berkeley: University of California Press.
O'Donnell, Guillermo and Philippe C. Schmitter. 1986. *Transitions from Authoritarian Rule*. Baltimore: Johns Hopkins University Press.
Olson, Mancur. 1965. *The Logic of Collective Action*. Cambridge, MA: Harvard University Press.
Owen, Roger. 1969. *Cotton and the Egyptian Economy, 1820–1914: A Study in Trade and Development*. Oxford: Clarendon Press.
Owen, Roger. 2000. *State, Power and Politics in the Making of the Modern Middle East*. London: Routledge.
Parsa, Misagh. 2000. *States, Ideologies, and Social Revolutions: A Comparative Analysis of Iran, Nicaragua, and the Philippines*. Cambridge: Cambridge University Press.
Posusney, Marsha Pripsein. 1997. *Labor and the State in Egypt*. New York: Columbia University Press.
Ramadan, Abdel Aziz. 1968. *Taṭāwur al-ḥarakat al-wataniyya fī miṣr, 1918–1936* (The Development of the Egyptian Nationalist Movement, 1918–1936). Cairo: Dār al-Kitāb al-'Arabī.
Rashid, 'Abd al-Majīd Muḥammad. 2007. *al-Kartha wal-wahm: mustaqbal siyāsat al-iṣlāḥ al-iqtiṣādi fi-Miṣr fi ẓill niẓām al-awlama'a* (Catastrophe and Delusion: The Future of Economic Reform Policy in Egypt in Light of Globalisation). Cairo: Al-Shurta.
Reid, Donald Malcolm. 2002. *Cairo University and the Making of Modern Egypt*. Cambridge: Cambridge University Press.
Richards, Alan and John Waterbury. 2006. *A Political Economy of the Middle East*. 3rd edn. Boulder: Westview.

al-Rifa'i, Abdel Aziz. 1968. *al-'Umal wal-ḥarakat al-qawmiya fi maṣr al-ḥāditha* (Workers and the Egyptian Nationalist Movement in Modern Egypt). Cairo: NP.

Rivlin, Helen Anne B. 1961. *Agricultural Policy of Muhammad 'Ali in Egypt*. Cambridge, MA: Harvard University Press.

Robbins, Lionel. 1932. *An Essay of the Nature and Significance of Economic Science*. London: Macmillan.

Rogers, Everett M. 1983. *Diffusion of Innovations*. London: Collier Macmillian.

Sa'd, Aḥmad Sādiq. 1990. *Dirasāt fī-l-ishtirākiyya al-miṣriyya* (Studies in Egyptian Socialism). Cairo: Dār al-Fikr al-Jadīd.

Sadat, Anwar. 1979. *al-Baḥth 'an al-dhāt* (The Search for the Self). Cairo: Al Ahram.

el-Sa'īd, Rif'at. 1972. *al-Yasar al-Miṣri, 1925–1940* (The Egyptian Left, 1925–1940). Beirut: NP.

Said, Muhammad. 1989. *Hizb al-wafd wal-ṭabāqa al-'āmila fī miṣr 1924–1952* (The Wafd Party and the Working Class in Egypt 1924–1952). Cairo: Dār al-Thaqāfa.

al-Sayyid, Mustafa Kamal. 1983. *al-Mujtama'a wal-siyāsa fi Maṣr: dawr jamā'at al-maṣāliḥ fī-l-niẓām al-siyāsī 1952–1981* (Society and Politics in Egypt: The Role of Interest Groups in the Political Order, 1952–1981). Cairo: Dār al-Mustaqbal al-'Arabī.

al-Sayyid-Marsot, Afaf Lutfi. 1977. *Egypt's Liberal Experiment, 1922–1936*. Berkeley: University of California Press.

al-Sayyid-Marsot, Afaf Lutfi. 2007. *The History of Egypt: From the Arab Conquest to the Present*. Cambridge: Cambridge University Press.

Sharaf al-Din, Aḥmad. 2007. *Asrār jadīda ḥawl mazbhat Kafr al-dawwār wa istishhād Khamis wal-Baqari* (New Secrets of the Kafr al-dawwar Massacre and the Martyrdom of Khamis and al-Baqari). Cairo: Hisham Mubarak Centre.

Shehata, Samer S. 2010. *Shop Floor Culture and Politics in Egypt*. Cairo: AUC Press.

Shuhyib, 'Abd al-Qādir. 1979. *Muḥākamat al-infitāḥ al-iqtiṣādi fī maṣr* (The Trial of Economic *infitāḥ* in Egypt). Cairo: Ibn Khaldūn.

Shukr, Abdel Ghaffar. 2004. *Munāẓamat al-shabāb al-ishtirākī: tajruba maṣriyya fī i'da'ad al-qāḍa 1963–1976* (The Organisation for Socialist Youth: An Egyptian Experiment in Leader Formation). Lebanon: Centre for Arab Unity Studies.

Skocpol, Theda. 1979. *States and Social Revolutions: A Comparative Analysis of France, Russia and China*. Cambridge: Cambridge University Press.

Soliman, Samer. 2011. *The Autumn of Dictatorship: Fiscal Crisis and Political Change Under Mubarak*. Stanford: Stanford University Press.

Sowers, Jeannie and Chris Toensing, eds. 2012. *The Journey to Tahrir: Revolution, Protest, and Social Change in Egypt*. New York: Verso.

Springborg, Robert. 1989. *Mubarak's Egypt: Fragmentation of the Political Order*. Boulder: Westview Press.

Stacher, Joshua. 2012. *Adaptable Autocrats: Regime Power in Egypt and Syria*. Stanford: Stanford University Press.

Sullivan, Denis and Sana Abed-Kotob. 1999. *Islam in Contemporary Egypt: Civil Society versus the State*. Boulder: Lynne Reinner.

Tarde, Gabriel. 1903. *The Laws of Imitation*. New York: Henry Holt Company.

Tarrow, Sidney. 1989. *Democracy and Disorder*. New York: Oxford University Press.

Tarrow, Sidney. 1998. *Power in Movement: Social Movements and Contentious Politics*. Cambridge: Cambridge University Press.

Tarrow, Sidney. 2005. *The New Transnational Activism*. Cambridge: Cambridge University Press.

Tignor, Robert L. 1998. *Capitalism and Nationalism at the End of Empire: State and Business in Decolonizing Egypt, Nigeria and Kenya, 1945–1963*. Princeton: Princeton University Press.

Tilly, Charles. 1978. *From Mobilization to Revolution*. Reading: Addison Wesley.

Tilly, Charles. 1992. *Coercion, Capital and European States: AD 990–1992*. Oxford: Blackwell.

Tilly, Charles. 1995. *Popular Contention in Great Britain, 1758–1834*. Cambridge, MA: Harvard University Press.

Tilly, Charles. 2004. Social *Movements, 1768–2004*. Boulder: Paradigm Publishers.

Tuchman, Gaye. 1978. *Making News: A Study in the Construction of Reality*. New York: Free Press.

Turner, Ralph H. and Lewis M. Killian. 1957. *Collective Behavior*. Englewood Cliffs: Prentice Hall.

Vatikiotis, P.J. 1969. *The Modern History of Egypt*. London: Weidenfeld & Nicolson.

Vatikiotis, P.J. 1991. *The History of Modern Egypt, From Muhammad Ali to Mubarak*. Baltimore: Johns Hopkins Press.

Wahba, Mourad. 1994. *The Role of the State in the Egyptian Economy, 1945–1981*. London: Ithaca Press.

Warriner, Doreen. 1962. *Land Reform and Development in the Middle East: A Study of Egypt, Syria, and Iraq*. Oxford: Oxford University Press.

Waterbury, John. 1978. *Egypt: Burdens of the Past, Options for the Future*. Bloomington: Indiana University Press.

Waterbury, John. 1983. *The Egypt of Nasser and Sadat: The Political Economy of Two Regimes*. Princeton: Princeton University Press.

Weber, Max. 1947. *The Theory of Social and Economic Organization*. New York: The Free Press.

Wickham, Carrie Rosefsky. 2002. *Mobilizing Islam: Religion, Activism and Political Change in Egypt*. New York: Columbia University Press.

Wickham, Carrie Rosefsky. 2013. *The Muslim Brotherhood: Evolution of an Islamist Movement*. Princeton: Princeton University Press.

Wickham-Crowley, Timothy P. 1992. *Guerrillas and Revolution in Latin America: A Comparative Study of Insurgents and Regimes Since 1956*. Princeton: Princeton University Press.

Wiktorowicz, Quintan. 2001. *The Management of Islamic Activism: Salafis, the Muslim Brotherhood, and State Power in Jordan*. Albany: SUNY Press.

Wiktorowicz, Quintan, ed. 2004. *Islamic Activism: A Social Movement Theory Approach*. Indiana: Indiana University Press.

Zaki, Moheb. 1999. *Egyptian Business Elites: Their Visions and Investment Behavior*. Cairo: Dar al-Kutub.

Zayani, Mohamed, ed. 2005. *The Al Jazeera Phenomenon: Critical Perspectives on New Arab Media*. Boulder: Paradigm Publishers.

Book chapters

Abdallah, Ismail. 1987. "Thawrat ulio wal-tanmiya al-mustaqilla" (The July Revolution and Independent Development). In *Thawrat thalātha wa ʿashrīn ulio: qaḍāyā al-ḥaḍr wa tahdiyat al-mustaqbal* (The 23rd of July Revolution: Current Cases and the Challenges of the Future). Cairo: Dār al-Mustaqbal al-ʿArabī.

Abdel Ghafar, Adel. 2015. "January 25th: The Day the Barrier of Fear Broke Down." In

Voices of the Arab Spring: Personal Stories of the Arab Revolutions, edited by Asaad Al Saleh. New York: Columbia University Press.

Abdel Khaleq, Gouda. 1978. "Aḥamm dalālat siyāsat al-infitāḥ al-iqtiṣādī" (The Most Important Indicators of the Infitāḥ Economic Policy). In *al-Iqtiṣād al-miṣru fī rub'a qarn 1952–1977* (The Egyptian Economy in the Quarter-Century 1952–1977). Cairo: Egypt Institute for Books.

Amin, Galal. 1968. "The Egyptian Economy and the Revolution." In *Egypt since the Revolution*, edited by P.J. Vatakotis. London: George Allen & Unwin.

Beinin, Joel. 2009. "Neo-Liberal Structural Adjustment, Political Demobilization and Neo-Authoritarianism in Egypt." In *The Arab State and Neoliberal Globalisation: The Restructuring of State Power in the Middle East*, edited by Laura Guazzone and Daniela Pioppi. Reading: Ithaca Press.

Beinin, Joel. 2009. "Workers' Struggles under 'Socialism' and Neoliberalism." In *Egypt: The Moment of Change*, edited by Rabab El-Mahdi and Philip Marfleet. London: Zed Press.

Binder, Leonard. 1969. "Egypt: The Integrative Revolution." In *Political Culture and Political Development*, edited by Lucian Pye and Sidney Verba. Princeton: Princeton University Press.

Collier, Davis. 1979. "Overview of the Bureaucratic Authoritarian Model." In *The New Authoritarianism in Latin America*, edited by David Collier. Princeton: Princeton University Press.

Edwards, Bob and John McCarthy. 2004. "Resources and Social Movement Mobilization." In *The Blackwell Companion to Social Movements*, edited by David Snow, Sarah Soule and Hanspeter Kriesi. Oxford: Blackwell Publishing.

Gamson, William and David Meyer. 1996. "Framing Political Opportunity." In *Comparative Perspectives on Social Movements*, edited by D. McAdam, J. McCarthy and M.N. Zald. Cambridge: Cambridge University Press.

Goldstone, Jack and Charles Tilly. 2001. "Threat (and Opportunity): Popular Action and State Response in the Dynamics of Contentious Action." In *Silence and Voice in the Study of Contentious Politics*, edited by Ronald Aminzade, Jack Goldstone, Doug McAdam, Elizabeth Perry, William Sewell, Sidney Tarrow and Charles Tilly. Cambridge: Cambridge University Press.

Goodwin, Jeff and James M. Jasper. 2004. "Introduction." In *Rethinking Social Movements*, edited by Jeff Goodwin and James M. Jasper. New York: Rowman & Littlefield Publishers, Inc.

Groenewgen, Peter. 2008. "Political Economy." In *The New Palgrave Dictionary of Economics Online*, edited by Steven N. Durlauf and Lawrence E. Blume, 2nd edn. New York: Palgrave Macmillan. www.dictionaryofeconomics.com/article?id=pde2008_P000114 (accessed October 1, 2014).

Hafez, Mohammed M. and Quintan Wiktorowicz. 2004. "Violence as Contention in the Egyptian Islamic Movement." In *Islamic Activism: A Social Movement Theory Approach*, edited by Quintan Wiktorowicz. Bloomington: Indiana University Press.

Handoussa, Heba. 1991. "Crisis and Challenge: Prospects for the 1990s." In *Employment and Structural Adjustment: Egypt in the 1990s*, edited by Heba Handoussa and Gillian Potter. Cairo: AUC Press.

Handoussa, Heba. 1991. "The Impact of Foreign Aid on Egypt's Economic Development, 1952–1986." In *Transitions in Development: The Role of Aid and Commercial Flows*, edited by Uma Lele and Nabi Ijaz. San Francisco: International Center for Economic Growth Press.

Ibrahim, Saad Eddin. 1994. "Egypt's Landed Bourgeoisie." In *Developmentalism and Beyond: Society and Politics in Egypt and Turkey*, edited by Ayse Oncu, Caglar Keyder and Saad Eddin Ibrahim. Cairo: American University of Cairo Press.

Katz, Elihu. 1968. "Diffusion (Interpersonal Influence)." In *International Encyclopaedia of Social Sciences*, edited by David Shils. London: Macmillan and Free Press.

Kerr, Malcolm. 1965. "Egypt." In *Education and Political Development*, edited by James Coleman. Princeton: Princeton University Press.

Klandermans, Bert. 1990. "Linking the 'Old' and 'New': Movement Networks in the Netherlands." In *Challenging The Political Order: New Social Movements in Western Democracies*, edited by Russel Dalton and Manfred Kuechler. Oxford: Polity.

McAdam, Doug. 1995. "'Initiator' and 'Spinoff' Movements: Diffusion Processes in Protest Cycles." In *Repertoires and Cycles of Collective Action*, edited by Marx Traugott. Durham, NC: Duke University Press.

McAdam, Doug. 1996. "Conceptual Origins, Current Problems and Future Directions." In *Comparative Perspectives on Social Movements*, edited by D. McAdam, J. McCarthy and M.N. Zald. Cambridge: Cambridge University Press.

Marfleet, Phillip. 2009. "State and Society." In *Egypt: The Moment of Change*, edited by Rabab El-Mahdi and Philip Marfleet. London: Zed Books.

Merton, Robert K. 1949. "On the Sociological Theories of the Middle Range." In *Social Theory and Social Structure*, edited by Robert K. Merton. London: The Free Press.

Oberschall, Anthony. 1996. "Opportunities and Framing in the Eastern European Revolts of 1989." In *Comparative Perspectives on Social Movements*, edited by Doug McAdam, John D. McCarthy and Mayer N. Zald. Cambridge: Cambridge University Press.

Reid, Donald Malcolm. 1998. "The 'Urabi Revolution and the British Conquest, 1879–1882." In *The Cambridge History of Egypt*, edited by M.W. Daly. Cambridge: Cambridge University Press.

Snow, David, and Robert Benford. 1992. "Master Frames and Cycles of Protest." In *Frontiers in Social Movement Theory*, edited by A.D. Morris and C.M. Mueller. New Haven: Yale University Press.

Soule, Sarah. 2004. "Diffusion Processes Within and Across Movements." In *The Blackwell Companion to Social Movements*, edited by D.A. Snow, Sarah Soule and H. Malden. Oxford: Blackwell.

Tarrow, Sidney. 2010. "Dynamics of Diffusion: Mechanisms, Institutions and Scale Shift." In *The Diffusion of Social Movements: Actors, Mechanisms and Political Effects*, edited by Rebecca Kolins Givan, Kenneth M. Roberts and Sarah A. Soule. Cambridge: Cambridge University Press.

Journal articles

Abdel Khaleq, Gouda. 1981. "Looking Outside, or Turning Northwest? On the Meaning and External Dimension of Egypt's Infitah, 1971–1980." *Social Problems* 28, no. 4 (April): 394–409.

Abdelrahman, Maha. 2013. "In Praise of Organization: Egypt between Activism and Revolution." *Development and Change* 44: 569–585.

Abu-Lughod, Janet L. 1965. "Urbanization in Egypt: Present State and Future Prospects." *Economic Development and Cultural Change* 13, no. 3 (April): 313–343.

Almeida, Paul. 2003. "Opportunity Organizations and Threat-Induced Contention: Protest Waves in Authoritarian Settings." *American Journal of Sociology* 109, no. 2 (September): 345–400.

Baiocchi, Gianpaolo and Brian T. Connor. 2008. "The *Ethnos* in the *Polis*: Political Ethnography as a Mode of Inquiry." *Sociology Compass* 2, no. 1: 139–155.

Beinin, Joel. 1977. "The Communist Movement and Nationalist Political Discourse in Nasirist Egypt." *Middle East Journal* 41, no. 4 (Autumn): 568–584.

Beinin, Joel. 1989. "Labor, Capital, and the State in Nasserist Egypt, 1952–1961." *International Journal of Middle East Studies* 21, no. 1 (February): 71–90.

Beinin, Joel. 2007. "The Militancy of Mahalla al-Kubra." *MERIP*, September 27. www.merip.org/mero/mero092907 (accessed October 1, 2014).

Beinin, Joel. 2011. "Workers and the Egyptian January 25th Revolution." *International Labor and Working-Class History* 80, no. 1 (September): 189–196.

Benford, Robert D. 1997. "An Insider's Critique of the Social Movement Framing Perspective." *Sociological Enquiry* 67, no. 4 (November): 409–430.

Benford, Robert and David Snow. 2000. "Framing Processes and Social Movements: An Overview and Assessment." *Annual Review of Sociology* 26: 611–639.

Bianchi, Robert. 1986. "The Corporatization of the Egyptian Labor Movement." *Middle East Journal* 40, no. 3 (Summer): 429–444.

Black, Bernard, Reinier Kraakman and Anna Tarassova. 2000. "Russian Privatization and Corporate Governance: What Went Wrong?" *Stanford Law Review* 52, no. 6 (July): 1731–1808.

Bruton, Henry J. 1983. "Egypt's Development in the Seventies." *Economic Development and Cultural Change* 31, no. 4 (July): 679–704.

Buechler, Steven. 1993. "Beyond Resource Mobilization? Emerging Trends in Social Movement Theory." *The Sociological Quarterly* 34: 217–235.

Bush, Ray and David Seddon. 1999. "Editorial: North Africa in Africa." *Review of African Political Economy* 26, no. 82 (December): 435–439.

Carroll, William K. and R.S. Ratner. 1996. "Master Framing and Cross-Movement Networking in Contemporary Social Movements." *The Sociological Quarterly* 37, no. 4 (Autumn): 601–625.

Chaichian, Mohammed. 1988. "The Effects of World Capitalist Economy on Urbanization in Egypt, 1800–1970." *International Journal of Middle East Studies* 21, no. 1 (February): 23–43.

Conell, Carol and Samuel Cohn. 1995. "Learning From Other People's Actions: Environmental Variation and Diffusion in French Coal Mining Strikes, 1890–1935." *The American Journal of Sociology* 101, no. 2 (September): 366–403.

Cooper, Mark. 1979. "Egyptian State Capitalism in Crisis: Economic Policies and Political Interests." *Middle East Studies Journal* 10: 482.

Craig, A.J.M. 1935. "Egyptian Students." *Middle East Journal* 7, no. 3 (Summer): 293–299.

Crecelius, Daniel. 1966. "Al-Azhar in the Revolution." *Middle East Journal* 20, no. 1 (Winter): 31–49.

De Mesquita, Bruce Bueno, Randolph Siverson and Gary Woller. 1992. "War and the Fate of Regimes: A Comparative Analysis." *The American Political Science Review* 86, no. 3 (September): 638–646.

Deeb, Marius. 1978. "The Socioeconomic Role of the Local Foreign Minorities in Modern Egypt, 1805–1961." *International Journal of Middle East Studies* 9, no. 1 (February): 11–22.

Della Porta, Donatella. 2005. "Making the Polis: Social Forums and Democracy in the Global Justice Movement." *Mobilization* 10, no. 1: 73–94.

Della Porta, Donatella and Lorenzo Mosca. 2007. "In Movimento: 'Contamination' in Action and the Italian Global Justice Movement." *Global Networks* 7: 1–27.

Denis, Eric. 2008. "Demographic Surprises Foreshadow Change in Neoliberal Egypt." *MERIP* 38 (Spring). www.merip.org/mer/mer246/demographic-surprises-foreshadow-change-neoliberal-egypt (accessed October 1, 2014).

Desai, Raj, Anders Olofsgard and Tarik Yousef. 2009. "The Logic of Authoritarian Bargains." *Economics and Politics* 21, no. 1 (March): 93–125.

Dessouki, Ali E. Hillal. 1981. "Policy Making in Egypt: A Case Study of the Open Door Economic Policy." *Social Problems* 28, no. 4 (April): 410–416.

Diani, Mario. 1996. "Linking Mobilization Frames and Political Opportunities: Insights from Regional Populism in Italy." *American Sociological Review* 61, no. 6 (December): 1053–1069.

Eaton, Tim. 2013. "Internet Activism and the Egyptian Uprisings: Transforming Online Dissent into the Offline World." *Westminster Papers in Communication and Culture* 9, no. 2 (April): 3–23.

Eisinger, Peter K. 1973. "The Conditions of Protest Behaviour in American Cities." *The American Political Science Review* 67, no. 1 (March): 11–28.

El Shafie, Omar. 1995. "Workers, Trade Unions and the State in Egypt: 1984–1989." *Cairo Papers in Social Science* 18, no. 2 (Summer): 1–43.

El Tantawy, Nahed and Julie Wiest. 2011. "Social Media in the Egyptian Revolution: Reconsidering Resource Mobilization Theory." *International Journal of Communication* 5: 1214.

Faksh, Mahmud. 1980. "The Consequences of the Introduction and Spread of Modern Education: Education and National Integration in Egypt." *Middle East Studies* 16, no. 2 (May): 42–55.

Fandy, Mamoun. 1994. "Egypt's Islamic Group: Regional Revenge?" *Middle East Journal* 48, no. 4 (Autumn): 607–625.

Francisco, Ronald. 1995. "The Relationship between Coercion and Protest: An Empirical Evaluation in Three Coercive States." *Journal of Conflict Resolution* 39, no. 2: 263–281.

Frandsen, Paul. 1990. "Editing Reality: The Turin Strike Papyrus." *Studies in Egyptology* 1: 166–199.

Freeman, Jo. 1973. "The Origins of the Women's Liberation Movement." *American Journal of Sociology* 78: 792–811.

Gamson, William A. 1975. "Review Symposium on Frame Analysis: An Essay on the Organization of Experience." *Contemporary Sociology* 4, no. 6: 599–603.

Garret, Kelly. 2006. "Protest in an Information Society: A Review of Literature on Social Movements and New ICTs." *Information, Communication and Society* 9, no. 2: 202–224.

Gillespie, Andra and Melissa R. Michelson. 2011. "Participant Observation and the Political Scientist: Possibilities, Priorities, and Practicalities." *PS: Political Science and Politics* 44, no. 2 (April): 261–265.

Ginat, Rami. 2003. "The Egyptian Left and the Roots of Neutralism in the Pre-Nasserite Era." *British Journal of Middle Eastern Studies* 30, no. 1: 5–24.

Goldberg, Ellis. 1992. "The Foundations of State-Labor Relations in Contemporary Egypt." *Comparative Politics* 24, no. 2 (January): 147–161.

Goldstone, Jack. 1980. "Theories of Revolution: The Third Generation." *World Politics* 32: 425–453.

Goldstone, Jack. 2001. "Toward a Fourth Generation of Revolutionary Theory." *Annual Review of Political Science* 4: 139–187.

Gorgas, Jordi Tejel. 2013. "The Limits of the State: Student Protest in Egypt, Iraq and Turkey, 1948–63." *British Journal of Middle Eastern Studies* 40, no. 4: 359–377.

Hamed, Osama. 1981. "Egypt's Open Door Economic Policy: An Attempt at Economic Integration in the Middle East." *International Journal of Middle East Studies* 13, no. 1 (February): 1–19.

Handley, William J. 1949. "The Labor Movement in Egypt." *Middle East Journal* 3, no. 3 (July): 277–292.

Handy, Howard. 1998. "Egypt: Beyond Stabilization, Toward a Dynamic Market Economy." *Occasional Paper no. 163*. Washington, DC: International Monetary Fund.

Hinnebusch Jr, Raymond A. 1981. "Egypt under Sadat: Elites, Power Structure, and Political Change in a Post-Populist State." *Social Problems* 28, no. 4 (April): 442–464.

Hinnebusch Jr, Raymond A. 1983. "From Nasir to Sadat: Elite Transformation in Egypt." *Journal of South Asian and Middle Eastern Studies* 7, no. 1: 25–26.

Hinnebusch Jr, Raymond A. 1993. "Class, State and the Reversal of Egypt's Agrarian Reform." *MERIP*, September–October: 20–23.

Holden, Robert T. 1986. "The Contagiousness of Aircraft Hijacking." *American Journal of Sociology*: 874–904.

Hussein, Mahmoud. 1972. "The Revolt of Egyptian Students." *MERIP* 11 (August): 10–14.

Ibrahim, Saad Eddin. 1975. "Over-Urbanization and Under-Urbanism: The Case of the Arab World." *International Journal of Middle East Studies* 1: 29–45.

Issawi, Charles. 1961. "Egypt Since 1800: A Study in Lop-Sided Development." *The Journal of Economic History* 21, no. 1 (March): 1–25.

James, L. 1947. "The Population Problem in Egypt." *Economic Geography* 23, no. 2 (April): 98–104.

Jenkins, Craig. 1983. "Resource Mobilization Theory and the Study of Social Movements." *Annual Review of Sociology* 9: 527–553.

Johnson, Harry G. 1965. "A Theoretical Model of Economic Nationalism in New and Developing States." *Political Science Quarterly* 80, no. 2 (June): 169–185.

Johnson, Peter. 1973. "Retreat of the Revolution in Egypt." *MERIP* 17 (May).

Joya, Angela. 2011. "The Egyptian Revolution: Crisis of Neoliberalism and the Potential for Democratic Politics." *Review of African Political Economy* 38, no. 129 (September): 367–389.

Khalidi, Rashid. 2011. "Reflections on the Revolutions in Tunisia and Egypt." *Foreign Policy*, February 24.

Khawaja, Marwan. 1993. "Repression and Popular Collective Action: Evidence from the West Bank." *Sociological Forum* 8, no. 1: 47–71.

Lachine, Nadime. 1977. "Class Roots of the Sadat Regime: Reflections of an Egyptian Leftist." *MERIP* 56 (April).

Lesch, A.M. 2011. "Egypt's Spring: Causes of the Revolution." *Middle East Policy* 18, no. 3: 35–48.

Loveman, Mara. 1998. "High-Risk Collective Action: Defending Human Rights in Chile, Uruguay, and Argentina." *American Journal of Sociology* 104, no. 2: 477–525.

McAdam, Doug and Dieter Rucht. 1993. "The Cross-National Diffusion of Movement Ideas." *The Annals of the American Academy of Political and Social Science* 528 (July): 56–74.

McAdam, Doug and Sidney Tarrow. 2011. "Dynamics of Contention Ten Years On." *Mobilization* 16, no. 1 (February): 1–10.

McCarthy, J.A. 1976. "Nineteenth Century Egyptian Population." *Middle East Studies* 12, no. 3: 33–34.

McCarthy, John D. and Mark Wolfson. 1996. "Resource Mobilization by Local Social Movement Organizations: The Role of Agency, Strategy and Structure." *American Sociological Review* 61: 1070–1088.

McCarthy, John D. and Mayer N. Zald. 1977. "Resource Mobilization and Social Movements: A Partial Theory." *American Journal of Sociology* 82: 1212–1241.

Masoud, Tarek. 2011. "The Road to (and from) Liberation Square." *Journal of Democracy* 22, no. 3: 20–34.

Meital, Yoram. 2006. "The Struggle Over Political Order in Egypt: The 2005 Elections." *The Middle East Journal* 60, no. 2 (Spring): 257–279.

Meyer, David S. 2004. "Protest and Political Opportunities." *Annual Review of Sociology* 30: 125–145.

Meyer, David S. and Steven A. Boutcher. 2007. "Signals and Spillover: Brown v. Board of Education and Other Social Movements." *Perspectives on Politics* 5: 81–93.

Meyer, David S. and Nancy Whittier. 1994. "Social Movement Spillover." *Social Problems* 41, no. 2 (May): 277–298.

Mitchell, Timothy. 1999. "Dreamland: The Neoliberalism of Your Desires." *MERIP* 210, vol. 29 (Spring). www.merip.org/mer/mer210/dreamland-neoliberalism-your-desires?ip_login_no_cache=90205cf5e7c2ad8f1dab4bddef9ab22a (accessed October 1, 2014).

Moaddel, Mansoor. 2002. "Discursive Pluralism and Islamic Modernism in Egypt." *Arab Studies Quarterly* 24, no. 1 (Winter): 1–29.

Mostafa, Tamer. 2004. "Protests Hint at New Chapter in Egyptian Politics." *MERIP*, April 9. www.merip.org/mero/mero040904?ip_login_no_cache=f78b5695fa9cbcb6e47487aa2a7f37b6 (accessed October 1, 2014).

Murphy, Emma C. 2001. "The State and the Private Sector in North Africa: Seeking Specificity." *Mediterranean Politics* 6, no. 2: 1–28.

Murphy, Emma C. 2011. "The Arab State and (Absent) Civility in New Communicative Spaces." *Third World Quarterly* 32, no. 5: 959–980.

Murphy, Emma C. 2012. "Problematizing Arab Youth: Generational Narratives of Systemic Failure." *Mediterranean Politics* 17, no. 1: 5–22.

Nagarajan, K.V. 2013. "Egypt's Political Economy and the Downfall of the Mubarak Regime." *International Journal of Humanities and Social Science* 3, no. 10 (Special Issue, May): 22–39.

Posusney, Marsha Pripsein. 1993. "Irrational Workers: The Moral Economy of Labor Protest in Egypt." *World Politics* 46, no. 1 (October): 83–120.

Posusney, Marsha Pripsein. 1995. "Egypt's New Labor Law Removes Worker Provisions." *Middle East Report* 194/195, Odds Against Peace (May–August): 52–64.

Posusney, Marsha Pripsein. 1999. "Egyptian Privatization: New Challenges for the Left." *Middle East Report* 210, Reform or Reaction? Dilemmas of Economic Development in the Middle East (Spring): 38–40.

Reid, Donald Malcolm. 1987. "Cairo University and the Orientalists." *International Journal of Middle East Studies* 19, no. 1 (February): 51–75.

Richards, Alan. 1991. "The Political Economy of Dilatory Reform: Egypt in the 1980s." *World Development* 19, no. 12: 1721–1730.

Ross, Michael. 2001. "Does Oil Hinder Democracy?" *World Politics* 53, no. 3: 326–361.

Ryan, B. and N.C. Gross. 1943. "The Diffusion of Hybrid Seed Corn in Two Iowa Communities." *Rural Sociology* 8: 15–24.

Schleifer, Abdallah. 2006. "The Impact of Arab Satellite Television on Prospects for Democracy in the Arab World." *Transnational Broadcasting Studies* 15.

Schmitter, Phillipe. 1974. "Still the Century of Corporatism?" *Review of Politics* 36, no. 1 (January): 85–131.

Shawki, Noha. 2013. "Understanding the Transnational Diffusion of Social Movements: An Analysis of the US Solidarity Economy Network and Transition." *Humanity and Society* 37: 131–158.

Shehata, Dina. 2011. "The Fall of the Pharaoh." *Foreign Affairs* (May/June): 26–32.

Shenton, Andrew K. 2004. "Strategies for Ensuring Trustworthiness in Qualitative Research Projects." *Education for Information* 22: 63–75.

Smith, Charles D. 1979. "4 February 1942: Its Causes and Its Influence on Egyptian Politics and on the Future of Anglo-Egyptian Relations, 1937–1945." *International Journal of Middle East Studies* 10, no. 4: 453–479.

Snow, David A., R. Burke Rochford, Jr., Steven K. Worden and Robert D. Benford. 1986. "Frame Alignment Processes, Micromobilization, and Movement Participation." *American Sociological Review* 51: 464–481.

Soliman, Samer. 1999. "State and Industrial Capitalism in Egypt." *Cairo Papers in Social Science* 21, no. 2.

Spencer, John H. 1937. "The Italian-Ethiopian Dispute and the League of Nations." *The American Journal of International Law* 31, no. 4: 614–641.

Strang, David and Sarah Soule. 1998. "Diffusion in Organizations and Social movements: From Hybrid Corn to Poison Pills." *Annual Review of Sociology* 24: 265–290.

Summers, Lawrence H. and Lant H. Pritchett. 1993. "The Structural-Adjustment Debate." *The American Economic Review* 83, no. 2 (May): 383–389.

Tamimi, Azzam. 1997. "Democracy in Islamic Political Thought." *Encounters: Journal of Inter-Cultural Perspectives* 3: 1–35.

Thompson, Edward P. 1971. "The Moral Economy of the English Crowd in the Eighteenth Century." *Past and Present* 50 (February): 76–136.

Tignor, Robert L. 1976. "The Egyptian Revolution of 1919: New Directions in the Egyptian Economy." *Middle Eastern Studies* 12, no. 3 (October): 41–67.

Tuchman, Gaye. 1976. "Telling Stories." *Journal of Communication* 26, no. 4: 93–97.

Utvik, Bjørn Olav. 2005. "*Hizb Al Wasat* and the Potential for Change in Egyptian Islamism." *Critical Middle Eastern Studies* 14, no. 3 (Autumn): 293–306.

Vitalis, Robert. 1990. "On the Theory and Practice of Compradors: The Role of Abbud Pasha in the Egyptian Political Economy." *International Journal of Middle East Studies* 22, no. 3 (August): 291–315.

Weinbaum, Marvin G. 1985. "Egypt's 'Infitah' and the Politics of US Economic Assistance." *Middle Eastern Studies* 21, no. 2 (April): 206–222.

Wolff, Sarah. 2009. "Constraints on the Promotion of the Rule of Law in Egypt: Insights from the 2005 Judges' Revolt." *Democratization* 16, no. 1: 100–118.

Zhao, Dingxin. 1998. "Ecologies of Social Movements: Student Mobilization during the 1989 Prodemocracy Movement in Beijing." *American Journal of Sociology* 103, no. 6 (May): 1493–1529.

Reports and papers

Badr, Ahmad Enas Zakariyya and Mohamed Saleh. 2009. "Impact of Global Economic Crisis on Tourism Sector in Egypt: A System Dynamics Approach." Information and Decision Support Center (IDSC), Economic Issues Program (EIP), Egyptian Cabinet.

Beinin, Joel. 2012. "The Rise of Egypt's Workers." *Carnegie Papers* (June).

Bibi, Sami and Mustapha Nabili. 2010. *Equity and Inequality in the Arab World.* PRR

No. 33. Cairo: Economic Research Forum, February. www.erf.org.eg/CMS/uploads/pdf/PRR33.pdf (accessed October 1, 2014).

Dobronogov, Anton and Farrukh lqbal. 2005. "Economic Growth in Egypt: Constraints and Determinants." Working Paper Series No. 42 (October). Washington, DC: World Bank. http://siteresources.worldbank.org/INTMENA/Resources/WP42SEPTEMBER2006.pdf (accessed October 1, 2014).

Dodge, Toby. 2012. "The Middle East After the Arab Spring." *London School of Economics (LSE) Ideas Report.*

Dunne, Michele and Mara Revkin. 2011. "Egypt: How a Lack of Political Reform Undermined Economic Reform." *Commentary for Carnegie Endowment for Peace.* http://carnegieendowment.org/2011/02/23/egypt-how-lack-of-political-reform-undermined-economic-reform/crn (accessed October 1, 2014).

The Egyptian Centre for Economic Studies. 1997. "Egypt's Economic Reform and Structural Adjustment Program (ERSAP)." Working Paper 19 (October). www.eces.org.eg/Uploaded_Files/%7BD83916F9-6CEF-4E7C-8F35-4A8CDC7AD78A%7D_ECESWP19e.pdf (accessed October 1, 2014).

El Tarouty, Safinaz. 2008. "Reinventing the Party: Reform and Internal Dynamics of Egypt's National Democratic Party." *PSI Papers in Culture, Ideas and Policy*, University of East Anglia Working Paper 2. www.uea.ac.uk/polopoly_fs/1.103897!s%20eltarouty%20final%20dec%202.pdf (accessed October 1, 2014).

Gray, Matthew. 2011. "A Theory of 'Late Rentierism' in the Arab States of the Gulf." Occasional Paper, Centre for International and Regional Studies (CRIS) 7: 1–44.

Halliday, Fred. n.d. "1967 and the Consequences of Catastrophe." *MERIP*. www.merip.org/mer/mer146/1967-consequences-catastrophe (accessed October 1, 2014).

International Finance Corporation. 2007. "Top Reformers in 2006/2007." *Doing Business*, www.doingbusiness.org/features/refomr2007.aspx (accessed October 1, 2014).

International Monetary Fund. 1976. *Arab Republic of Egypt*, Staff Report for the 1976 Article X IV Consultation (August).

International Monetary Fund. 2010. "IMF Executive Board Concludes 2010 Article IV Consultation with the Arab Republic of Egypt." Washington, DC: IMF, April. www.imf.org/external/np/sec/pn/2010/pn1049.htm (accessed October 1, 2014).

Korayem, Karima. 1997. "Egypt's Economic Reform and Structural Adjustment (ERSAP)." Working Paper No. 19. The Egyptian Center for Economic Studies (ECES) (October): 21–22.

Lachine, Nadime. 1978. "The Open Door Policy of Anwar Sadat." *Association of Arab American University Graduates*, Information Paper 21: 7–28.

Lagi, M., K.Z. Bertrand and Y. Bar-Yam. 2011. "The Food Crises and Political Instability in North Africa and the Middle East." *New England Complex Systems Institute* (August 10).

Mansour, Tamer. 2011. "Egypt and the Financial Crisis." Faculty of Economics and Political Science Paper, Cairo University (December). http://mpra.ub.uni-muenchen.de/37370/2/MPRA_paper_37370.pdf (accessed October 1, 2014).

Nathan Associates. 2004. "Changing International Trade Rules for Textiles and Apparel." Report submitted to Egyptian Ministry of Foreign Trade and USAID (January).

OECD. 2003. "African Economic Outlook: Egypt, 2003." www.oecd.org/countries/egypt/2498037.pdf (accessed October 1, 2014).

Rojas, Fabio and Michael T. Heaney. 2008. "Social Movement Mobilization in a Multi-Movement Environment: Spillover, Interorganizational Networks and Hybrid Identities." John F. Kennedy School of Government Paper, Harvard University (February).

Subramanian, Arvind. 1997. "Egypt: Poised for Sustained Growth?" *IMF Growth and Development* (December).

Subramanian, Arvind. 1997. "The Egyptian Stabilization Experience: An Analytical Retrospective." *IMF Working Paper 97/105*. Washington, DC: International Monetary Fund.

Umar, Khālid ʿAlī. 2008. *al-Ḥaqq fī-l-tanẓīm: al-huriyya al-niqābiya bayn al-utur al-tashrīʿiya wa mabadiʿī al-maḥkama al-dusturiyya wal-mumārasa al-ʿamaliyya* (The Right to Organize: Freedom to Unionize between the Legislative Framework, Principles of the Constitutional Court and Actual Practice). Publication of the Hisham Mubarak Law Centre. http://hmlc-egy.org/node/59 (accessed October 1, 2014).

United Nations Development Program. 1990. *Human Development Report 1990*. New York: Oxford University Press. http://hdr.undp.org/sites/default/files/reports/219/hdr_1990_en_complete_nostats.pdf (accessed October 1, 2014).

United Nations Development Program. 2003. *Egypt Human Development Report 2003*. Cairo: United Nations Development Program and Institute of National Planning.

United Nations Development Program. 2008. *Egypt Human Development Report 2008*. Cairo: United Nations Development Program and Institute of National Planning.

United Nations Economic and Social Commission for Western Asia. 2012. "Egypt Demographic Profile 2012." www.escwa.un.org/popin/members/egypt.pdf (accessed October 1, 2014).

Welch, Dick and Olivier Frémond. 1998. "The Case-by-Case Approach to Privatization: Techniques and Examples." Washington, DC: The World Bank (International Bank for Reconstruction and Development). http://elibrary.worldbank.org/doi/pdf/10.1596/0-8213-4196-0 (accessed October 1, 2014).

World Bank. n.d. "Egypt Poverty Headcount Ratio at Urban Poverty Line." http://data.worldbank.org/indicator/SI.POV.URHC/countries/EG?display=graph (accessed October 1, 2014).

World Bank. 1976. "Arab Republic of Egypt, Report No 870." Washington, DC: World Bank.

Newspapers, magazines and online portals

Abdel Ghafar, Adel. 2012. "The First Hours of the Egyptian Revolution." *New York Times Lede Blog*, January 25. http://thelede.blogs.nytimes.com/2012/01/24/the-first-hours-of-egypts-revolution/ (accessed October 1, 2014).

Abul Magd, Zeinab. 2011. "The Army and the Economy in Egypt." *Jadaliyya*, December 23. www.jadaliyya.com/pages/index/3732/the-army-and-the-economy-in-egypt (accessed October 1, 2014).

Al Ahram Newspaper. March 31, 1968.

Al Ahram Online. 2011. "General Hassan al Roiny Speaking to the Protestors in Tahrir Square." *Al Ahram Gate Online*, February 6.

Al Ahram Online. 2011. "Egyptian Minister of Solidarity Abdel Khaleq Will Also Take on Food Prices in Latest Reshuffling." *Al Ahram Online*, December 3. http://english.ahram.org.eg/NewsContent/3/12/28359/Business/Economy/Egyptian-Minister-of-Solidarity-Abdel-Khaleq-will-.aspx (accessed October 1, 2014).

Al Ahram Online. 2014. "Mubarak-era Egyptian Steel Tycoon Ahmed Ezz Released on Bail." *Al Ahram Online*, August 7. http://english.ahram.org.eg/NewsContent/3/12/107956/Business/Economy/Mubarakera-Egyptian-steel-tycoon-Ahmed-Ezz-release.aspx (accessed October 1, 2014).

Al Akhbar Newspaper. January 31, 1977.

Al Mosawar Magazine. 1981. Interview with President Hosni Mubarak. October 30.

Al Tali'a Newspaper. February, 1966.

Al Umaal Newspaper. June, 1967.

Al Umaal Newspaper. February 19, 1970.

Al Wafd Newspaper. December 29, 2010.

Amin, Galal. 2007. "Nothing Trickles Down." *Daily Star Egypt*, November 15.

Anderson, Betty. 2011. "The Student Movement in 1968." *Jadaliyya*, March 9. www.jadaliyya.com/pages/index/838/the-student-movement-in-1968 (accessed October 1, 2014).

Anonymous. 2011. *Kul ma turīd an ta'rifah 'an thawrat 25 yanayer* (All You Need to Know About the 25th of January Revolution). Cairo, January. https://docs.google.com/document/d/1qU3TnumUD5ZzZN9CEBbDRIzNvcjbOtJX5CkcBcC9OjI/preview?sle=true (accessed October 1, 2014).

Asher-Shapiro, Avi. 2012. "IMF Amnesia in Egypt." *Muftah*, September 7. http://muftah.org/imf-amnesia-in-egypt/ (accessed October 1, 2014).

Atalah, Lina. 2012. "Farwell Samer Soliman." *Egypt Independent*, December 23. www.egyptindependent.com/news/farewell-samer-soliman (accessed October 1, 2014).

Business Insider. 2011. "Hosni Mubarak's Pinstripes Are Actually His Name Repeated Over And Over." March 4. www.businessinsider.com.au/hosni-mubarak-pinstripes-2011-3 (accessed October 1, 2014).

The Cairo Post. 2014. "Mubarak-Era Prime Minister Atef Ebeid Dead at 82." September. http://thecairopost.com/news/124779/news/mubarak-era-prime-minister-atef-ebeid-dead-at-82 (accessed October 1, 2014).

Constitution of the Arab Republic of Egypt. 1971. www.constitutionnet.org/files/Egypt%20Constitution.pdf (accessed October 1, 2014).

Cornwell, Rupert. 2006. "Milton Friedman, Free-Market Economist Who Inspired Reagan and Thatcher, Dies Aged 94." *Independent*, November 17. www.independent.co.uk/news/world/americas/milton-friedman-freemarket-economist-who-inspired-reagan-and-thatcher-dies-aged-94-424665.html (accessed October 1, 2014).

Dawoud, Khaled. 2001. "Message to the 'Castle'." *Al Ahram Online*, September 13–19. http://weekly.ahram.org.eg/2001/551/eg4.htm (accessed October 1, 2014).

Dreyfuss, Robert. 2011. "Who's Behind Egypt's Revolt?" *The Nation*, January 31. www.thenation.com/blog/158159/whos-behind-egypts-revolt (accessed October 1, 2014).

The Economist. 2012. "Let Them Eat Baklava: Today's Policies are Recipes for Instability in the Middle East." *The Economist*, March 17.

Egypt Independent Staff. 2011. "Egypt's Minister of Defense Joins Protesters in Tahrir Square." *Egypt Independent*, January 30. www.egyptindependent.com/news/egypts-minister-defense-joins-protesters-tahrir-square (accessed October 1, 2014).

El-Mahdy, Rabab. 2011. "Orientalising the Egyptian Uprising." *Jadaliyya*, April 11. www.jadaliyya.com/pages/index/1214/orientalising-the-egyptian-uprising (accessed October 1, 2014).

El Sharnoubi, Osman. 2013. "Revolutionary History Relived: The Mahalla Strike of 6 April 2008." *Al Ahram Online*, April 6. http://english.ahram.org.eg/NewsContent/1/64/68543/Egypt/Politics-/Revolutionary-history-relived-The-Mahalla-strike-o.aspx (accessed October 1, 2014).

El-Wardani, Salma. 2011. "Money, Power and Law-Twisting: The Makings of the Real Ezz Empire." *Ahram Online*, May 7. http://english.ahram.org.eg/News/11480.aspx (accessed October 1, 2014).

England, Andrew. 2007. "Wealth Disparities Cloud Progress." *Financial Times*, December 10.

Fahmy, Magdi. n.d. *Dawr al-tabaqah al-ʿamila fī-l-ḥarakat al-waṭaniya* (The Role of the Working Class in the Nationalist Movement). *al-Tāliʾa*, 39–40.

Howeidy, Amira. 2002. "Solidarity." *Al Ahram Online*, April 4–10. http://weekly.ahram.org.eg/2002/580/eg4.htm (accessed October 1, 2014).

Hussein, Salma and Salma El Wardani. 2011. "All the King's Men: Who Runs Mubarak's Money?" *Ahram Online*, May. http://english.ahram.org.eg/NewsContent/3/12/8793/Business/Economy/All-the-king%E2%80%99s-men-Who-runs-Mubaraks-money-.aspx (accessed October 1, 2014).

Kim, Sung Un. 2012. "Egypt Court Sentences Former Housing Minister for Corruption." *Jurist*, March 30. http://jurist.org/paperchase/2012/03/egypt-court-sentences-former-housing-minister-for-corruption.php (accessed October 1, 2014).

Kirkpatrick, David. 2015. "Mubarak Sons Released From Egyptian Jail." *New York Times*, January 26.

Martin, Douglas. 2008. "Charles Tilly, 78, Writer and Social Scientist, Is Dead." *New York Times*, May 2.

Muhram, Riyad. 2011. "*Dhikra intifādāt al-khubz 18–19 January 1977*" (The Memory of the Bread Intifada, 18–19 January 1977). *Al Hewar*, www.ahewar.org/debat/show.art.asp?aid=241223 (accessed October 1, 2014).

Myers, Steven Lee. 2003. "Egypt Sanctions Massive Demonstration Against Iraq War." *New York Times*, February 28.

New York Times. 1990. "Arab League Headquarters to Return to Cairo." *New York Times*, March 12. www.nytimes.com/1990/03/12/world/arab-league-headquarters-to-return-to-cairo.html (accessed October 1, 2014).

Owen, Roger. 2011. "Remembering Ahmad Abdalla." *Al Ahram Online*, June 6. http://english.ahram.org.eg/ṭ/NewsContentP/4/13783/Opinion/Remembering-Ahmed-Abdalla.aspx (accessed October 1, 2014).

Qamhawy, Hassan. 2001. *al-Iṣlāḥ al-iqtiṣādī: injizāʾāt ḥaqīqiya aw farīda ghaʾiba?* (The Economic Reform: Real Achievements or Absent Duty?). *al-Ahrām al-iqtiṣādī*, December 31. http://economic.ahram.org.eg/Ahram/2001/12/31/INVE1.HTM (accessed October 1, 2014).

Rizk, Younan Labib. 2000. "A Diwan of Contemporary Life." *Al Ahram Weekly*, February 24.

Sami, Aziza. 1999. "Eid Abdel-Rahman."*Al-Ahram Weekly*, July 23–29.

Shabāb, Muḥammad. 2011. *Maḥmūd al-Gammal: Nahb al-arḍī fī himāyat al-niẓām* (Mahmoud el Gammal: The Robbery of Land with the Protection of the Regime). *al Wafd*, February 17.

Shoukri, Ghali. 1987. *al-Thawra wal-thawra al-muḍḍadda fī Miṣr* (Revolution and Counterrevolution in Egypt). Cairo: Kitāb al-Ahallī, no. 15 (September).

Shukrullah, Salma. 2011. "Egyptian Revolution Youth Form National Coalition." *Ahram Online*, February 9. http://english.ahram.org.eg/ṭ/NewsContent/1/64/5257/Egypt/Politics-/Coalition-of-The-Revolutions-Youth-assembled.aspx (accessed October 1, 2014).

Suha, Yahya. 2014. "*al-Dīb: 25 Yanayer Muʾamara Amrīkiya Qaṭariya Turkiya ikhwāniya tastahdif Maṣr*" (El-Deeb: 25th of January was a US Qatari Turkish Brotherhood Conspiracy Targeting Egypt). *Al Dostor*, September 27. www.dostor.org/684910 (accessed October 1, 2014).

Time Magazine. March 19, 1974.

Watson, Ivan and Mohamed Fadel Fahmy. 2011. "Army Officers Join Cairo Protest." CNN, April 9. http://edition.cnn.com/2011/WORLD/meast/04/08/egypt.protests/ (accessed October 1, 2014).

Theses

Abdel Tawab, Salah. 1997. "Patterns and Dynamics of the Pre-University Education in Egypt: A Developmental and Demographic Perspective." M.Phil thesis, Cairo Demographic Center.

Farid, Ahmad. 1960. "*al-ʿAllāqat al-maṣriya al-briṭniyah wa atharahā fī taṭāwur al-ḥarakat al-waṭaniya fī maṣr*" (Egyptian British Relations and its Impact on the Nationalist Movement in Egypt 1914–1952). Ph.D. dissertation, Faculty of Arts, Cairo University.

Helmy, Amina Amin. 1988. "*Dawr ṣundūq al-naqd al-dawlī fī al-duwal al-namiʾa maʿa al-ishāra ilā al-tajriba al-maṣriya*" (The Role of the IMF in Developing Countries with a Focus on the Egyptian Experience). M.A. thesis, Faculty of Economics and Political Science, Cairo University.

al-Mahdi, Nawal Abdel Aziz. 1976. "*al-Ḥaraka al-ʿumaliya wa atharahā fi tatāwur masr al-siyāsī, 1930–1945*" (The Labor Movement and its Impact on the Development of Egyptian Politics, 1930–1945). Ph.D. dissertation, Faculty of Economics and Political Science, Cairo University.

Shehada, Hani. 2012. "Social Movement 2.0: An Analysis of Mobilization Through Facebook in the 2011 Egyptian Revolution." M.A. thesis, International Institute of Social Studies, Netherlands.

Speeches

Abdel Nasser, Gamal. 1958. Speeches, 23 January. *Biblioteca Alexandria.* Nasser digital repository. http://nasser.bibalex.org/home/main.aspx?lang=ar (accessed October 1, 2014).

Sadat, Anwar. 1980. Speech on the Occasion of National Doctors Day, March 18. *Bibliotheca Alexandria Sadat Digital Archive.* http://sadat.bibalex.org/speeches/browser.aspx?SID=924 (accessed October 1, 2014).

Government cables and communiqués

Egypt State Information Service. n.d. "First Announcement by SCAF." www.sis.gov.eg/Ar/Templates/Articles/tmpArticles.aspx?ArtID=44081 (accessed October 1, 2014).

Foreign Office. 1943. Cable no. 141, 892. "Education and Student Employment."

Foreign Office. 1947. Cable no. 141, 1223. "British Propaganda: Effendi Class." C.W. Austin to Sir Ronald Campbell.

US Embassy, Cairo. 2007. "Prominent Independent MP on Presidential Succession." Cable 07CAIRO974. April 4. https://wikileaks.org/cable/2007/04/07CAIRO974.html (accessed October 1, 2014).

Index

Page numbers in *italics* denote tables, those in **bold** denote figures.